Brian and Alison M[...] [...] Sydney, Australia, and met at university. Alison is a teacher; Brian is an international yachtsman, and a qualified naval architect. They were married in London in 1985.

The Cochin Connection

TWO AGAINST THE DRUG TRADE:

A TRUE STORY

Brian and Alison Milgate

SPHERE BOOKS LIMITED

SPHERE BOOKS LTD

Published by the Penguin Group
27 Wrights Lane, London W8 5TZ, England
Viking Penguin Inc., 40 West 23rd Street, New York, New York 10010, USA
Penguin Books Australia Ltd, Ringwood, Victoria, Australia
Penguin Books Canada Ltd, 2801 John Street, Markham, Ontario, Canada L3R 1B4
Penguin Books (NZ) Ltd, 182–190 Wairau Road, Auckland 10, New Zealand

Penguin Books Ltd, Registered Offices: Harmondsworth, Middlesex, England

First published in Great Britain in 1987 by Chatto and Windus Ltd
Published by Sphere Books Ltd 1988

Printed and bound in Great Britain by
Richard Clay Ltd, Bungay, Suffolk
Set in Monophoto Ehrhardt

Contents

List of illustrations   vii
Authors' note   ix
Maps   x

PROLOGUE   16 April 1983   1
    Saturday in Edacochin, southern India   3

PART ONE   January to 18 April 1983   11
  1   Sailing Away   13
  2   'The' James Charles Howard   23
  3   Pandora's Box   35
  4   *Hetty Mitchell*   44
  5   A Case for Cochin Customs   58
  6   A Turn of Events   71

PART TWO   19 April to 3 November 1983   77
  7   Alison Alone   79
  8   On the Run   92
  9   Diplomatic Dilemma   104
 10   A Cowardly Confrontation   108
 11   Two Faces of Canberra   118
 12   An Ambiguous Ambassador   123
 13   From Pillar to Post   132
 14   A Timely Objection   139
 15   A Verdict of Suicide   145
 16   The Rae Memorandum   156
 17   The Blinds are Down   164
 18   Intelligence at Work   176
 19   Bahamas or Bust   182

PART THREE   5 November 1983 to
  14 March 1984   187
20 Parliamentary Procedure   189
21 Howard Meets the Press   198
22 At Large in London   212
23 Winter in America   216
24 Clearing the Way   230
25 Back in Cochin   235
26 Alison at Law   246
27 The Trial   256
28 The 'Money Sack'   265
29 Angels at Work   273

EPILOGUE   15 March 1984 to September 1986
  The Connection is Broken   285

Illustrations

1 Brian and Alison Milgate
2 Jim Howard
3 Jyl Gocher aboard *Steppenwolf*
4 *The Steppenwolf*
5 Jim Howard and Jyl Gocher taking coconut cocktails
6 Brian Milgate in the Edacochin boatyard
7 Alison Milgate on the verandah of the Bolghatty Hotel
8 The *Hetty*
9 US Customs take custody of the *Hetty*
10 Part of drug concealment on the *Hetty*
11 The *Hetty* crew being led away
12 The crew of the *Hetty*: (a) Donald Dickinson (b) Stephen Marriott (c) Peter Jackson (d) William Charlesworth
13 Consul General Ian Tricks with Brian and Alison Milgate
14 The *Tiger Rag*

Authors' note

The remarkable contents of this book are true. Behind it is an enormous volume of supporting documentation: copies of communications, court documents, copies of Indian Customs Department records, newspaper reports and research gathered by journalists in seven countries, in addition to copies of restricted Australian government telexes released under the Freedom of Information Act, the Howard tapes, shipping records, the *Hetty* logbooks, US Coast Guard records and police computer intelligence. Many of these documents have been quoted in the book.

Over the fifteen months in which the story took place, events were sometimes centred on only one of us. As these occasions arise we have chosen to alternate the telling of events between us, with Alison writing some chapters and Brian others.

A third aspect has been written into the book. These sequences provide the reader with an understanding of events that were going on elsewhere in the story at that time – events which unfortunately we were not aware of at the time they were happening.

Brian and Alison Milgate
Fethiye, Turkey, September 1986

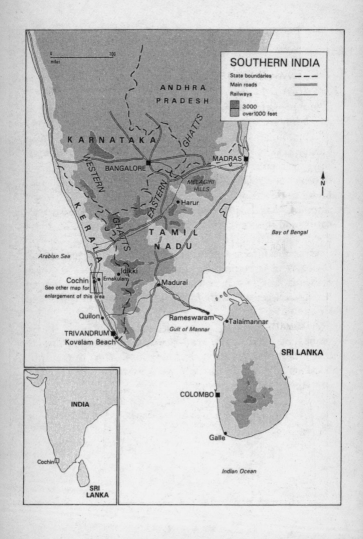

SOUTHERN INDIA

State boundaries ---
Main roads
Railways

3000
over 1000 feet

ANDHRA PRADESH

KARNATAKA

WESTERN GHATTS

BANGALORE

MADRAS

EASTERN GHATTS

MELAGIRI HILLS

Harur

KERALA

TAMIL NADU

Arabian Sea

Idikki

Cochin
Ernakulam
See other map for
enlargement of this area

Madurai

Bay of Bengal

N

Quilon

TRIVANDRUM
Kovalam Beach

Rameswaram
Gulf of Mannar

Talaimannar

SRI LANKA

COLOMBO

Galle

Indian Ocean

INDIA

Cochin

SRI LANKA

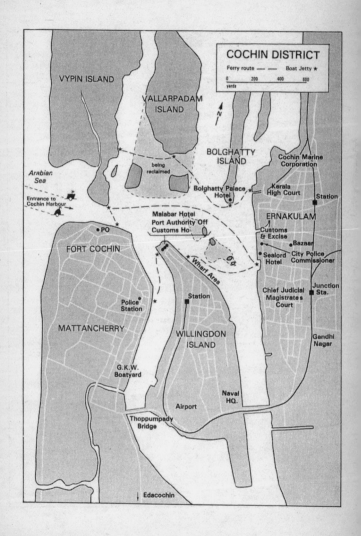

COCHIN DISTRICT

Ferry route —— Boat Jetty ★

0   200   400   600
yards

VYPIN ISLAND

VALLARPADAM ISLAND

BOLGHATTY ISLAND

Cochin Marine Corporation

Arabian Sea

being reclaimed

Bolghatty Palace Hotel

Kerala High Court

Station

Entrance to Cochin Harbour

ERNAKULAM

Malabar Hotel
Port Authority Off
Customs Ho

Customs & Excise

PO

FORT COCHIN

Bazaar

City Police Commissioner

Sealord Hotel

Wharf Area

Junction Sta.

Chief Judicial Magistrate's Court

Police Station

Station

WILLINGDON ISLAND

Gandhi Nagar

MATTANCHERRY

G.K.W. Boatyard

Naval HQ.

Airport

Thoppumpady Bridge

↓ Edacochin

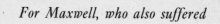

For Maxwell, who also suffered

PROLOGUE
16 April 1983

Saturday in Edacochin, southern India

The old bus careered along the rutted, serpentine road. From the windowless cabin we look out on a coastal strip of rural land that was green and colourful. All round us were paddy fields and coconut groves. Although it was early morning, a man was still turning the dry earth with oxen and plough, women gathered water at the wells and coolies toiled at their labours.

Suddenly the bus jolted to a halt. The driver turned off the ignition and the rattling metal frame fell silent. The more inquisitive passengers crowded towards the front of the bus, some of the men stepping down through the door. From where we sat we could see a procession approaching.

At the head of the group was a young bull elephant and his mahout; behind came many of the local villagers, awed by the ceremonial beast and excited by the events which it heralded. Further back in this colourful parade came the painted faces of players, and the dancers and musicians who would entertain those who gathered for the annual festival. Excited children ran among the procession, occasionally darting off to pick a wild flower for the garlands that would adorn them on this special night. Bringing up the rear were two of the musicians, one striking a drum in time to the slow march, the other a gong.

Tabla drums beat out their rhythm from the small Hindu temple towards which the procession was heading, echoing across the miles of coconut palms and rice paddies, and calling the people to the small shrine where the village priest waited. During the day the temple clearing had been cleaned and meticulously decorated. Tea stalls had been erected, and the wooden stakes which had been driven into the ground would be set aflame at sunset to provide the light needed till

3

dawn. The essence of Hinduism in India has been enacted in festivals of this kind for thousands of years and to these village people tonight's festival would end a week of devotions and special offerings dedicated to their gods. Within a month the monsoon rains would come.

We sat in the bus quietly watching it all, drawn by the charged atmosphere, and looking forward to the evening because we had been invited to attend the ceremony.

It was almost 9 p.m. when we entered the temple clearing. We were greeted warmly by the villagers who had become known to us since we had rented a small boatyard nearby as a place to repair our yacht. Only very few of them could speak English, but in place of words, smiles and vigorous handshakes indicated that we were welcome guests, regardless of our faith or caste.

The colourful scene around us was lit by a pale light which came from burning tapers set on the perimeter of the clearing. Villagers had seated themselves, or squatted in native fashion. Others mingled with their neighbours, enjoying the dancers' costumes and repertoire, the tunes of the musicians, and the antics of the mystics and wandering sadhus. Tired as we were, we too were able to forget the day's troubles and soon were absorbed into the happy festivities on this tropical night. Our hosts brought us tea and chatted to us about local events, after which we settled into our seats close to the stage and watched the play.

The drums rose to a final crescendo. On the tiny makeshift stage and in the magnificence that their exaggerated make-up and costumes brought them, Rama the hero-god was locked in mortal combat with Ravana the villain. To and fro their conflict raged. Just as all seemed lost for the hero, the heroine made an entry from behind the scenery. After an exclamation of shock and horror, and with time-honoured theatrical style, she promptly dispatched the villain. The audience delighted in this action and all sighed in unison; nobody, it seemed, liked the villain. The symbolic victory of righteousness over evil brought this Ramlila play to an end.

After thanking our hosts and the performers, we headed back to our yacht for some sleep.

The path from the Hindu temple to the boatyard where our yacht had been hauled from the water meandered for a kilometre through the rural houses and beside the brackish canals and waterways. We walked along the sandy path in silence, both of us lost in our own thoughts. In the moonlight the fronds of the coconut palms towering above us cast eerie shadows on the dry earthen path which was still warm from yesterday's heat. It was difficult to imagine the deluges of tropical rain which would shortly inundate the parched grey fields, flooding them for the three months of the wet season. We knew that repairs to our yacht had to be completed before the monsoon rains came to Cochin.

The village through which the now familiar path brought us was all but deserted. Those who had not attended the festival had long ago bolted their shutters and retired for the night. To avoid several pariah dogs who diligently guarded their territorial patch we turned down a narrow path we knew would lead us to the water's edge and near to our boatyard. Our access was by way of an adjoining boatyard, where a small common gate usefully served as a back entrance to the property, a convenient passage to the village's only telephone in a house close by.

Reaching the bamboo gate Alison suddenly halted. I drew alongside and felt for the latch which I thought Alison could not find in the darkness, but her hand was already there, poised. She turned to ask me if I had heard anything. I didn't reply, but instead stood quietly listening for the sound which Alison had heard. The distant strains of classical Indian music reached my ears, and somewhere two dogs were barking, while from the direction of the river came the sound of water lapping gently against a moored boat.

Still motionless in the darkness, I was about to answer when another, closer noise reached us, the low cough of a habitual smoker, followed by the clatter of metal – somebody was in the boatyard. In the fading moonlight I could just see the outline of our yacht, propped securely at the head of a short ramp which sloped down to the sea wall. No other boat was careened in the yard, nor was the yard open to the public, so it was strange that anybody should be there, especially at such a late hour. I touched Alison softly on the arm and raised a finger to my lips before we set off once more on the path which led to the water's edge.

Out of sight of the boatyard we talked softly. Alison had heard a voice, and seen somebody walking away from the gate. We both wondered who it could be, and why they would be awaiting our return. I decided that if I crept along the wall to the bottom of the ramp, perhaps I could get a look into the yard. I told Alison to wait for me, but as I turned to go she tightened her hand around my wrist, wanting to come.

'Okay,' I whispered, 'but we must be cautious.' With one hand touching the wall I led the way deep into the shadows, my mind racing through the possibilities of who might be in the boatyard.

At the foot of the ramp we paused to listen. Hearing nothing we crossed to the other side of the opening. Again we waited.

'Hear anything?' I whispered in Alison's ear.

'No. Did you?'

'Only the sound of water lapping against a boat. Perhaps there's one beyond the end of the wall.'

We stopped short of the end of the sea wall. The sound of small waves lapping against a boat was much louder now. Very slowly I ventured into the moonlight and peered around the corner. There, on the small indented beach, pulled up a few feet onto the sand, was a big yellow inflatable dinghy which was all too familiar to us. Tilted over the stern was a powerful outboard motor. And sitting on the bow keeping watch through the bushes on the boatyard's front gate was an Indian boatman, his long fishing knife beside him in readiness. How many more were here? I wondered.

I could feel Alison close behind me. Curiosity had brought her to look, and she also would realize who the intruders were. Best that we should get ourselves far away from this lonely boatyard without delay, and well before we lost the cover of the night. From the position of the moon I estimated the time to be around three o'clock. In two hours when the dawn came we could be miles away.

Retracing our steps, we had almost reached the ramp when the sounds came again – the same cough and the same clatter of metal. A gruff rebuke came from deeper within the boatyard, followed by a woman's voice hissing an inaudible reply. Then the riverfront fell quiet, though from far off the sounds of laughter and singing still carried on the light breeze. On the beach we stood frozen, pressing our backs into the stones of the retaining wall as if trying to disappear completely.

Alison was the first to move. Her intention was obviously to leave by the way we had come. We went round the corner and were back on the path when I reached out for Alison, my hand unsteady, and both of us stopped – someone had moved further along the path, and I could smell the smoke from their cigarette. Had this person been set to watch the back entrance of the yard? Might this have been the person whom Alison had seen walking back into the boatyard some minutes earlier when we had first approached this gate?

Keeping our eyes on the figure just visible in the darkness, we carefully retreated, backing away again into the shadows of the stone wall. Small waves broke gently on the shore beside us. From the east the light breeze still blew across the mile-wide waterway, rustling the palms and combining with the distant temple drummers to unsettle us. Our predicament was frightening, we had walked right into a trap. But those who lay in wait were not yet aware they had us trapped. Our only two exits were effectively blocked, and we would certainly be discovered if anybody came down the ramp to go to the inflatable dinghy, or wandered to the water's edge to relieve themselves. We had no way of defending ourselves against armed intruders on this secluded riverfront. Waiting somewhere out on the waterway might be one of the thousand or more small fishing trawlers that motored every day into the Arabian Sea to work a coastline long ago fished out. Would they be waiting on this early morning to take our bodies in two hessian bags far out to sea, add several stones for ballast, and dispose of the bags with no questions asked? We had heard that was the procedure for a murder in Cochin. And the price began at US $100.

Tears formed in Alison's eyes. 'What now?' she whispered, her voice betraying her fear. But I couldn't reply. If only there was somewhere to hide! But yes, there was. It would be a cheeky move, the mere thought of it chilling me, and it was chancy, though perhaps not as great a risk as the alternatives – making a run for it past the watchers, or tempting our luck by swimming into the tide, or remaining on the beach to face detection.

Beckoning Alison to follow me, I set off along the beach. On the other side of the wall was an old timber hull that had been pushed into an out-of-the-way place and left in the hope that it might one day be repaired. I looked at Alison and wondered how I could explain, without words, my bold idea that we could climb over the wall and hide beneath the old hull, right under their noses.

Taking Alison's hand I sank down with her to squat on the beach, but while I was scratching out my plan in the sand, a new sound interrupted – the throbbing of a diesel engine. This would be the small passenger ferry which had departed the previous evening from deep within the Cochin backwaters, and regularly brought village folk and their produce to the city in time for the early-morning market. The deep pulses of the diesel's engine became increasingly loud. Soon the ferry would pass by, and the boat's wash would break on the shore and disturb the stillness of the night. The sound of this vessel which daily plied the vast waterways seemed curiously normal. Now was the right time to make our move.

With no time to explain further, and hoping that Alison would follow my direction, I pulled myself up to the top of the wall and lay flat on the stones before easing myself down into the boatyard and under the hull. As I had reckoned, it provided a good shelter. Seconds later Alison climbed under the hull and I reached out to touch her in a gesture of comfort. For moments I softly stroked her back, the movement calming us both. I could feel Alison's heart pounding, and so was mine. We listened to the wash of the passing ferry crashing onto the sand, and waited for any soft footfall, all the time gathering our courage to face the terrifying encounter which would come if we had been observed climbing over the wall.

Minutes passed. The throbbing of the diesel engine faded, the muted sounds of Indian classical music returned. To the left of our hiding place stood a small thatched-roof workshop, beyond which was the main entrance gate. In the centre of the yard and almost directly ahead of us was our yacht, *Tiger Rag*, its bulk dominating the small boatyard. To get a better view of the scene, or anyone else entering our chosen corner, I carefully inched my way along the upturned hull and lay in the shadow the moonlight had formed from the bow. The undersides of our yacht were now clearly in view, and there, sitting on a chair, was the woman whose voice we had heard earlier. She was not a patient person, and as she sat her foot tapped continually, pausing only for the moment when she searched through her bag for another cigarette. Again came the sound of rattling metal; the hollow brass bangles adorning her wrists turned out to be the source of the dull clatter of metal we had heard earlier. Then her coughing began again.

From out of the inky shadow of the yacht's hull loomed the bulky figure of a man. Arrogantly drawing himself up alongside the woman, he addressed her with a hushed fury. 'Can't you keep quiet? You know that if these two get out of Cochin it will mean big trouble for us! They've got to be shut up for good!'

The woman made no reply. A match flamed from under the yacht, revealing the man's face, his nostrils flaring as he sucked at the end of a cigar. Seconds later another match flamed, again lighting his face – this time revealing a hideous disfigurement that identified him.

An hour must have passed before we heard the noise of the powerful outboard motor retreating down the river, and we were able to emerge cautiously from the fading shadows of concealment into the first blush of a new dawn. Shaken from our ordeal we gathered a few items from our yacht and headed down the village path, through the coconut groves, and onto the only road that led the 12 miles to the city of Cochin. There we would merge into the press of people that is India.

It had been over three months since we had come to India, and in this time a highly dangerous situation had developed. It was a situation which common sense told us to run right away from, but at the same time our moral instincts were pushing us further into danger.

PART ONE

January to 18 April 1983

I

Sailing Away

Alison and I met and became friends at Sydney University in 1974. We shared lunchtimes on the front lawn of the campus, but our busy lives denied us the time to continue the friendship.

Alison graduated as a Bachelor of Arts with a diploma in education after studying anthropology and geography. Before she could consider herself ready for teaching, she felt she should travel. She spent 1976 observing the life and people of other lands. Returning from her journeys across Asia she stayed a short time with friends who owned a farm on the southwestern coast of Western Australia. Her first teaching appointment was at a high school north of Perth, and in the eighteen months that she spent there, Alison found teaching a joy. In 1979 she went to New Zealand to be the geography mistress in a private girls' boarding school situated in rural Wairarapa. In the ample school holiday time she toured both islands from top to bottom, often riding her pushbike.

The need to be with her family took her back to Sydney, and on this occasion she taught at a suburban high school; two tough years experiencing the disillusionment of city youth. To relax at weekends Alison began sailing small boats on the bays and rivers to the south of Sydney, near her home. In the latter months of 1981 she bought shares in a traditional Indonesian sailing boat and set off on a six-month adventure that took her through the islands of the eastern archipelago of Indonesia. On her return to Australia she took up a temporary position at a high school in Darwin, the only city on the vast expanse of northern Australia.

It was in Darwin that I met Alison again. I had just finished sailing *Tiger Rag* around New Guinea and the yacht had been taken out of the water at Darwin Sailing Club to undergo the final preparations necessary for its next long voyage. I was teaching navigation classes in the evenings when Alison came into my classroom as a new pupil on the first day of a new course, and by the end of the navigation course we were in love.

Those years of lost contact had been rewarding for me as well. In 1977 *Tiger Rag* was completed in Sydney and became officially registered. It represented three years of weekend and evening work. I had designed and built the nine-metre yacht to be at her best in the heavy ocean conditions of the southern hemisphere. After a broken period of study I had qualified as a naval architect and set up my own business, and was involved with projects, organizations and government bodies close to Sydney harbour. Designing yachts suitable for ocean racing occupied much of my time, but on Sundays I would race an 18-foot skiff on the sparkling summer waters of the beautiful harbour. With a firm grip on the 12-foot tiller I would steer the skiff hard on the fresh afternoon sea breeze to the Beaschel buoy near the southern entrance headland to Sydney harbour. Once around the buoy the two crewmen would set a huge spinnaker, and with all three of us extended on trapeze wires, the bow of the powerful skiff would lift out of the water and we would begin a series of long tacks down the harbour, dodging ferries, ships and pleasure boats. Often we reached more than 20 knots in short bursts that took us as fast as we could go on the race to the finishing line. I lived in an old house above Sydney harbour and would often look out over the bay to *Tiger Rag* tugging at her moorings. I was determined that some day I would take a break and slip quietly away for a couple of years of good sailing.

In the summer of 1978 I temporarily closed the door on my career, sold my Lotus sports car and bade farewell to my friends. Cruising *Tiger Rag* through the Micronesian group of islands in the western Pacific was a few years in paradise. In late 1980 I returned to Australia to consider my other ambition – to compete in the *Observer* single-handed transatlantic yacht race. This race, held every fourth year, sets off from Plymouth in England, crosses the Atlantic Ocean and finishes at Newport, New York. The next race was in 1984. For a long time it had been my wish to compete in this race and in 1980 circumstances put the opportunity of doing so within my reach – I had a fast and capable yacht and more than enough successful competitive experience.

When I met Alison again I was preparing *Tiger Rag* for her long sail to England, where the yacht would be brought up to competitive trim for the race across the Atlantic Ocean. I showed her the letter that the Royal Western Yacht Club in Plymouth had sent accepting my entry for the race, and she realized my excitement at the prospects which lay ahead for me. I planned to be ready to leave Australia in July 1982, but as the time approached I began to wonder how I could leave Alison behind.

Alison, herself an enthusiastic sailor, solved my dilemma for me. 'You're not going without me!' she decided.

'You just want more navigation lessons,' I joked.

She replied firmly, 'I'm coming anyway.'

Leaving ourselves plenty of time for the long voyage to England, we set out from Australia on 29 July 1982. It was wonderful to be on the sea again. Our days were spent in the company of sea birds, pods of dolphins and seasonally migrating whales. The seas were mostly kind to us, and the winds fair.

Our log entries included our impressions of Indonesia, a poem about migrating whales in the Alas Strait, and an account of Komodo Island where we bravely stalked the Komodo dragon, only to run like rabbits when a tiny monkey scampered onto the beach. On many days we set our biggest spinnaker, though north of Java we experienced heavy weather and during that exhilarating week *Tiger Rag* scurried along before a following sea. There were many idyllic anchorages for us – Timor, Sumba, exotic Bali and lesser-known islands of the Lingga Archipelago.

We crossed the equator and called at Singapore, then

made a diversion into the South China Sea where we swam in crystal waters over beautiful coral gardens. We sailed along the west coat of Malaysia and across the Malacca Strait to the tip of Sumatra, then had a tough beat over the thousand-mile emptiness of the Bay of Bengal. Being out of sight of land for two weeks brought with it a feeling of ocean, a sense of mental space. The routines of navigation, which had to be carried out three times a day, the preparation of meals and the tasks of sailing the yacht occupied our time and drew us closer together.

With the help of Alison's by now accurate navigation we fetched up southern tip of Sri Lanka, and an afternoon sail ended in a safe anchorage in Galle harbour for a well-earned rest. It was Christmas 1982.

On New Year's Eve we put to sea for our crossing of the Indian Ocean, but before the first day of the new year was over we were caught in the spirals of a tropical depression. Out of season and without warning, the storm came from the southwest; a day later it had turned fully around to the northeast. Many times we tapped our barometer, willing it to rise, but for four days it stayed down. With each day the waves got bigger – huge hollow waves which climbed up from far away till they towered threateningly above our little sloop, sometimes to come crashing down in a thunderous roar, deluging the yacht and throwing it about like a cork. For four days we braced ourselves against the awesome power wrought by this tropical depression, anxious and cold in the turmoil of our cabin, listening helplessly to the deafening gale howling through our rigging.

On the first day we tried to run before the wind and out of the shipping lane which we had been crossing, but the confused seas had risen to an alarming height and for safety we had to haul in our tiny storm sail and lay hove to, bow on to the breakers. Against our mounting exhaustion we maintained a tiring vigil to watch for any passing ship that might have been on a collision course, unable to see a small white yacht amid the mountainous breaking crests.

The third day was the worst for us, a day of horrific and unabated ferocity – and damage to *Tiger Rag*. We were below when a rogue wave picked the yacht up and flung her, rudder first, into a trough and onto her beam-ends. The extent of the damage was not at first apparent, but we had at least one smashed porthole and a broken radio aerial, and within hours we could see the bruises where our bodies had been bumped. Between watches we slumped onto the saloon floor, jamming ourselves between bulky bags of sails, trying to sleep, praying for respite.

Finally, on the fourth day, the gale moved off to the east where it ravaged the northwest coast of Sri Lanka. Sanity eventually returned to the ocean as the winds eased and the seas started to contain their fury. After the danger had passed we were able to sleep, and then assess the full extent of the damage.

Tiger Rag was built to last, built to withstand broach or capsize. Her strength had often impressed us. But now the rudder shaft was bent, causing the steering quadrant to shatter, which meant that we had no steering. We fitted the emergency tiller, only to find the shaft so bent that the rudder was still unable to turn.

The following day the sun came out and the sea conditions calmed still further, and we had recovered enough to patiently construct a steering oar which we hoped could guide us back to Galle harbour. It looked an untidy arrangement – dinghy oars and wooden locker covers stoutly lashed together – and it took all of one day to make, though with patience we got the device to work.

The going was slow. The wind, what little of it that now blew, came from the southeast quarter, the direction we wanted to go, and a persistent current pushed us northwards almost as fast as we made our slow progress eastwards. In frustration the pilot books were consulted, in addition to the on-board geography teacher.

Our alternative to Galle harbour, which lay 300 miles to the southeast and into the wind, was the port of Cochin, situated on the southwestern coast of India. It was a shorter distance away than Sri Lanka, but well to the north of our position. We had heard favourable reports of Cochin from other yachtsmen, the pilot book made good reference to it, and our atlas presented Cochin in bold lettering. Alison knew it as 'The Jewel of the Arabian Sea', a major trading port built centuries ago at the entrance to a myriad of waterways. As the only important harbour on India's southwest coast, Cochin would have considerable maritime activity, we thought, including boat-repair facilities.

And so we eased the sheets, trimmed the sails and set *Tiger Rag* on a course for India.

We smelled India before we saw the lights. It reached us on a gentle land breeze, intruding into the clean sea air around us in the way land usually does; the pungent odour of humanity. Next followed the lights, but dawn intervened before we were in sight of the outer fairway buoy marking the entrance to Cochin harbour.

For thirty minutes the port officer hardly moved. Before him on the saloon table of *Tiger Rag* lay forms piled high: the headache of paperwork that must be completed in triplicate for every ship that calls at India. The young official dutifully shuffled carbon paper in between form after form. He worked methodically, knowing that in due time the Port Authority dory that had brought him would return to pick him up, and perhaps he would be required to clear in another incoming vessel.

We sat opposite him. Gathered in front of us was another pile of documents – passports, ship's registration papers, clearances, exemption certificates and the like. The official business was now almost done; the pile of completed forms was much higher than those still to be seen to.

'Would you like some tea?' Alison asked. 'We have China or China.'

The officer laughed. Yes, he would like to drink China tea. Most of the tea he drank was only tea dust, he said, since the best Indian tea is exported.

Alison worked with ease in the small galley to prepare the

morning tea, her movements no longer impeded by the constant motion of the yacht. Less than an hour before we had come to rest off a harbour building with a prominent clock tower, dropping our anchor in the designated area indicated by the customs patrol boat which had escorted *Tiger Rag* inside the harbour entrance.

The young officer breathed heavily on his official stamp, then belted it onto a document that he passed across the table.

'Welcome to Cochin, captain. Here is your port permission. Report, please, to our office twenty-four hours before you intend to leave. Anchorage for foreign yachts is allowed at Bolghatty Island. It's not very far. I will direct you. When you approach you will see two foreign sailboats. Another one is here undertaking full refitting works.'

We only began to appreciate the extent of the harbour we were in when we motored up the main channel. The narrow entrance was spectacular. On each side were several giant Chinese fishing nets, and fringing the entrance, coconut trees gave shade to the decaying buildings of old Fort Cochin further back. Then a vast expanse of water cluttered with numerous islands opened up before us, its vastness dominated by a busy maritime world – foreign cargos, warships, oil tankers, tugs and workboats, trawlers, ferries, local primitive sailing lighters unloading a huge dhow, an antiquated floating dredge, bunkering barges, fishing boats and public rowboats.

On the shoreline in clusters were the wharves, warehouses and serving facilities. Somewhere here we would find the place to repair the broken rudder, of that we felt certain.

Following the port officer's instructions we turned north when we saw the masts, leaving the worst of the harbour congestion behind. *Tiger Rag's* diesel beat out a steady rhythm as it pushed us ahead and towards two yachts anchored snugly off a long, narrow island adjacent to the mainland. A grand building dominated the island's entire southern end and as we approached we were able to read a faded timber hoarding, barely visible below two thick, leafy

trees: BOLGHATTY PALACE OF CONVENI-
ENCE. Our anchor dropped through the surface of the
murky green water, followed by tens of metres of anchor
chain, singing a tuneless cacophony as it rattled and clattered
out over the bronze bow roller. In a well-established routine
Alison made the anchor line fast while I shut down the
diesel.

A head appeared from the hatchway of the yacht anchored
nearest, followed by a stout body, suntanned and healthy.
Another body followed, also stout and suntanned. There
was a brief discussion, after which the man pulled up the
line attached to the yacht's dinghy, and they rowed over and
gave us a hearty welcome. Rolf and Helga were German;
they had arrived a week before, and soon they would sail
west across the Indian Ocean, homeward bound. They had
come to give us a rundown on the where, why and how of
the local community.

Among cruising yachts this customary introduction given
to a new arrival in port is often most helpful, though varying
in emphasis according to the nationality of the teller –
Americans concentrate on the bars and liquor stores, the
British know the local regulations, the French and Italians
specialize in the restaurants – but the information given by
Rolf and Helga was more practical, exactly what was most
useful.

After making *Tiger Rag* shipshape we went ashore. As
always after many days of restricted movement, both of us
wanted to walk for miles and miles. Clutching an empty
basket and sufficient rupees we headed for the market,
hungry for the grapes and the fresh ripe mangoes Helga had
told us about. As we walked we took our first look at Cochin,
the home of over a million people who today all seemed to
be out in the streets. Those not hawking, begging or working
were on the move – walking, running, crammed into bright
red buses, clinging to the back of chaotically painted lorries,
piled one, two, three on countless motor scooters, or hanging
on grimly inside battered autorickshaws.

Following a roughly drawn map we turned right onto a

narrow road, oddly named Broadway, which led to the commercial sector and was thick with people, busy industrious people who smelled of the coconut oil that smoothed their hair, of the *bidis* they smoked and of the chilli they ate. The women were dressed traditionally in colourful saris, the men in shirts and lungis; almost all wore plastic sandals. Their cleanliness was in marked contrast to the unhidden public squalor. Coolies, their heads laden with sacks of rice or baskets full of vegetables, weaved by on their way to the market. Assured we were on course we strolled on, taking in the sights, sounds and smells of the street traders and people of the bazaar.

We paused to watch the work of a street barber who, with deft strokes of his blade, whisked away the stubble from the neck which had been stretched tight in sacrifice to his skill. The betel-stained pavements were the venue for street tailors treadling ancient machines, tea boys slopping glasses of steaming milky *chi*, shoe repairers sitting cross-legged mending sandals and buckets, spice ladies squatting on woven mats behind small mounds of this spice and that, and old men repairing umbrellas. Behind the street traders were the shops of the well-to-do merchants. We passed groups of hardware stores and grocery shops and, turning into Cloth Bazaar Road, found the material and silk shops. From the stench of fish wafting down from the end of this street we guessed that the produce market we sought should be off to our left.

The street took us past a gaudy religious temple complex. Outside it beggars sat, hoping for a few coins dropped by worshippers generous to the tragic plight of lepers, the deformed and the crippled, and their ragged children – all unfortunates born into a poor country which cannot stretch its national budget to provide a welfare system.

Nearby, Cochin's market stalls were abundant. Well serviced by the fertile rural hinterland, the market offered a quality and variety that amazed us – benches topped with healthy green vegetables, coconuts stacked high like cannonballs, stalls hung with yellow and green bananas, baskets of tomatoes, eggs and nuts, together with endless displays of choice tropical fruit.

That night back at the anchorage we feasted on delicious fresh mangoes and discussed the experience of our very long day, now almost past. After we at last turned in to our comfortable bunk, Alison asked when we would begin our rudder repair, a big job. 'Tomorrow,' I said – we would start first thing in the morning.

2

'The' James Charles Howard

'Someone is calling *Tiger Rag*.'

Alison backed down the companionway steps into the cabin and pulled at my big toe, which stuck out from under the cockpit where I was busy unbolting a difficult section of the steering mechanism. It must be Mr Nair, I assumed, the man we had seen the previous day about the rudder. However, he had told me that he wouldn't be coming here till 14 January, which was tomorrow.

Alison looked through the porthole. 'This one ain't no Indian,' she remarked.

Indeed, the man on the end of the Bolghatty Island wharf looked like a one-man Wild West show, having a large frame made to seem even taller by fancy cowboy boots, tan military trousers and matching long-sleeved shirt buttoned at neck and wrists, a huge cigar, dark sunglasses and a big straw hat to top it all off.

When he began calling *Tiger Rag* again, Alison rowed ashore to see what he wanted.

Amazing place, this, I thought later as Alison came up on deck with the coffee. It was dusk and we were lounging on comfortable cushions in *Tiger Rag*'s teakwood cockpit. The evening haze now hung veiled over the water, adding a mystical atmosphere to the scene by accentuating the domes and minarets of the skyline. Primitive boats were being poled along the mainland shore. They were crude vessels, simply built of coconut trunks lashed together with coir rope made locally from the fibre of coconut husks. On each boat a man would run forward carrying a long bamboo pole which he pushed into the water until it found the solid mud bottom. He strained against it while walking slowly aft, making the

23

boat move forward until he had walked right aft; then he would rush forward to repeat it all again. Another man stood over a massive steering paddle.

Would I like a life like that? I wondered. It was simple and uncomplicated, and when the steering on their boats broke they only had to go and chop down another tree.

Closer to our anchorage was Bolghatty Island, and the hotel. With the sun setting behind it, it was a picturesque sight. Built as a maharajah's palace, it later became the residence of the British governor of Kerala till the demise of the Raj in 1947. It must have been the British who had thoughtfully planted the trees which covered the spacious grounds. The trees were not native to India but had taken to the climate and grown unpruned, to become big and healthy specimens. Since independence, the palace had become an expensive hotel, a little shabby and run down, and not much used, but still retaining much of its earlier magnificence. Later in the evening we were expected there – the man on the wharf this morning had asked Alison if we would like to join him and his wife for drinks.

Alison nudged me, but I had already seen them and immediately recognized the man from Alison's description. He sat with a woman at a corner table on the far side of the tiled veranda; they were the only foreigners there. Now clothed all in black, the man had his legs crossed as if to show off his cowboy boots. On the table was the straw hat.

'Hello there. Glad you could join us. I'm Jim Howard.' The man stretched out his right hand in introduction, sweeping his left hand towards the woman. 'This is Jyl, but call her Jilly.'

We introduced ourselves and sat down. Jim took a cigar from the attaché case at his side and began to pull away the cellophane wrapper, turning casually to instruct Jilly to order some cold beer. His voice was a drawl, affected somehow, and when he spoke to Jilly it had a certain edge to it.

The woman obeyed his command without comment. She looked in her early thirties, a little older than us but obviously

24

much younger than Jim Howard, whom we guessed to be approximately sixty. Her arms were noticeably tanned and muscular, her dark hair was severely swept back off a hard face, giving her a hawkish appearance, and her eyes were hidden by dark sunglasses although the sun had set long ago.

'How are ya gettin' on?' Jim began, stroking his fingers through his thinning gingery hair as he spoke. He had a yacht here in Cochin, he said, in dry dock being refitted. We told him that we had a bit of work to be done here too, repairs to damaged steering. We would be sending to England for some parts, others would be made locally.

The beer came, and Jim Howard continued his efforts at being an entertaining host. Commanding the conversation, he spoke about his yacht, his voyages, his exploits and his achievements. It was easy to see he was happy to talk at length of his life and career.

He was an Australian; his father had been a real-estate businessman there, he told us, and his brothers had died in the war. But much of his life had been spent in South Africa, till they threw him out, he said, for political reasons. Married twice, he had three sons. At the age of nineteen he had joined the army and served in Korea as an army doctor, but he had given up the stethoscope for the camera. He told us that he had become world-famous as a combat photographer, and before he retired he had been 'the' James Charles Howard who had immortalised a few moments in history by his photographs – the self-immolating Buddhist monk in Saigon in 1964, the killing of Kasim in 1962, the troubles in Uganda and, earlier, in the Congo. He had made a lot of money during his career and now wanted to do some business in Cochin. He was also planning to write a book on the district, and Jilly was going to help. They had sailed his luxury ketch to Cochin, and now it was being refitted, though apparently not to his satisfaction.

We listened to Jim's expansive patter while the waiter, in response to a nod from Jilly, brought another round of beers. Jilly had excused herself earlier and gone to change in their upstairs suite of the hotel, returning shortly after in a pale dress and without her dark glasses. Large brass bangles adorned both her wrists. An unhappy look was on her face, and her eyes were red-rimmed. Again she sat aloof, uninterested, maybe bored from having heard Jim's yarns too many times, or perhaps the two of them had had a fight earlier in the day.

While Jilly ordered the waiter to bring plates and assorted dishes of food to the table, Jim moved the conversation to politics. His political views were very right-wing, and he believed that war was a necessary tool for world economies. Tapping his cigar over the ashtray he spoke with conviction about the evils of Communism, pausing to gauge our response before drawing the conversation deeper towards his ideals. When the cause is good one knows no fear, he said, adding that he had not known fear – Idi Amin had jailed him, as had the Algerians, and in Vietnam he had had a close brush with death. Napalm, he told us, pointing to an ugly disfigurement around his left temple.

'Don't forget your pill, Jim,' Jilly interrupted.

Jim fiddled with the combination lock of his attaché case. 'I'm a medical guinea pig,' he remarked, pulling out his pill bottle as if proud of the medication. 'Interferon.'

Neither of us commented. We knew that the drug was a new 'miracle cure,' for cancer, but the man across the table appeared robust enough, his disease apparently under control.

Dinner was brought by the hotel's young and nervous management trainees – a casual affair that offered vast servings of steaming and spicy Indian food. Jilly had ordered her favourite dishes and brightened up when her plate was piled high with dhals, biriani, curried vegetables, fried fish and buttered naan. Jim, on the other hand, told us that he didn't care at all for Indian food, and hungrily described his preference for blood-red steak. Alison winced, and so did I; both of us are vegetarians.

After the plates had been removed Jim lit another cigar and told us about 'his' Cochin. They had arrived in September the year before and had only been allowed anchorage in the harbour proper. Too uncomfortable, Jim complained, and too many idiot port officers. Worse still, they had been made to anchor the ketch directly in front of the customs house. Then Jim had found the Bolghatty Hotel, taken a permanent room, and with the help of his Cochin lawyer had begun to press the authorities to allow foreign yachts to anchor away from the harbour chaos and in seclusion off the large, pleasant grounds of the palace. After his victory, the ketch was contracted to a Cochin dry dock for a refit, and it was here that Jim expected to reap the benefits of India's Third World status – the pay rate for a tradesman was below five US dollars per day. Since then Jim and Jilly had entertained the crews of the few yachts who came up to the hotel anchorage, just as we ourselves were being entertained, evidently trying to establish Cochin as a select stop-over for yachtsmen in transit.

However, Jim's vision of Cochin had soured somewhat. After his victory over the local authorities he had made a brief business trip to Europe, and on his return, in December the previous year, he had been dissatisfied with the work being done on his ketch. The yard had charged him for the very best craftsmen available, he complained bitterly, glancing across the table at Jilly, but he had found that only simple village carpenters had been used instead.

I discussed the technical refit problems at length, wanting to repay their hospitality. As a naval architect I understood most of the difficulties the yard was experiencing due to the ketch's sophisticated construction methods, and I politely offered to call at the yard, thinking that I might be able to come up with one or two helpful suggestions.

'Naval architect, eh?' Jim seemed pleased, his mind busy calculating the possibilities. 'Yes,' he muttered, almost under his breath, 'you just might be able to help me teach that bastard Jacobs a lesson. Nobody gets the better of Jim Howard.'

The next day they came in the inflatable dinghy at noon, as they had said they would, Jim driving the outboard motor hung over the stern, Jilly sitting in the bow, head held high into the wind, like an obedient dog. When the dinghy came alongside *Tiger Rag* we climbed down into it, Jim twisted the throttle and away we sped.

Alison and I hadn't been along this part of the island before. As we skimmed over the water we saw neatly white-washed groups of small houses with locally styled red tile roofs dotted among the coconut palms. Thatch fences separated the dwellings, and the orderly dirt paths dissecting the island had been swept clean. The whir of the outboard motor was a lure for the children who ran to the water's edge to wave and squeal at the spectacle speeding up their river. The dinghy was bright yellow, the outboard motor red, and it went twice as fast as anything afloat in Cochin.

The waterway narrowed, and past the end of an old stone retaining wall that jutted out from the mainland we turned sharply to our right and towards two big timber masts. Jim Howard's yacht *Steppenwolf* was lying with its bows facing the dry-dock gates, and as the dinghy approached we were able to take it all in – a big timber ketch in a traditional style but of a modern construction not suitable to a tropical climate. She looked very tired indeed and far from shipshape – her masts were slack, halyards loose, sun awning torn and stanchions askew. The hot Indian sun had opened up her topside planking and part of the gunwhale strake was missing, perhaps rotted away. Lying in the mud the way she was, with no copper sheathing on the hull, she might expect a serious problem from Toredo worms. All told, it looked to be a lot more work than Jim had intimated last night.

On deck a team of industrious Indian tradesmen were busy at an enormous task. As Jim climbed aboard they cowered noticeably, and the cheerful banter we had heard earlier over the sounds of chisels and saws stopped at the sight of the big man. Perhaps his black clothes, cigar and hat intimidated them. Or was it just his air of imposing authority?

A shrill hooter broke the spell. Seven of the eight workers on deck downed tools and filed forward and down the gangplank into the yard, while another four followed from the decks below; 12.15 was obviously the start of the lunch break. One man remained on deck, a cautious distance from Jim Howard. 'Good morning, master.' His words came through a nervous smile.

'Morning, JP. All going well, eh?' Jim introduced him to us.

Jayaprakash, known to all as JP, was the master carpenter on this job. Fortyish, slightly built and dressed in khaki working clothes, he gave the impression of being a worried man. In one of the barrack-style buildings on the shore were his workmates, and a tiffin box was no doubt awaiting him there, but I sensed that he dared not make a move off the ketch till Jim Howard dismissed him.

Jilly took Alison below while I remained on deck to watch the inspection. An impressive new aft cabin was almost completed. Most of the carpenters had been occupied there, and their tools were scattered around. Each piece of timber had been exactingly chiselled and the standard of their workmanship was high. The master carpenter spoke uncertain English, but he was confident in his work, explaining correctly each of the steps he would take to finish the aft cabin.

Jim Howard, however, had lost interest. He stood on the aft deck staring across the yard to a small building at the head of the dry dock, which had an air-conditioning unit installed in one of its windows. 'Mr Jacobs in today, JP?'

JP shook his head.

Jim chuckled. 'He must still be in hospital, eh?'

The inspection continued below decks. Afterwards Jim dismissed the master carpenter to his lunch and sauntered to the saloon table where Jilly and Alison sat chatting.

'What do ya think of her?' Jim asked Alison, beaming proudly. She smiled politely, but did not answer. Jim pulled a handkerchief from his pocket and dusted the wood shavings from a settee before settling down. Comfortable amid the rich teak panelling of his yacht's interior, he lit a cigar and waited until he had our full attention.

'There's an opportunity here for you two,' he began, his voice resuming the affected tone of the previous evening. He told us he had to go to England for extensive medical treatment and that, in his absence, 'they' – he jerked his thumb back in the direction of the yard and sucked on his cigar – would spoil his boat. He needed somebody to carry out the more involved tasks that he didn't trust the Indians to do. And Jacobs, the manager, would cheat like hell unless somebody was around to keep him honest. If we could help him then he could help us, Jim said. By purchasing the parts we needed for our steering from England and shipping them by air freight to us, he would save us a lot of trouble. We had a few days to think his offer over, he went on, and he would agree to any fair arrangement.

When he had finished putting the persuasive touches to his proposal a silence fell on the cabin, heightened by the patter of bare feet across the deck above. Then the hooter sounded again and the workers on deck resumed their sawing and tapping, but while the big man was here, the carpenters working below decks discreetly waited outside.

'We'll talk it over and let you know tomorrow, Jim,' Alison said.

Sunday 16 January started with a glorious morning. We breakfasted on *Tiger Rag*'s deck and looked out at the hotel's splendid grounds, open to the public only on Sundays. Courting couples walked arm-in-arm; the young women wore their best saris, their hair slicked with coconut oil and entwined with strands of stringed flowers, while the young men wore flared trousers with sharp creases, and shirts that had been heavily starched. In the afternoon large family groups would gather to sit under the trees, an ice-cream stall might be set up and the wealthier would be able to buy bottles of beer or glasses of spirits and proudly sit on the tiled veranda for a while.

On a small beach next to the hotel's jetty two young Indian boys had begun to scrub furiously to remove the weed from the bottom of the yellow inflatable dinghy. Watching from the timber jetty 10 yards away was Jilly. She sat on a moulded plastic chair, a large black umbrella in one hand and a teacup in the other. Earlier we had watched with much amusement when she had come down the path from the hotel, a tall woman who stood head and shoulders above the entourage who followed in single file behind – small boys carrying buckets and scrapers, a waiter in white shirt and trousers bearing a tray, and two khaki-uniformed porters bringing a table and a chair. With her umbrella she had poked and directed until all was arranged to her fancy.

'She's done that before,' Alison commented with a laugh as we set off to join her.

I stroked hard before pulling the oars back through the rowlocks to let our dinghy glide gracefully to the jetty, where Alison made it fast. After greeting us, Jilly invited us to tea. She clapped her hands twice and the waiter came running up; Jilly ordered more chairs, more tea, and he trotted away in the direction of the hotel. Jim was in his room, playing computers. He hated Sundays, she said, so if we wanted to see him we must go up to room 44.

I left Alison with Jilly and made my way to the hotel. A carved hardwood balustrade highlighted the curved marble stairs leading to the upper floor. Once there might have been three or four enormous bedrooms on this level, but now there were six suites. In the centre of the building the formal dining room had been retained. A huge wooden table with chairs for fifty diners stood over an old Indian carpet, and a dozen original etchings hung on the wall, all of them now unfortunately water-damaged. A latticework veranda led to room 44.

After I had knocked on double oak doors, a bolt slid back, the doors opened and Jim let me in. The room was exceptionally large, perhaps the best in the hotel. Along one wall untidy piles of papers and books were stacked. A ship's compass, radio, numerous bottles of pills and some electronic equipment unfamiliar to me lay in a distant corner. Two single four-poster beds stood on opposite sides of the room, both unmade. A door led off to a room beyond. On the table near the front wall was a sophisticated microcomputer which Jim had been operating, its wheels whirring and clicking. On the ledge of the bay windows lay a pair of binoculars. The room commanded a broad view of the docks as far as the naval headquarters. On the jetty below I could see Alison, and Jilly below her umbrella, and further away *Tiger Rag* was visible.

'Great view, Jim. Does it make you feel like a maharajah when you wake up each day?' I asked.

Jim Howard laughed as he stood looking out at the peaceful scene. 'You've built yourself a pretty little boat,' he said. In making the compliment his voice had taken on the affected tone that I could now recognize as part of his persuasive routine. Jim knew that I had come about the offer he had made us, but I guessed that his unspoken rule was to have me bring up the subject. I wanted him to wait, however, to see just how keen he was, and had prepared myself to play his verbal games.

Jim reminded me he would be off to London later in the week – 'Doctors, hospitals, and endless bedpans,' he scoffed, 'and a little bit of business too.' His partner, Richard, was an American, Jim informed me, and their latest venture was being backed by an Australian, a powerful man with endless wealth.

His eyes then fell on an accounts book on the floor, and suddenly he went to it, picked it up and hurled it into the corner. Pill bottles went flying, one rolling across the bare timber floor. I wasn't sure if this display of temper had been spontaneous or a calculated show for my benefit.

'Jilly isn't keeping the financial accounts in order,' Jim complained angrily.

I picked up the wayward pill bottle and returned it to the others in the corner. The bottles contained Valium.

Jim saw my casual interest in the labels and commented in a tone of disgust, 'Jilly likes her pills.'

I decided that now was the right moment to bring up Jim's offer, which Alison and I had discussed at length. Jim was a wheeler-dealer, we had decided, a high flyer who wanted things to go all his way, but his ketch was a real mess and technical know-how was needed to get it right. I told Jim the terms on which we were prepared to work for him.

Firstly, our involvement must end on 31 March; that would leave us plenty of time to repair *Tiger Rag* and be away before the monsoon season began. Secondly, Jim was to purchase the steering equipment we required from England, as he had originally suggested, and air-freight it to Cochin. Thirdly, we expected to be paid a small weekly allowance to cover our basic expenses. In return we would work on his ketch every day except Sunday, and carry out the more difficult repairs. Once a week we would report progress to Jilly.

Jim lit a cigar. I could see that he could hardly conceal his delight. 'Make it April 30 finish, and ya got yourself a deal, sir,' he drawled, holding out his hand, ready to shake on settlement. But I stuck fast to my original offer. He again tried to squeeze a little more time from me, without success, then let it drop. Another ploy, I thought, fully expecting him to bring it up again in a little while.

He strode to the telephone and barked an order for cold beer to the receptionist, then sat down on the chair beside his computer. The display screen was still lit with an instruction. He explained that the computer was to keep his records, but it looked to me more like a rich man's new toy. When an Indian voice interrupted from outside the room saying that the beer had come, Jim left his chair to unlock the doors. Some text came up on the computer screen and from where I sat I was surprised to read military listings. After a moment the text lapsed and a new instruction came up.

Jim signed the bill and brought the beer over. 'Last offer April 30,' he tried.

I shook my head, unimpressed by his persistence.

He explained that he would be coming and going over the next few months and if we could stay till the end of the refit, then deliver his ketch to the Maldive Islands, we would be paid handsomely.

While I drank cold beer I looked out of the window at Alison, still chatting with Jilly. I knew that by spending extra time in Cochin we would jeopardize our itinerary to sail to England for the 1984 yacht race – we had to cross the Indian Ocean before the southwest monsoon began in May – but I wanted to let Jim think that I was at least considering his offer. On an impulse I reached out for a note pad and pencil that lay next to the binoculars on the window ledge and asked Jim for his timetable.

'Back last week of February,' he said slowly, 'then away again a week later, on business, for about six weeks. My ketch must be out of Cochin before the monsoon season closes the harbour here on May 31. I'll need to be in Australia then.' When he had finished speaking he waited hopefully.

'March 31, take it or leave it.'

He let my words hang for a minute or so before he replied, 'You're a hard man to do business with, Mr Milgate. But you got yourself a deal.'

3

Pandora's Box

Saturday 29 January was a very hot day. Even the crows seemed to have succumbed to a midday lethargy.

Leaving Jim's ketch at lunchtime I walked with Alison and JP, the master carpenter, through the ramshackle dry dock. In times past the Cochin Marine Corporation had held contracts for the construction of small ships and trawlers, employing as many as 200 men. But India's central government no longer favoured Kerala State with subsidies for small ship building, so the dry dock had fallen on hard times; the banks were threatening foreclosure, the management was worried and the workers were nervous.

The local café was inappropriately named the Elite Hotel. It was the best of three cafés that served the industrial area dominated by the Tata oil-storage depot and a rambling railway siding. Lunch, served between noon and two o'clock, consisted of a traditional southern Indian midday meal. Up two steps and inside the door the owner sat at a wooden desk selling tickets at two rupees each. The floor was earthen, trampled down and swept clean; the tables were rickety and bare, and the benches hard. A hole had been cut into the wall to allow patrons to reach the brass tap of the water barrel and a sliver of soap, and come away with thoroughly scrubbed hands held high like a surgeon before sliding in behind a table to await the procession. First came a bare-footed waiter with a stainless steel cup of hot water, followed by a man with a banana leaf which the customer washed with the water. A plate stacked high with hot boiled rice would be upended onto the leaf, then, one by one, came the dhals, vegetables, curries, *rasam*, pappadam and curd.

All round us the ritual was underway, and Indian hands were very busy squashing rice and dhal into their fists and flinging it into hungry mouths. A withered old man with a toothy grin presented Alison with a shiny fork, and we joined the fray. As I had been there before, I was left to eat with my fingers. After we had eaten our fill, we folded the leaves and took them to the side window to throw the remains into a trough. Nearby the crows waited raucously for their lunchtime pickings. Hands were again washed, then tea ordered.

Sitting over our steaming *chi* we talked. In the nine days since Jim Howard had left for London, JP and his workers had been noticeably more at ease, but it still had taken all week before JP had relaxed enough to talk freely with us. He was a woodworker, as his father had been, and married with three young children and a widowed mother to support, he really needed this job. But the dry dock manager had caused him misery, as had Jim Howard and 'madam', as he called Jilly. Before 'the accident' happened, 'madam' would come every day for inspection and sit with Mr Jacobs in his office and drink whisky. When Master Jim came back from abroad last December, 'the devil got hold of him,' JP told us, and Jim had thrown one of the carpenters into the water. It had taken JP a long and distressing day to get his workers to go back on the ketch again. And that very night Mr Jacobs 'met with a serious accident'. Sombody had beaten him up, JP explained, 'more work of the devil inside Master Jim'.

Alison and I were sceptical, but JP was insistent. He told us that he had heard this from Georgie, who worked for Mr Jacobs, and Georgie always knew what was going on.

'Sounds like quite a story,' I said to Alison that night; it was probably exaggerated in the telling but we felt there was some truth in it. Hadn't I already seen a display of Jim's temper? And we knew he didn't like this man Jacobs. Again we laughed over JP's account of the devil-man Jim throwing the worker into the sea, then the whole thing was forgotten.

Another strange tale was to unfold for us that week. It began when we took a trip upriver to see Jim Howard's lawyer, Joseph Vellapally. He was interested to meet us and had extended an invitation, via Jilly, to join him for tea on Sunday afternoon.

The rich and respectable lawyer lived in a modern, expensively furnished waterside bungalow opposite the naval officers' residences on Willingdon Island. It was one of the finest homes in Cochin. As we sat on Vellapally's patio, the lawyer told us he represented Jim's interests in Cochin, and he would be pleased if we were in any way able to assist in resolving Jim's differences with Cochin Marine Corporation, and Mr Jacobs.

Vellapally told us that before Jim Howard's arrival in Cochin, there had once been difficulties with a foreigner over a yacht. Back in 1980, a German who had made money in the Middle East came to Cochin to build a fine and proper yacht. A sharp entrepeneur had manoeuvred him to a boatyard south of Cochin, However, the German discovered the fellow to be a trickster and sought assistance from Vellapally, who specialized in maritime law. The culprit absconded soon after and the yacht was towed downriver to Cochin Marine Corporation's dry dock, under the management of Mr Jacobs, who was, we were interested to learn, a close friend of Vellapally's. Work progressed smoothly until the German became short of money. Meanwhile, the lawyer had mentioned the German's plight to an American friend of his called Gordon Gold, who was able to make an arrangement with the German and lend him money. 'In the end the work was all too much for the poor German,' Vellapally recalled. 'He went quite mad and had to be taken away.'

Two days later the same story came up again, and we heard another side of it.

When I arrived at the dry dock, I found JP studying a tattered old photograph of a yacht similar to Jim's. He had helped to build it, he told me with pride. I wasn't at all surprised by this, since the aft cabin built above us was almost a copy of the one in the photograph. I prompted JP to tell me what had happened to the German in the photograph, and learned that JP's friend Georgie had taken the snapshot before the German had locked himself in a hotel room for four days, terrified by death threats and claiming that he had been set up and cheated out of his yacht. Then he had mysteriously disappeared. 'Too much trouble here,' J P said, shaking his head.

But J P had been very serious, I said later that day when I related the tale to Alison.

'The man seems possessed by devils,' Alison lightheartedly remarked. 'Where does he get it from?'

I didn't know what to answer, but Alison had another aspect to add to the bizarre story. When she had chatted to Jilly on the Bolghatty Hotel jetty some days before, they had talked about Cochin. Jilly had told her that a good friend of Jim's, an American named Gordon Gold, possessed a yacht that had been built by Cochin Marine Corporation a few years ago. We began to wonder what sort of man Gordon Gold was, and how many other of Jim's friends were linked with the Cochin Marine Corporation.

In the two weeks following Jim Howard's departure for England things settled down, and February began in a subdued mood.

While we were waiting for Jim to air-freight the parts we needed for *Tiger Rag*'s steering repairs, we remained anchored off Bolghatty Island. Later we would have to find a suitable boatyard where we could haul *Tiger Rag* out, but now we wasted no time in getting down to work on Jim Howard's ketch *Steppenwolf*. There was much to be done – fitting a diesel generator and a small desalinisation unit, removing the 50-foot main mast for maintenance, repairing the electrical circuitry and trying to find a sailmaker who could repair the ketch's sails, among other things.

Late one afternoon, early in February, Jilly called us to the Bolghatty Hotel to say that she was taking a short holiday. We found her sitting at her usual corner table on the veranda. I ordered cold beers for us and another whisky for Jilly. She was off to a hill station in Idikki District, she told us, to spend the extended Sivarathi holiday weekend with her French friends, Alice and Christie. As we talked, a splendid

Indian evening glow came upon us and we were able to relax and appreciate the beauty of the tropical sunset. The sky was a constantly changing panorama of colour, and I wondered how anyone could tire of such loveliness.

But my thoughts turned back to Jilly. After Jim had gone away she had become bright and cheerful, and occupied herself with forays into the town. But now she looked tense and nervous, constantly smoking cigarettes and tearing up an empty cigarette packet until all that remained was a mound of tiny pieces. Then she similarly destroyed a matchbox. '*Tepati*!' she shouted impatiently to a passing waiter, interrupting Alison's account of an upholsterer she had found who could mend the soft furnishings on Jim's ketch. When the waiter came running with a box of matches for Jilly, I asked for the bill and we excused ourselves and left.

'What's got into her?' Alison asked as we walked down the path to the jetty.

'Perhaps she's run out of Valium,' I suggested.

At Cochin Marine Corporation our comings and goings were now a workaday occurrence. The injured manager, Mr Jacobs, began to make an appearance for two hours each day. He walked leaning heavily on a crutch, the bruising still visible on his face, as was the bulge where the doctors had wired his smashed jaw together. For many months yet he would have to take his food through a straw.

I met him in his office to discuss the work on *Steppenwolf*. He tried to be pleasant, though it was difficult for him to speak, and I felt sympathy for the man since it was clear that he was still in pain. More than just beaten up, his body had been thoroughly battered. Surely Jim's jealousy shouldn't have provoked such hostility? In conversation I mentioned Jim's name. Jacobs paled, then lost his composure. His body swelled up as if growing in strength before he erupted into a volley of inaudible rage spat out through clenched teeth. I left the office as soon as I could, shocked by the intensity of his reaction.

As I walked back to Jim's ketch, a man fell into step beside me, but waited until he had my attention before he spoke. 'You must forgive Mr Jacobs his anger,' he said clearly. He introduced himself as Georgie and informed me that he drove the Corporation's workboat. I shook his hand, interested to meet JP's friend at last. Georgie had an easy-going, relaxed manner and gave the impression that he was someone of importance about the place. Perhaps he was of high caste; certainly his tasteful clothes, solid gold watch and clipped speech set him poles apart from the other workers here. At the gangplank I thanked him for the apology, adding that I had not been offended by Mr Jacobs. He smiled warmly, then took his leave.

Watching Georgie walk away I realized why JP had been so sure of him, and realized as well that deeper than JP's demons, devils and satanic embellishment lay a Pandora's box.

But we didn't preoccupy ourselves with past conspiracies, gossip or skeletons in other people's closets. Our lives were too busy and interesting for that. Though isolated matters continued to come to our notice, they seemed insignificant at the time. One of them was the telegram.

The telegram had been in a pile of engine manuals which Jim had dumped untidily under the chart table of his ketch before he left. I was looking for information on the ketch's life raft, and read it before I knew what it was ... JOIN HETTY PORT SAID. FEBRUARY ONE LATEST ... Addressed to Jim Howard, the telegram had been sent from London the week before Jim left Cochin, and the sender's name was Merkley. At the time I was puzzled by its meaning, but busily rummaged on down the pile.

It was at about this time, halfway through February, that I first met a tall American businessman. I had taken the yellow dinghy to the Malabar Hotel jetty on Willingdon Island in order to collect some generator parts. When I returned to the jetty, a tall thin man was sitting there staring out through the harbour entrance. So out of place did he seem that I said aloud, half in jest, 'You look like a man who's waiting for his ship to come in.' My words took him by surprise, but he recovered quickly and suggested a cool drink. His business was export, he told me; last time in India he had sent out musical instruments, this trip it was to be furniture, and he was very interested in exporting frozen seafood to Europe. Later that day Alison saw the same man together with Jilly in the town.

These little events passed us by, but Saturday 19 February was a day full of surprises.

During the morning I was busy on Jim's ketch when I noticed a definite change in the workers' mood. From the timetable Jim had given me, I expected him back in Cochin any day now, and thought he might be in the office. JP was not about so I wandered to the main building to look for him. Passing Mr Jacobs' room I overheard part of a heated conversation – raised voices coming from behind the thin office walls. One voice I recognized as the constrained mumble of Mr Jacobs, saying that he didn't want to be involved anymore; the other voice was that of a loud American. Rather than the New York brogue of the tall businessman I had recently met on the Malabar Hotel jetty, the accent I could hear came from the southern United States. I lingered for a moment to listen, then, catching sight of Georgie watching me from an adjacent building, I waved to him and moved on.

I found JP in the machine shop. 'Mr Gold has come back to Cochin,' he said in a very subdued voice.

Alison joined me for lunch that day and afterwards we set off to *Tiger Rag*. When we got to the Bolghatty Hotel we noticed that another yacht had arrived, a steel-hulled yawl, and waiting by our dinghy was a hotel porter with a message from Jilly. A moment later Jilly came hurrying down the path, looking most disturbed. 'Holiday doesn't seem to have done her much good,' Alison commented quickly before Jilly arrived.

'Jim's back. But I can't get in touch with him,' Jilly panted. She handed me the paper she had been waving about and asked me its meaning. It was a message from the Cochin Radio station for relay to Jyl Gocher, Bolghatty Hotel: . . . WAITING OUTSIDE. CONTACT BEFORE MONDAY 2182 OR VHF 16 . . . Signed Jim Howard. The message had been sent from a ship, and the codes referred to radio frequencies.

I asked Jilly if she had called Cochin Radio.

'Of course I did,' she spluttered indignantly before going into a tirade on how she'd got nowhere and how all Indians were stupid.

But they were not stupid, it was just that Jilly didn't understand marine radio procedure. Somewhat curious myself, I offered to call and find out what it was all about. There was also something else she was anxious for us to do. Could we go out to the yacht that had come in today and bring the captain in? A Mr Gold was waiting inside the hotel to see him. Though first we should telephone, Jilly implored. But the number was engaged, so we left Jilly and rowed out to the yacht.

Passing by the yacht's stern we read its American home port. We ahoyed several times before a greying man in his late fifties staggered onto deck and invited us aboard. We gave him Jilly's message, but he looked bewildered. 'Come aboard anyway while I change,' he said, and placed a half-empty bottle of Indian rum and two glasses at the head of the hatchway. 'Help yourselves,' he shouted, before going below.

At the hotel again, Alison and I went straight to the telephone while the yawl's captain went to find Jilly. Cochin Radio's number was busy again, so we went to the hotel's veranda. Sitting with Jilly at her usual table were four foreigners – I had met the tall American businessman and the yawl's captain, but the other two were strangers. Jilly announced us as Alison and Brian, who 'worked for Jim', before turning her attention back to the gold-bedecked man sitting close by her side, whom she introduced as Mr Gordon Gold. The fourth man, a Filipino captain, gave his name as Ysmael.

Thirty minutes passed before we decided to try Cochin Radio's number again. While we persevered with making the call we discussed the group we had left on the veranda. It was clear from their conversation that friendship had not brought them together, and that this gathering was some strange sort of business meeting which Jim Howard was meant to attend.

Cochin Radio's number was found to have gone out of order, so on a hunch, I rang the officer of the harbour master to enquire if there was a ship anchored at the fairway buoy and due to dock on Monday. I spoke to the assistant harbour master, who read through his daily logbook. 'Here it is. A British freighter, name of *Hetty Mitchell*, standing off the fairway buoy. They radioed this morning to say that they were on a scheduled voyage from Spain to Malaysia, but had altered course for Cochin because they were having engine trouble and needed major mechanical repairs. Permission was granted for the *Hetty Mitchell* to enter Cochin and dock p.m. Monday at number four buoy.'

We were astonished by the news. Given that Jim Howard had told us he was due to be back in Cochin about now, we had not expected him to arrive as he shortly would – on board a merchant ship not even scheduled to call at India!

4
Hetty Mitchell

Hetty Mitchell, the small freighter waiting outside Cochin, was owned by Primrose Investments Ltd, a company registered in Tortola, British Virgin Islands, and solely owned by a Mr Richard Merkley.

For most of her humdrum working life *Hetty Mitchell* had belonged to the long-established London shipping firm of H. R. Mitchell & Sons. In September 1982, Mitchell's was declared bankrupt and its six-vessel fleet of coastal freighters, none of which had travelled further than Kiel or Rotterdam, came on the market. Mitchell's main trade had been to carry dangerous cargoes like explosives and most of the ships had been especially built for this work. But the *Hetty Mitchell* was different. She had been designed for general cargo work and then converted to comply with Board of Trade regulations. This had involved creating a cavity between the engine room and the hold by building a second bulkhead forward of the engine room bulkhead. The concealed space, two feet deep, 25 feet wide and 16 feet high, was accessible only through an inspection hatch of standard plating which was bolted to the bulkhead.

Mitchell's lifeless ships had been moored at Tilbury docks on the Thames while the receivers advertised them for sale. Fred Stanley, *Hetty Mitchell*'s captain of seven years, had remained on board as shipkeeper. Captain Stanley was at home on the water, fifty of his sixty-five years having been spent on the sea.

One by one the vessels were brought up, and the receivers had tentatively accepted a telephone offer of £36,350 for the *Hetty Mitchell* when on 4 December 1982 they had a further request for an inspection of the ship. Captain Stanley later recalled that a biting breeze had been blowing up the

Thames when a white Honda Civic pulled up and two men representing Primrose Investments got out – a Mr Richard Merkley and a Mr Jim Howard.

'They came from Tortola in the British Virgin Islands, they told me, and they were fascinated by the ship's range of forty days between bunkers. Both of them were even more intrigued by *Hetty Mitchell*'s layout and the secret compartment created that didn't show on the ship's plans.'

Learning that the ship was under offer, Howard and Merkley proposed doubling the price and paying immediately. Merkley signed a cheque for £72,700 on behalf of Primrose Investments. Captain Stanley was asked if he could deliver the *Hetty Mitchell* to Singapore. The tired old ship would be refitted there, and then, as Merkley told the captain, the ship could be sold at a profit to an acquaintance of Howard's.

Captain Stanley agreed to make the voyage, but he would need a crew of three, he explained – a deck hand, an engineer and a properly certified mate. He suggested, and they agreed, that Robert Turnbull, his friend and the ship's former mate, be signed on for the passage. Merkley was to send an engineer and a seaman from the Virgin Islands.

But instead of four persons aboard the *Hetty Mitchell* for its voyage to the Far East, as Captain Stanley had envisaged, there turned out to be seven. First aboard were Stephen Marriott and Willie Charlesworth, both flown by Merkley from the Virgin Islands. Marriott, Primrose Investment's engineer, was an English drifter who had no more training than his motorbike-mechanic father had given him. Charlesworth was a big, tough, 33-year-old Canadian yachtsman who had run out of money and been stranded in the Virgin Islands. Richard Merkley brought aboard a pretty, dark-haired Californian woman to meet the captain. Shelley Fern, signed on as cook, was Stephen Marriott's girlfriend and a one-time flame of Merkley's.

After Christmas 1982 work was to get underway to make the *Hetty Mitchell* shipshape. But Marriott turned out to be incapable of doing his duty, not even able to start the ship's

engine. A worried Captain Stanley contacted Primrose Investments. 'It simply won't do,' Captain Stanley insisted. 'We
must have a proper engineer.'

On 11 January 1983 Adrian Impey was signed on as chief
engineer. He was the *Hetty Mitchell*'s former engineer and
grateful to have been plucked from the thousands of un-
employed British seamen. The following day Captain
Stanley's friend, the short, round and dry-witted Robert
Turnbull, caught the train up from Kent, and three days
later the ship sailed. On board there were six, but Richard
Merkley sent a telegram that day to the seventh – Jim
Howard – who would join the *Hetty Mitchell* in Port Said,
Egypt.

In Bilbao, Spain, the ship picked up a cargo of 14.75
tonnes of explosives to be delivered to Port Kelang, Malaysia.
The charter had been prearranged in London to help ease
the expenses of the voyage.

The *Hetty Mitchell* was two days behind schedule when
she arrived in Port Said. Apart from three days of fairly
rough weather and a twenty-seventh birthday for Shelley
Fern, the passage had been uneventful. An enthusiastic
Marriott had begun to learn the engine-room operations
from Engineer Impey. The ship was now eighteen days out
of London and still a little short of halfway to Singapore so
they took on bunkers, ensuring the ship enough fuel for the
remainder of the voyage.

When the *Hetty Mitchell* had arrived at Port Said, Jim
Howard clambered aboard with his suitcases. After the purchase of the ship had been completed in December he had
flown back to Cochin, only to take off again the following
month, though not to a London hospital as he had announced, but direct to Port Said. He was aboard the *Hetty
Mitchell* as supernumerary – a position of authority representing the interests of the present owners, Primrose Investments.

On 5 February the *Hetty Mitchell* was recorded as having
passed through the Suez Canal with the convoy of that day.
Somewhere safely past Newport Rock the pilot gave Captain

Stanley his clearance papers and was taken off. The stern lights of the bigger, newer and faster ships of the convoy faded into the night while the lights of Port Suez were still receding astern. Soon the inconspicuous little British freighter was alone, and Captain Stanley had set course for Malaysia.

*

Within sight of Cochin harbour entrance a clock tower stands as a sentinel to the bygone era of British rule. Huddled round it, as if afraid to venture further into the 200 square miles of interlocked lagoons and canals of the hinterland, is a cluster of buildings that include the customs house and the offices of the Port Authority. Situated on the western perimeter of these buildings on Willingdon Island is the Malabar Hotel.

There are two reasons why this hotel is uncommon in southern India – one is its staid British architecture, seemingly contrary to Indian tastes, the other is that it can boast a five-star rating. One star is for its restaurant, another for its bar, the third is because each room has a telephone (regardless of whether it works or not), the fourth is for the telex facility and the fifth is for its swimming pool. On Saturdays the pool is closed, while they fill it up. On Sunday morning the rich Cochinites come to swim, early, because no chlorine is used in the pool, and the colour of the water becomes markedly greener as the day progresses. The hotel also boasts a splendid timber jetty with a pagoda-style roof and latticework sides. From tables there one can order tea with lemon or cream.

On Monday afternoon, 21 February, Alison and I sat at one of these small tables drinking tea. The breeze was falling away, the tide slackening and the afternoon becoming more tranquil. While waiting earlier in the Port Authority office we had studied a harbour chart mounted on the wall and now we played at identifying from memory each of the big red mooring buoys. Number four buoy, set aside for the *Hetty Mitchell*, was still vacant.

An ocean-going pocket tug held fast to number three buoy was swinging easily in the last of the ebb tide. The tug was pleasing to the eye. It flew an Indian courtesy flag from its topmast to indicate that it was a visitor, and on the stern flagstaff flew her country's flag, which neither of us could identify. We could read GEORGETOWN lettered on the transom, but the flag was not Malaysian. At the time we didn't realize the significance of the tug being in Cochin.

A big freighter came through the harbour entrance shepherded by two small tugboats. 'The *Hetty Mitchell*?' Alison suggested, but after seeing the hammer and sickle on the funnel she could only laugh.

The next ship to come in was the one we had waited to see. Embossed on the bows were the words HETTY MITCHELL; and at that time we knew nothing more about that ship, except that Jim Howard was aboard and that it needed major engine repairs. But without tugs or assistance she came through the narrow entrance at about nine knots. She looked like a tidy little freighter, painted navy blue with white superstructure aft and mustard-coloured derricks and booms forward. In mid-channel she easily turned hard to starboard and manoeuvred gently to number four buoy.

'Diverted hundreds of miles off course for major engine repairs?' Alison sounded sceptical.

Because we were busy moving *Tiger Rag*, it was two days before we were able to get to Cochin Marine Corporation.

In the previous week two harbourside boatyards had agreed to haul *Tiger Rag* out of the water, but at the last moment both had changed their minds, without explanation. In the end we had had to make use of the basic facilities at a rural boatyard in Edacochin, a place which Jim Howard's lawyer, Joseph Vellapally, had repeatedly recommended. Now that *Tiger Rag* was hauled out we were growing ever more anxious to learn when we would be receiving the air-freight package of steering parts which Jim Howard had agreed to send from England.

The moment we arrived at Cochin Marine Corporation

we sensed Howard's presence. We found him on his ketch, below decks, sitting at the saloon table smoking a cigar and talking to a scruffy chap whom he introduced as Steve Marriott, the *Hetty* engineer. Jim's greeting to us was friendly and he was pleased with the progress we had made on his ketch. He asked if we had seen 'his' new ship, suggested we go there that night for drinks and, still in the same breath, told us to come at five o'clock to his hotel. Then he climbed the companionway steps, and from below decks we could hear the noises of the workers fade as Jim's footsteps tapped along the deck. The scruffy engineer looked vacant, then grabbed his pack of cigarettes and bolted up the companionway ladder to follow Jim Howard.

That night we arrived punctually at the Bolghatty Hotel, and found Jim and Jilly sitting on the veranda having an argument. Jim's language was harsh and spiteful, their disagreement bitter. We could have left them to it and come back later, but I steered Alison on. There was one thing that I was most anxious to discuss with Jim.

When she saw us Jilly fell quiet, but Jim quickly changed his mood and cordially invited us to sit down. I waited only as long as politeness allowed before asking him what he had done about the steering equipment he had agreed to purchase for *Tiger Rag*. Without flinching, he told us that his accountant in London had the arrangements in hand, adding that he would be leaving Cochin aboard the *Hetty*, but would give us the air-freight details before he left. Jim asked us again to stay longer in Cochin, and again we refused.

In the evening twilight the bright-yellow dinghy sped us across the harbour to where the *Hetty Mitchell* was moored to number four buoy. Jim proudly showed us round, calling the *Hetty* 'his' ship, and introducing us to 'his' crew. Stanley, the old captain, was quietly spoken in contrast to Turnbull, the mate, who was jolly and talkative. Impey, the chief engineer, was peeved about something, and the other three members of the crew were uncommunicative, keeping much to themselves. They had been together continuously for six weeks now, long enough to have established a clear pecking order.

The men gathered on the bridge to talk about seagoing matters. Captain Stanley was interested to hear about the Malacca Straits and Singapore, where he had never been. I wanted to know what had brought the ship to Cochin. But when I bluntly asked them, neither the captain nor the mate answered, but looked instead at Jim Howard.

'A coupling on the scavenger pump requires repair. And the engine-room ventilator too. Cochin Marine will come and look at it tomorrow,' he replied.

My suspicions were aroused, and it was more than just my maritime training that told me things didn't fit into place. The repairs needed didn't justify seeking a 'port of refuge'; quite apart from which, Mr Jacobs would surely be the last person Jim would trust, and it was well known that there were many better shipyards in Cochin. More intriguing still was why the ship had been diverted to Cochin. Why not Colombo or Galle, both of which had been closer to the *Hetty Mitchell*'s route?

Depite my suspicions, this was not the time to press my questions. I could feel an undercurrent of tension, and clearly I should mind my own business. Stanley, the old man sitting quietly by the navigation table, might officially be the captain, but it was Howard, puffing at his cigar, with one arm draped over the wheel, who was in command here.

*

Buildings that remain open twenty-four hours a day, seven days a week, take on their own identity. Some are public and transient, like railway or bus stations, others are semi-public, like hospitals, or the Cochin customs house. From time to time all manner of people from any part of the world pass through the corridors of the sprawling two-floored customs house – seafarers of all ranks, businessmen, the shipwrecked, the prosperous, and even smugglers. Indian workers in small groups loiter in the corridors to chat a while, a relief from the monotony of the day and from their desk, straining under a plethora of paperwork.

Inside the customs house there is an office on the upper

level where few willingly go. On the timber nameboard above the doorway is written: OFFICE of the SUPER-INTENDENT OF INTELLIGENCE – M. A. MENON. The sign is old and faded. Wooden swing doors fill half the doorway, and beyond in the large room are several desks. Along one wall are cupboards, closed and padlocked, while along another are pinned graph charts of contraband seized over many years and snapshots of culprits who have been apprehended. The window in the far wall is blocked to the room by a screen, but even so, it is noticeable that the desks are bare of all paperwork. Behind the screen, usually in bright sunlight, is the desk of the superintendent, whose habit it is to sit with the window wide open. Archutha Menon, superintendent, is in his sixties, short in stature and with just a tuft of hair above each ear on a remarkable, elliptical, shiny bald head. There is a nervousness about the man that makes one instantly distrust him. Unlike the other senior officers, M. A. Menon has always lived locally and, having been born to parents of low caste, was forced to work his way up the hard way. After forty years in the Customs Department he now rules over a network of collaborators and paid informers that enables him to exert his authority, bullying blackmarket hustlers and picking off petty smugglers at his whim. Archutha Menon willingly tells all this, adding with a chortle that in forty years he hasn't had a blot on his record. When he talks there is a cynicism in his words, a bitterness even, and definitely a chip on his shoulder.

On Monday 28 February we had not yet met Superintendent Menon, and only much later were we to learn that he was then busy acting on a big tip-off.

It had started on Friday 25 February in the bar of the Malabar Hotel where two Indians had been drinking, waiting for someone to meet them. A third man arrived and they had sat in the corner and talked. The barman, with no other customers, busied himself by taking them a dish of nuts, wiping down their table and all the tables nearby, listening all the time to their conversation. Late that afternoon when he had finished his shift, Superintendent Menon had a tip-off, and the barman was a few rupees richer. The two Indians came from the north and were thought to be underworld dealers in drugs. The third man was well known to the Malabar staff – Jim Howard.

Menon had been very interested and the name of Jim Howard he had heard before. He traced Howard to the *Hetty Mitchell* and ordered a surveillance to begin. The north Indian contacts were identified, and when he learned that Howard was no stranger to Cochin – first arrival September, departure October, second arrival December, departure January, and third arrival February – Menon had lifted his telephone and got to work.

Twenty-four hours later his network had come good. Howard had been getting sums of money sent to him in Cochin from banks in London and Hong Kong. In the previous six weeks alone it added up to US$25,000. There had been more in 1982 and the woman accompanying him had recently cashed over $5000 in traveller's cheques, using almost every bank in town. On Sunday the Cochin Marine Corporation's workboat was seen alongside the *Hetty Mitchell*. Superintendent Menon knew Cochin Marine Corporation was always closed on Sundays, so when the *Hetty Mitchell* filed first thing the following morning for a clearance to sail that day, Menon had enough suspicion to have the ship searched.

*

That same Monday Alison and I were totally unaware of the troubles around Jim Howard and the *Hetty Mitchell*. When we arrived at Cochin Marine Corporation JP revealed that Jim's ship was due to sail in the afternoon. It couldn't be so, I argued, the engine hadn't been repaired yet. 'Yesterday,' JP said, Georgie had just told him so.

But the previous day had been a Sunday, and the dry dock was deserted on Sundays. A little checking proved JP right – somebody had come in on Sunday to open up the machine shop for a few hours and do some welding. Georgie then had gone to the ship in the Corporation's workboat.

Alison and I were beginning to feel edgy about Jim Howard and would be happy when he left, though we didn't want him to leave before giving us confirmation that *Tiger Rag*'s steering parts had been sent from England. But had it been Jim's intention to leave Cochin without giving us those details? Twice we had been to see him at the Bolghatty Hotel, and twice Jyl Gocher had turned us away, saying that Jim was too busy with his computer to see us. If Jim now thought he could keep us waiting in Cochin to suit his programme he was quite mistaken. I decided to have it out with him before he left. Ships come and go from Cochin harbour according to the tides. The tide would be flooding all day and I knew the *Hetty Mitchell* wouldn't leave till the ebb.

It was almost dark when I pulled the dinghy alongside the ship and climbed the Jacob's ladder. Nobody was atop the ladder so I set off towards the aft accommodation, but on the midship deck two Indian men approached me. When they saw that I was a foreigner one man pointed to a long cabin below the bridge, which I knew was the captain's quarters. The door was open and I could see several people inside.

'Passport, please.' In response to the official request I warily handed across my passport, glad that I had brought it with me. Inside the captain's dayroom nobody spoke. A bright bulb shone from the ceiling above a table, and sitting in its light on a settee were Jim and Jilly, both staring at the floor. Jim looked up and saw me, but said nothing. The old captain sat on a hard-backed chair watching a man sitting at the table listing the serial numbers of Indian currency. Wide open on the table was Jim's attaché case and from where I stood I could see, stacked inside, tidily banded bundles of 100-rupee notes. The other person in the dayroom was Robert Turnbull, the ship's mate, who sat well away from the circle of light, almost in darkness, near the captain's sleeping quarters. When my passport was handed back to me the official turned back to face the room.

I could have left then, but the scene intrigued me. I walked around the edge of the room to where Robert Turn-

53

bull was sitting. If challenged I would say that I had come to speak to him. The atmosphere was loaded and my footsteps were soft and cautious as I approached him. 'Customs officers,' Turnbull whispered. 'They've searched parts of the ship but found nothing. They've got Jim for violation of currency regulations. It's illegal here for any person aboard a foreign ship about to leave port to be in possession of large denominations of Indian currency.'

The picture of Jim Howard walking around town with his case stuffed full of bundles of money certainly fitted the man's brazen style, and must have been sending the imaginations of the Indian authorities wild. But why so much money? There may have been more than 10,000 rupees on the table – more than the man recording the serial numbers would earn in a whole year. The man standing, who appeared to be the one in charge, was slowly and methodically questioning Jim.

The mate and I sat outside the main area and were all but forgotten. Turnbull told me that the main interrogation was over, having begun a little after four when the Rummage Squad was searching the ship. Looking across at Jyl Gocher I could see that she wore a calm expression which hid her feelings well. But Jim Howard was pale and looked frightened, even guilty. He kept asking to be allowed to talk with his lawyer. In contrast, Captain Stanley looked detached and unaffected by it all. He sat patiently, answering without hesitation all questions put to him.

Before I left the *Hetty Mitchell* I listened to Turnbull's recollections of Richard Merkley, the man Jim Howard had said was his business partner. (Turnbull had met Merkley in the days before the freighter had left England.) The mate also spoke of Engineer Impey's allegation that Jim Howard had been tampering in the engine room, after which Howard had ordered that the ship alter course for Cochin.

When I eventually climbed back down the rope ladder and off the ship I felt relieved to be in the night air and away from the tension. The customs officers were still grilling Howard, so the question I had come to ask remained unanswered. But I had resolved to have nothing more to do with the dubious Jim Howard.

*

Things might have been different for Jim Howard if he hadn't lost his temper. The Customs Rummage Squad hadn't found the drugs that Superintendent Menon was sure were hidden on the *Hetty Mitchell*, but it did find that certain regulations of the Customs Act had been broken, and that was enough to hold the ship.

Jim Howard might have settled the problems if he had shown more patience. But he was kept waiting in the corridors of the customs house all of 1 March and some of 2 March. Then he lost his patience. He burst into the office of the head official – Additional Collector M. G. Venugopalan – thumped his big fists on the officer's desk and called him a black Indian bastard. The insulted head official didn't even know who Jim Howard was. In Africa, where Howard had lived for most of his adult life, such intimidation might have worked, but in India it was the worst possible thing he could have done, because from that moment Additional Collector Venugopalan declared war on him.

The case was taken out of Superintendent Menon's control and began to get the additional collector's exacting scrutiny. Probes were sent out to Interpol and the Australian government, and Menon's squad were called in and questioned. How well had the ship been searched? Who was this man James Howard who kept coming and going from India? What role did he have on this small English freighter? Why did he have so much Indian currency aboard, with the ship due to sail that night? Why had the ship been illegally taking fuel in drums instead of through official bunkering sources? Why did James Howard have the two passports that were found on the *Hetty Mitchell*? And, lastly, what business did Jim Howard have with two underworld drug dealers?

It was several days before the facts in the Jim Howard/*Hetty Mitchell* case began to be gathered at the customs house. Primrose Investments, the owner of the *Hetty Mitchell* and confirmed as registered in the British Virgin Islands, was thought to be a sizeable operation since the company's bank accounts in London, Hong Kong and Singapore held more than $10 million in cash deposits.

The question of the *Hetty Mitchell*'s fuel-bunkering irregularities became clearer. Regulations certainly had been breached. Instead of using official sources, Howard had sought out a waterfront dealer from whom he purchased seventy 200-litre drums of fuel, and had then begun loading them onto the ship from trawlers which had no customs permission to go alongside a foreign vessel. An additional $10,000 had been sent to Howard from Singapore for the ship's Cochin expenses and there was speculation that Howard's intention was to extort money from Primrose Investments. Howard had obtained an official-looking receipt for 52,000 rupees for the fuel, but the government-controlled bunkering price was only one third of this sum.

As for the 'major engine repairs' for which the ship had been diverted to Cochin, it was found that Cochin Marine Corporation had received an incredible 30,000 rupees for an unspecified minor repair to the *Hetty Mitchell*'s machinery. But when the time came for the Customs Tribunal to look into the Howard/*Hetty Mitchell* case, the telegrams sent to Interpol and to the Australian government requesting information on Jim Howard still remained unanswered.

Captain Stanley was the first of the accused to be brought before Additional Collector Venugopalan to face charges against the ship. Captain Stanley explained his situation aboard the *Hetty Mitchell* to the Customs Tribunal, and in a recorded statement spoke of Jim Howard's behaviour in Cochin, claiming that 'as he [Howard] had been appointed supernumerary I could not restrain him, and he acted totally out of his wits'. Realizing that the captain's position was subordinate to that of Jim Howard as supernumerary, Venugopalan fined him 1500 rupees.

Jyl Gocher was called next. For her involvement in currency infringements aboard the *Hetty Mitchell* she was fined 2500 rupees.

Jim Howard was last to be called. His lawyer, Joseph Vellapally, did all the talking. Howard's recorded statement began, 'I represent Zenith Enterprises of 70/71 New Bond Street, London, and my company intend to purchase the vessel *Hetty Mitchell*.' But Howard was unable to provide any proof that this company existed. Howard was next questioned over his two passports – one British, issued at Pretoria, South Africa, and one Australian, issued at Colombo, Sri Lanka. They were identical except for one detail – one gave, as place of birth, Bristol, the other one gave London – but Howard told the customs officer that Bristol was a suburb of London, and he was believed. However, he could give no satisfactory explanation of why he had so much Indian currency aboard the *Hetty Mitchell* when she was due to sail.

The Customs Tribunal found Howard guilty. Fines on him and the ship were severe – 80,000 rupees – and the seized currency of 12,300 rupees was confiscated.

Additional Collector Venugopalan ordered a second search of the *Hetty Mitchell* and Superintendent Menon's squad went in again, but this time Howard was expecting to be rummaged and nothing was found. The ship and Howard were eventually given permission to sail, despite allegations that Rummage Squad officers had been bribed during the second search. The *Hetty Mitchell* officially cleared Cochin harbour port control on 13 March 1983.

5

A Case for Cochin Customs

In the early 1500s the intrepid navigator Vasco da Gama came to Cochin. Around that time the Portuguese established diplomatic relations with the local district maharajahs along the Malabar coast, and their trading and diplomatic involvement continued for over 400 years. This incursion into India resulted in interbreeding with the local population and the introduction of Roman Catholicism into a predominantly Hindu society. Traces of non-Indian ancestry can still be seen in some of the inhabitants although for several generations their families have lived integrated into the ways of Indian culture.

Maxwell Fernandez was such a person. He emerged like an apparition on the foredeck of Jim Howard's ketch, wearing a Nehru-style *kurta*, sunglasses and a red motorcycle helmet. In a highly pitched voice he called, 'Hello, people, hello, people.'

Maxwell Fernandez didn't like the sun so Alison took him below decks. He told us that he worked as a subeditor for a current-affairs magazine called *The Week* and from his back pocket he pulled a folded copy. 'Inside the cover my name is printed,' he said, trying to establish his credentials.

We skimmed through the magazine. Maxwell removed his helmet and sunglasses, blinked severely and then, for no apparent reason, broke into a long unrestrained smile. He had come to interview us for an article he was doing on Western yachtsmen, he informed us, and without waiting for a response he began asking us personal questions.

Instead of answering, Alison explained that we weren't the owners of *Steppenwolf*. We had come only to complete repairs to the yacht and thus fulfil our commitment to the owner, Jim Howard. Alison suggested to Maxwell that his readers would be more interested in the stories Jim Howard had to tell than in us.

Another smile broke over his face, and he told us that the 'famous man' had already given him much of his time. Alison put on her best look of surprise and, half turning to me so that I could see her expression of feigned naïvety, asked, 'Is Jim really famous?'

'Oh yes,' the journalist replied. He told us that Jim Howard was in the *Who's Who of Photographers*. Jim had taken him up to his room at the Bolghatty Hotel and shown him his press clippings, his membership of the Royal Photographic Society and his Headliner's Award for the photograph 'Grim Harvest'. They had drunk beer – journalists together. Jim had promised that on his return to Cochin he would address a gathering at Maxwell's press club. When Maxwell had finished his enraptured account of Jim's greatness we politely excused ourselves and went back to finish our work on *Steppenwolf*.

After Maxwell Fernandez had departed we agreed that his explanation of wanting to do a story on us seemed like a cover for asking us personal questions. But the motives which lay behind his curiosity we didn't know.

Except for its serious implications, the customs raid on *Steppenwolf* that same afternoon certainly was a comedy of errors.

We could see the group coming from far away, sixteen men loaded to the gunwhales of a 15-foot public rowboat. When it came close to the Cochin Marine Corporation dry dock and alongside *Steppenwolf*, there was a scramble to climb on board. But as the customs men pushed to one side, the rowboat tipped from under them and slid away from the side of the ketch, leaving the men of Superintendent Menon's Rummage Squad straddled precariously between the two. Then there followed great shouting and haggling over the rowboat fare amid the general melee. The customs launch which had brought them from their Willingdon Island headquarters had apparently broken down off Bolghatty Island, so the rowboat had been commandeered to complete the journey. Georgie was sent in the Corporation workboat to take the disabled launch in tow.

The search of *Steppenwolf* then began. Nudging and pushing each other, the customs men opened and closed everything. A short time later a man whom we took to be their leader arrived in a government jeep to find his men lying on the ketch's deck like lizards in the sun. When the key to the locked storeroom on shore provided for *Steppenwolf*'s use was found, the customs men all pushed into the small room together. It took quite a time to get them out again.

Eventually a truck arrived and we saw boxes of equipment being loaded, among them sets of deep-sea scuba-diving equipment and a compressor to fill the air bottles. The equipment seized belonged to Jim Howard and was brand new, still in its original packaging. The only thing seized from the ketch was a small notebook which we'd never seen before, found behind the chart table. The notebook listed movements of merchant and naval ships in and out of Cochin harbour.

When the Rummage Squad struck a second time, a few days later, it was in room 44 of the Bolghatty Hotel. Coming so soon after the dry-dock rummage, it sent wild rumours of what had happened around a now animated Cochin Marine Corporation. One of the carpenters at the dry dock later told us the news. He lived on Bolghatty Island and his cousin, a porter at the hotel, had been made to carry the seized items down to the customs launch. They had taken Jim Howard's computer and several items of sophisticated electronic equipment, and in one of the rooms they had found, set up, a complete photographic darkroom. Jyl Gocher was taken off to the customs house for questioning, the carpenter told us.

We were too far removed from all these happenings to know what was behind them, though since the arrival of the *Hetty Mitchell* we had become suspicious of Jim Howard. However, we had seen no direct evidence that might incriminate him or his associates. Now that the work we had agreed to do on *Steppenwolf* was completed, our involvement with Jim Howard and Jyl Gocher was over, and we intended to concentrate on repairing *Tiger Rag*.

The morning after Jyl Gocher's interrogation by Cochin customs, she left Cochin unexpectedly. Her undisclosed destination was Singapore.

*

Number 26 Eastern Mansions, Jalan Kechil, Singapore, is a multibuilding residential complex with swimming pools, tennis courts, extensive gardens and other luxury amenities. In March 1983 two men occupied one of the apartments there – which can only be afforded by those in the very highest income bracket.

One was Donald Dickinson, a 31-year-old New Zealander, former manager of a boating facility in the Virgin Islands. He was waiting for the delayed *Hetty Mitchell*, still on its way to Singapore.

The other man, an American citizen, was a director of Primrose Investments of Tortola, British Virgin Islands – Richard Merkley. He was born and raised in New York State where his mother still lives; his father is dead. In 1970, when he was seventeen, he left home. Since then he hasn't communicated with his family, though in 1981 he visited his kid brother Thomas at his home in Berkeley, California. At that time, however, Richard was involved in a scam on the coast nearby at a place called Half Moon Bay.

Merkley likes the sun, which was what had taken him to the Caribbean, until it became too hot for him. In Haiti he got into trouble with the police. Soon after, a yacht he owned, the *SS Flying Carpet*, was searched and found to have a very large quantity of drugs aboard. Later his name was to come up on police files in drug cases involving bigger ships, the *Falcon* and the *Able Fox* among them. When Merkley left the Caribbean he kept his ties in the area active. In 1984 his company still operated there, and a small salvage tug he owned was registered close by in Georgetown,

Guyana. When Mexico nationalized its banks, in 1982, his substantial deposits there were frozen by regulations.

Since going to the Far East his fortune had improved remarkably. In August 1982, when his old acquaintance Jim Howard had come to Singapore with his new girlfriend, Jyl Gocher, and stayed in his apartment, the deal struck between them, and the need to purchase a small ship, was enough to make Merkley fly to the chill of an English winter. At least he would not have to forgo his comfort, since a girlfriend named Dolores would put him up in her Kensington Gardens flat in London.

That winter was behind him and now Merkley waited in his Singapore apartment for a telephone call. It came on 22 March. Nepline Stn Berhard, a Malaysian shipping agency, rang to tell him that the ship *Hetty Mitchell* would dock the following morning at Port Kelang to unload its cargo of explosives.

Early the next morning Merkley and Dickinson drove north through the island and across the Causeway Bridge over the Johore Straits separating the island of Singapore from the mainland of Malaysia. On the expressway they travelled north to Kuala Lumpur, then west to Port Kelang.

That night aboard the *Hetty Mitchell*, the crew-member Shelley Fern kept Engineer Impey company on the bridge through the long anchor watch. Captain Stanley and Mate Turnbull turned in early while Merkley, Howard, Dickinson, Marriott and Charlesworth went out on the town. Dickinson was signed on as supernumerary that day.

On 24 March at the Port of Singapore Authority, which uses a computer to keep watch on one of the busiest ports of the world, Boustead Shipping Agency filed a foreign-arrival report for the British freighter *Hetty Mitchell*. On that same day Captain Stanley, Mate Turnbull and Engineer Impey, the *Hetty Mitchell*'s original crew, were signed off and given air tickets for home. Dickinson, now appointed captain, Howard, Marriott, Charlesworth and Shelley Fern stayed on board.

The ship was then moved to Thornicroft Shipyard for

refit. Vosper Thornicroft records show the *Hetty Mitchell* was represented in Singapore by a Mr 'Murtley' and was with them from 25 March to 21 April. The works manager remembered the little freighter. 'Mr Murtley insisted that only he himself was to supervise the work. Nobody was allowed on board without Mr Murtley's permission. When the ship was refloated she had trouble in the engine room. The engine scavenger blower wouldn't run. It looked like they had removed part of the ventilator ducting themselves, but couldn't put it back together properly.'

The manager couldn't offer an explanation of why they should have attempted such a job themselves.

*

On the upper level of the rambling Cochin customs house are the rooms of the senior officials. Closest to the stairs is the office of the most senior operations officer, Additional Collector M. G. Venugopalan. In his early forties, he has climbed a long way up the ladder to get to the rank of additional collector of customs. After university he entered government service and promotion came easily to him. He is intelligent, ambitious and adaptable, but his record shows that two years earlier, a transfer brought him south to Cochin after his involvement in a matter of corruption in the district of Calicut. In India corruption is commonplace, at times the only way for someone in an official position to get ahead financially. A good officer might not be dismissed for such activities, and a first offender could be either demoted or transferred. Venugopalan's indiscretions had brought about his transfer to Cochin and the ambitious officer now badly wanted to build up a little more credit to his reputation.

In the last days of March an attendant took an envelope into the additional collector's office. The answer to the urgent requests to Interpol for information on the antecedents of James Charles Howard had finally come. There were two pages of paper and a small photograph enclosed in the envelope. Venugopalan must have been annoyed that the information had taken almost a month to arrive, and noted that it had been sent from Australia on a date after the *Hetty Mitchell* had docked in Singapore. But one reference he read on the documents must have delighted him: REF IP5373/83. SUBJECT JAMES CHARLES HOWARD, DATE OF BIRTH 30/8/1923, HAS SEVENTEEN (17) CRIMINAL CONVICTIONS IN AUSTRALIA.

For almost a month Venugopalan had been working at trapping Jim Howard, the man who had so rudely burst into his office and insulted him. At first he wasn't sure just what Howard was up to, but he suspected that whatever it was, it was no good. Venugopalan and Superintendent Menon had enlisted the clandestine support of Maxwell Fernandez, the journalist who had interviewed Jim Howard, from whom he established that Howard had once been a reputed combat photographer.

Then Jyl Gocher disappeared the morning after Venugopalan had tried to interrogate her, following the Bolghatty Hotel rummage. Superintendent Menon traced Gocher to the state capital, Trivandrum. She had caught a plane to Colombo, Sri Lanka, there to connect with another so that she could join Howard in Singapore. Furthermore, Menon found that an American had stayed in Gocher's room that last night in Cochin – Gordon Gold – whose immigration records showed he regularly visited Cochin. Gold had given his home address as South Africa and was somehow connected with a multinational conglomerate involved in the fertilizer and chemical business in India. It was known that Cochin Marine Corporation had built the yacht Gordon Gold now owned. He too had unexpectedly left Cochin.

As Additional Collector Venugopalan and Superintendent Menon got deeper into the case it became apparent to them that a drug-smuggling network was operating from Cochin. While their investigation had been concentrated on the *Hetty Mitchell*, all the foreigners they had since come to suspect of being involved in the drug network had left Cochin. Indeed, all had left within days of each other, around 28 February, the same time as the *Hetty Mitchell* had first filed for a sailing clearance – the tall American businessman had flown on to Europe; the yawl, with its American captain aboard, had sailed west; another yacht, English-registered but with a Filipino as captain, had sailed south, and a small salvage tug, registered in Georgetown, Guyana, had also put to sea.

When Superintendent Menon had finally turned his attention to the tugboat he found no legitimate reason for it to have called at Cochin, and further inquiries led him to reveal later that he had traced the ownership of the tug back to a Mexican salvage company owned by a Mr Richard Merkley. Menon also revealed that he 'understood the tug had been used to take a large quantity of heroin from Cochin'.

*

Edacochin is the name of an area on the southwestern border of the Cochin District which occupies the entire end of a long, flat, narrow barrier island connected to the mainland by two bridges. There is one road that snakes through the length of the island and a traveller on that road might see Edacochin as a large and disorderly coconut plantation lacking the uniformity of a planned forest or a planted grove. Numerous sandy paths weave in and out of the trees, connecting the small mud-brick houses built in the available open spaces.

It is said that India has one third of the world's coconut trees, and as the country is only tropical on its narrow coastal plains, it can be imagined just how prolific these palm trees are. But a visitor to the tropical areas will seldom see a coconut rotting on the ground where it has fallen, or any trunk left to lie where it has fallen, uprooted by a tropical storm; the coconut palm is far too useful for that. It provides food, oil, sweets, soap, rope, matting, building materials, copra, thatch for roofing and fencing as well as the alcoholic drinks toddy and arrack. In our boatyard on the riverfront at Edacochin there were several such 70-foot high coconut trees.

We were working there on *Tiger Rag* during the morning of 31 March, Maundy Thursday, a public holiday in Keraia. A six-inch hole had been cut in the hull and all the damaged steering removed. To be certain we could sail from India in time to avoid the monsoon season we decided not to continue to hope that our steering parts would eventually arrive from England, and instead had started to have all the parts we required made locally. When Jim Howard had left Cochin aboard the *Hetty Mitchell*, it had been under clouds of suspicion, and he had avoided seeing us. However, Howard was scheduled to return to Cochin very soon and we intended asking him then to pay us for the work we had now finished on *Steppenwolf*.

While we worked on *Tiger Rag* that holiday morning we didn't know that Superintendent Menon's Rummage Squad were on their way to Edacochin. They had been ordered to search *Tiger Rag*, but when they had left their Willingdon Island base in their customs launch nobody had thought to check the tide. A passing ferry pulled them off a sandbank and they retreated downriver. Undaunted by the setback the squad packed themselves into jeeps and were soon speeding down the island to execute their orders. But they got lost along the myriad of paths, then separated from each other. In dribs and drabs they eventually arrived and regrouped at the boatyard gate, ready to search *Tiger Rag*. While their leader explained that our association with Jim Howard had brought us under suspicion, his men emptied every locker on the yacht. Then they all scrambled off to the nearby house where we had rented a room for storage. The owner of the house, a dignified old man named Shri Anthappam, was ordered to open the door. He smiled, stepped up to the door and pushed – it hadn't been locked.

We were asked to explain the contents found inside – bags of sails, a big basket of ropes, two spars, one life-raft, our self-steering vane, two bags of our winter clothing, our grey rubber dinghy and other items needed to sail *Tiger Rag*. The man who led the squad nodded his head and told us in stilted speech that he must restrain our access to the storeroom. The items were listed and Restraint Order S14.209.83 was issued. But the goods were not taken away. The leader asked us if we had a padlock, and when it was produced the room was locked and the key taken.

Before they left, we were told that the additional collector wanted us to call on him at the customs house at 10 a.m. on Saturday, when we could discuss the release of our sailing equipment with him.

On that Saturday morning, 2 April, we were shown into a long room on the upper level of the customs house. A conference table and many chairs indicated the purpose of the room. On the walls were framed pictures of Indira Gandhi, Jawaharlal Nehru and other solemn-faced Indian dignitaries. Glass cabinets along the walls held displays of some of the more ingenious methods chosen by smugglers – false-bottomed suitcases, boxes with secret compartments, diamonds hidden in a toothpaste tube and other clever methods of disguising contraband.

Perusing the displays helped to pass our waiting time, a relief from the agitation we were both feeling. It was our association with Jim Howard, a man we had only spoken to half a dozen times, that must have brought this attention to us. We hadn't broken any laws or regulations, indeed the restraint order on our sailing equipment had been meant to make us immediately obedient to the customs chief we were waiting to meet. It was just a heavy-handed assertion of authority, and similiar injustices can be read of daily in Indian newspapers.

Two men came into the room. The first, the younger of the two, had a yellow pallor, slow shrewd eyes and an air of determination in his movements. The older man who followed him seemed to be the subordinate. He was short and bald and gave us a nervous grimace. They took chairs opposite us; the younger man cordially introduced himself as Additional Collector Venugopalan and his companion as Superintendent Menon. The younger man poured himself a glass of water and considered us, then the bald superintendent began to ask a steady stream of questions. What were we doing in Cochin? How long did we intend to stay? What were our occupations? Did we have a verifiable means of support? What foreigners did we associate with?

Alison had brought a folder of papers – passports, ship's papers, acceptance for the 1984 *Observer* single-handed transatlantic yacht race, bank receipts and the like – and handed the documents one by one to the superintendent. Once he had read each paper he passed it to his superior officer. Wherever the documents fell short of a clear explanation, Alison filled in the detail. Our information and backgrounds could be easily verified, she said, adding vehemently that we had broken no laws and had nothing to hide.

Perhaps the additional collector had detected an air of indignation in Alison's declaration of innocence, because his earlier seriousness soon dissolved into exclamations of apologetic disbelief that we could have possibly thought that we were under suspicion. His explanation was that we had been invited to the customs house only because we would be able to assist his superintendent in an inquiry that was being undertaken into the matter of drug smuggling from Cochin.

We saw surprise on Venugopalan's face when I suddenly leaned forward and bluntly asked, 'Why then was it necessary to impose a restraint on our access to *Tiger Rag*'s equipment?'

The officer tried hard to retain a friendly look, explaining that it was just a trivial thing and that in any case we should look upon it as a favour to us from the Customs Department. Thieves and tricksters were abundant in India but they wouldn't steal from us while his department were protecting our goods. When we needed the equipment we only had to ask and an officer would be sent to release whatever we wanted. I realized that it would not be wise to argue with Venugopalan; the power he held was much feared by others, and we had witnessed a little of it ourselves.

It was Superintendent Menon who set out to justify the action his superior officer had ordered. With an air of indifference he told us that in India people were uncooperative with the authorities when it came to an investigation, and often duress was a tactic that he had to employ to get co-operation. While we did not think that restraint of property was an acceptable method of gaining our assistance, we reconfirmed for the officers that we were totally opposed to drug smuggling and although we had seen no crime committed, we would help their investigation where we could.

We began by explaining our whole association with Jim Howard and Jyl Gocher, and our recollection of other foreigners we had seen them associating with in Cochin. The officers sat quietly as Alison recounted our first meeting with Howard and Gocher at the Bolghatty Hotel, and gave our opinions of their characters. I chipped in to emphasize a point here or there, but the whole story, including details of our work on *Steppenwolf*, didn't take Alison more than thirty minutes. There wasn't much to tell. With no stunning revelations forthcoming the officers relaxed and revealed aspects of what they had uncovered – including Howard's past criminal record.

Then their questions turned to personalities and probabilities. Asked how it was that Jyl Gocher had been able to sit calmly knitting through Venugopalan's attempted interrogation on the day he had sent the Rummage Squad to raid the Bolghatty Hotel, we suggested that perhaps she might have sedated herself with Valium tablets, which we had seen in room 44 at the Bolghatty Hotel. To a question why there would be an advantage for a ship carrying a dangerous cargo to be used for smuggling, we suggested a possible explanation which hadn't occurred to them. Since a vessel carrying explosives can allow no fire or welding aboard, all equipment requiring repair on the *Hetty Mitchell* had to be taken ashore. Once ashore, drugs could have been concealed in equipment repaired without the knowledge of the captain or any other crew not involved. Was this why a Sunday had been chosen as the day to carry out the work on the *Hetty Mitchell*'s equipment at Cochin Marine Corporation? It seemed that we were providing a few explanations missing from their enquiry into drug smuggling.

But we were most surprised by another line of investigation concerning Jim Howard that was introduced by Venugopalan. He asked us, had we ever seen Jim with military personnel? Had we seen him recording shipping movements in Cochin? Did we know the subjects of the photographs that had been developed in the darkroom set up in room 44? What were all those sophisticated electronic gadgets meant to do? And where were the floppy disks for Jim's computer? Did we think that Jim might be a spy?

At the conclusion of the meeting both Alison and I were dazed by the information that had been revealed by the customs officers in the course of our discussions, information necessary for us to know in order to be more helpful in answering their questions – but decidedly information that we would have been better off never having heard at all.

Now that the Easter holiday had begun with a feeling of despair, nothing could shake away the sense of foreboding. Alison and I talked and talked. Our immediate priority was to get *Tiger Rag* seaworthy. Now that we had cut the damaged rudder from the hull we couldn't leave Cochin until a new rudder, stock, bearing and stuffing box had been made and installed, and *Tiger Rag*'s sailing equipment released to us. We decided also that it might be in our best interests to do a little discreet investigating of our own. We hoped to come up with some information that we could trade with the customs chief to ensure that *Tiger Rag*'s sailing equipment might be returned to us without complication. We went back over all the small happenings that had struck us as being odd since we had met Jim Howard, in addition to what we had been told at the Customs Department. All things combined to convince us that a drug-smuggling network was operating from Cochin.

The thought of being in this nest of dangerous men was unnerving enough, but the customs officers were provoking a situation that looked set to become nasty. The customs chief had it clear in his mind that a crime had been committed, and had informed us that he had enough on Jim Howard to issue a warrant on smuggling charges.

6

A Turn of Events

On 12 April the Customs Prevention Section at Trivandrum airport, Kerala, reported to Superintendent Menon that Jyl Gocher had arrived on a flight from Colombo, Sri Lanka, and that when she had gone through customs and immigration she was alone. Superintendent Menon wasted no time in relaying this information to his chief, Additional Collector Venugopalan, who soon after gave the superintendent his orders – Jyl Gocher was to be picked up at the Bolghatty Hotel and brought to the customs house before she had time to call Howard's lawyer, Joseph Vellapally. Her passport was to be confiscated. If James Charles Howard should be following, a warrant must be ready to serve on him at the earliest possible moment after his arrival in India. The charge was smuggling.

*

I was in a bright mood when I walked into the boatyard at Edacochin. That morning I had picked up the rudder bearing and the stuffing box that had been machined to fit *Tiger Rag*, then delivered them to an engineering shop who were to weld and assemble a new shaft and rudder. As I walked beneath *Tiger Rag*'s hull I gave it an affectionate pat, as well as a promise. 'Soon, old girl. You'll be back in the water very soon.'

Another heartening thing which occurred while I was out that morning was the arrival of a junior customs officer from Willingdon Island to open our storeroom. Alison had brought out some equipment that we needed for the yacht. Early in the week we had gone to see Venugopalan and asked him for access to the storeroom. He had asked more questions about whom Jyl Gocher had associated with in Cochin, especially just before the *Hetty Mitchell* arrived. The information we gave him wasn't incriminating, but we identified the people we had seen her with.

Late that afternoon we were startled to see Jyl Gocher being led right up to where we stood under *Tiger Rag*, packing the toolbox. One of the plucky young girls from the village had brought her from the road, but when the girl saw we had no pleasure in receiving the foreign lady she scurried back to the entrance gate to join her friends.

'You've got to help me,' Jyl said without emotion.

Anger welled up inside me. 'Get out, Gocher,' I ordered. 'Bring no more trouble here.'

To Jilly we had always been friendly, and when she saw our hostility she sat down heavily on a log, put her face in her hands and started to sob in despair. 'Please help me. You don't understand. The customs men have taken my passport. But I promise I've left Jim for good, and I must get away from here.'

Jilly hadn't taken her hands from her face and we noticed that she had taken off the gold wedding ring she wore, for effect. But the compassion she expected from us now that the Customs Department were closing on her heels we weren't able to give. We had done a lot of work on Jim Howard's ketch, only later to realize that he had intentionally cheated us by not buying the steering parts he had promised us.

'Where's Jim?' Alison asked.

Jilly said he was still in Singapore. They'd had a fight there and she'd left. Then the customs men had picked her up at the Bolghatty Hotel and questioned her all day. They knew a lot about Jim, she told us in a frightened voice.

Alison suggested the obvious. 'Go and see that lawyer Vellapally, or go instead to the Australian high commission, or ring your family.'

Jilly began to sob. When she had calmed down she told us again that we didn't understand her situation, and began to explain. Her long personal confession continued well into the night. It was obvious that Jilly was under a lot of pressure, and very frightened. Certainly she had thought of us as naïve – her 'good little children' was how she liked to refer to us. We guessed it was because we were so opposite to her; we took pleasure from the simple things around us, and didn't mind working hard. She spoke openly, telling us many things about her past and about Cochin. Most of what she said was astonishing, and incriminating, but it fitted the characters whom we had seen with her and Jim, though we remained sceptical about some more sensational aspects relating to Jim Howard.

Alison helped her confession along by talking to her in that understanding kind of way which schoolteachers use when talking to errant children – part reassurance and part encouragement.

Jilly told us that she couldn't go back to Australia, since two years before, in Melbourne, she had been caught by the Australian police with a quantity of drugs. According to her, however, one telephone call to Jim was all that had been needed to get her release. We were doubtful about that, but she was insistent. 'Jim works for the Australian government,' she repeated time and time again. She had been with him in Singapore a year ago and met his contact there, 'an attaché working in the Australian high commission'. Jim had many contacts in the Australian government, Jyl continued. When he was on his way back to the Maldive Islands the year before, somebody in the high commission in Colombo had informed Jim that she had stayed a few nights on Gordon Gold's yacht, then anchored in the Maldive Islands. She recalled how angry Jim had been over that.

When I brought down mugs of hot coffee and a plate of food I had prepared, Jyl was talking about *Steppenwolf* and said Jim had promised it to her for helping him in Cochin. A $100,000 ketch for a few months' work! I let out an involuntary whistle. Alison threw me a stern glance, but I hadn't broken Jyl Gocher's rambling confession.

'Jim wouldn't sign the ownership papers over to me. That was what the fight in Singapore was about. I want to take the boat, but Jim expects me to stay in Cochin for another big job before he will sign *Steppenwolf* over.'

Eventually she lay down on the sandy earth, completely exhausted, and fell asleep. Alison threw a rug over her and we left her there. Perhaps tomorrow she would take Alison's advice and move her possessions out of the Bolghatty Hotel and into a room at the YWCA, and then have the courage to offer a full confession to the authorities in exchange for leniency.

In the morning when we woke, Jyl Gocher had gone.

The next time we saw her was three nights later, on 16 April, the night we attended the Hindu temple festival at Edacochin and watched the actors play out the ritual struggle of good against evil. Unknown to us as we walked home that night along the sandy paths to the Edacochin boatyard, Jim Howard, Jyl Gocher and a number of Indian thugs were waiting for us in the boatyard.

But luck was on our side and we were alerted to the danger just in time. Seeing the big yellow inflatable dinghy, we realized Jim Howard was back from Singapore, and though we didn't know what had brought Jim and Jyl to reconciliation, or what intentions he had for her, we did know that this midnight visit was not a social one. After we had climbed over the boatyard wall we heard his threatening words above the distant beating of temple drummers as we hid in the boatyard beneath an upturned old timber hull – Jim Howard wanted us 'shut up for good'.

*

'Tomorrow. We'll go first thing in the morning.' I walked to the bed and sat down heavily. Alison was still frightened, uncertain of what the future held in store for us, and remained standing by the window of the small hotel room looking out over a wide tree-lined street across to a waterway which was the harbour entrance.

Earlier that morning, when we had fled from the boatyard ambush, Alison had urged me to go straight to the police, but I had been reluctant. We had no proof. Besides, it was a Sunday, the official day off in India, and the police duty officer might not have been able to speak English. I reminded her of what Jilly had told us about Jim Howard working for the Australian government. Even if there was only a breath of truth in it, that made his activities in Cochin all the more sinister.

These circumstances had led us to book into the Seagull Hotel in Fort Cochin – clean, inexpensive and, above all else, very private.

After a while Alison came and sat next to me on the hard bed. She looked around the room, resigning herself to the long wait until we could go to the police. The most useful thing we could do was to write out a statement, I suggested, not just about what had happened the night before, but about what we knew of Jim Howard's activities. Alison looked thoughtfully at me, much more settled now, before she stood and crossed the room. After delving into her basket she turned and held up her diary. 'This is important to us now. We must think it all through.'

The next morning we paid an early visit to the Cochin customs house. We were informed that Superintendent Menon was 'out of station', and that Additional Collector Venugopalan would be tied up all day with official duties. We then caught the ferry from Willingdon Island to the mainland where the Cochin central police station was situated, and after a long wait, we were ushered in to see the commissioner, C. T. Antony. After listening to our report of the boatyard ambush he told us very abruptly that we must be mistaken.

'Jim Howard is a famous man, my friend in fact. How could you say such unpleasant things about such a nice man? Get out of this office and stop making trouble before I get angry.'

We tried to assure the commissioner that we were telling the truth, and pleaded that he must listen to us. But he told us that nobody from 'his police' would take our story seriously and we should forget about it and get out of his office before he had us arrested.

Feeling a mounting terror, we caught a ferry and returned carefully to the Seagull Hotel at Fort Cochin. By early afternoon we anxiously began to ring the customs house.

After three attempts on the telephone the tension became too much and we hired a public rowboat to cross over to Willingdon Island. We walked to the customs house and went straight up the stairs that led to Additional Collector Venugopalan's office. The attendant recognized us from our previous visits and welcomed us. With his few words of English and much animated gesticulating he was able to let us know that his master was talking to a big man, scar on the side of his face and a straw hat – Jim Howard. Uncertainly we slipped back along the corridor to a waiting room, where we could hide and listen.

Around six o'clock we heard Jim Howard's unmistakable drawl coming down the passage. All the office workers had gone home and this level was deserted. At the head of the stairwell the two men stopped to talk further. We could not catch all their words, but the tone of the conversation we heard certainly surprised us.

When we went in to see the additional collector he was very distant towards us, despite our previously cordial contact. We asked him about Jim Howard's visit and were astounded when Venugopalan told us there had been a mistake. 'The man who has a criminal record is named John Howard,' Venugopalan said. 'This man Jim Howard is a good fellow after all.' He told us that the investigation was now over, and that the case was closed.

Alison was visibly shaken by the unexpected change in Venugopalan. Only days before, he had confidently told us what the customs investigation into the drug-smuggling network had uncovered, and further confided that Jim Howard was involved in it 'up to his neck'. Had Jim Howard got to Venugopalan to make him suddenly change his mind? Or had Venugopalan waited till he held all the cards before initiating the terms by which he would declare the case closed? We didn't know.

Venugopalan had a smug look on his face and I turned on him angrily. 'There's a major drug-smuggling operation going on here, and you won't do a thing about it. But we'll make sure a higher authority outside Cochin puts a stop to it.'

PART TWO
19 April to 3 November 1983

7

Alison Alone

Forty hours on an uncomfortable Indian train served only to add to my despair. I had left Brian and a horrifying situation in Cochin hundreds of miles behind. Brian had become very concerned for my safety and had insisted that I get out of Cochin. At first I wouldn't go, not unless he agreed to leave with me, but he had implored me to be an emissary and go to the Australian consulate in Bombay and tell outside authorities what was going on in Cochin. Brian would remain at the boatyard to watch over *Tiger Rag*. In the end I left for Bombay on the first train after our confrontation with the customs chief, Venugopalan.

In the 'ladies only' carriage of the Janata Express, comfort was not a consideration. Women and children with possessions and food enough for the long journey had crammed themselves onto the flat wooden benches. I was hemmed into a narrow window seat alongside sacks of wheat, metal trunks and slumbering children. The open warmth of my fellow-travellers was not constrained by the lack of a common language. Small helpings of cooked rice or fried snacks were gingerly proffered, enhancing the camaraderie of shared space. Shy giggles became my company as the locomotive clacked across the barren Deccan plateau, pulling its overladen carriages.

Many hours of thought and mental preparation consumed the long train journey. I tried hard to anticipate the meeting I hoped to have with the Australian consul. Could I make these bureaucrats understand that an international smuggling ring had been set up in Cochin? Would they realize that these criminals might do anything to protect the huge drug shipments that were now en route to overseas destinations? And that it would be simple for them with their underworld connections to bribe the necessary officials, simple even to murder us?

The view from the window of the train was changing with Bombay now only a couple of hours away, and the urban sprawl flashing by the carriage window heralded the approach of the city. The shanty colonies were more prolific than I had imagined, and the face of Bombay, marked by lines of poverty, hunger and dirt, clearly showed. Littered among the *chawls* were giant film hoardings, a colourful part of the Bombay scene, while waking in their roadside dormitory were thousands of the homeless. Soon they would unobtrusively vanish into the city, the shutters of the shops would roll up, and the full pace of life would return to the footpaths. Morning had come to the capital of Maharashtra State.

Bombay's Victoria Terminus is a 24-hour event; like India, it never sleeps. The sun had barely risen when the long, rambling train wheezed to a stop. When I stepped from the train and out of my mesmerism I was engulfed by a bedlam of noise and the colourful mosaic of station life. A monumental and grandiose structure, Victoria Terminus was built in 1888, a legacy from the British Raj. Two million travellers pass beneath its gothic arches each day.

There were still several hours until the Australian consulate would open its doors for business. Before then I would have to do something about myself, since I felt as grubby and crumpled as a traveller could feel. My map showed the luxury Taj Mahal Hotel in the direction I needed to go and I set off on foot. The cool of the morning refreshed me and I paused at the Gateway of India, a grand arch with an outlook across Bombay harbour. How I longed to feel the freedom of the sea, and yearned for the peace and solace I hoped to find there again one day!

Set in from the promenade behind me was the Taj Hotel, and I approached with a sense of purpose, smiled at the commissionaire resplendent in his crisp uniform, and passed through the ornate glass doors into a scene which was in arrogant contradiction to the one from which I had just stepped. A spacious marble rest room provided me with a venue for a good wash, change of clothes and freshen-up before going into the splendid breakfast room. My parting smile to the doorman was one of thanks, and with fresh determination I walked off in the direction of the consulate offices.

Consul Ian Tricks showed me into his office. Clean-shaven, florid-faced, safari-suited, he was everything I expected an Australian diplomat in India to be. First he read the official forms I had completed, raising his eyebrows as he read. Then he requested my passport and thoroughly examined it before asking how he could help. I explained that we had been told by customs officials in Cochin about a drug-smuggling network operating there. I told him that a ship, a tug and two luxury yachts had left Cochin recently, carrying what was thought to be an enormous quantity of narcotics.

Consul Tricks asked if this was being investigated by the police. I answered that officers of the Cochin customs had uncovered the network and were investigating, but suddenly, three days ago, their investigation was stopped. We didn't know why. Then we went to the police, but the commissioner wasn't prepared to listen.

Consul Tricks asked why we didn't just leave Cochin. I produced *Tiger Rag*'s registration papers and passed them across to the consul. When he had read them I told him about the reasons for our journey to England, and the storm that had damaged our steering and led us to India, and Cochin, for repairs.

'But the repairs haven't been finished yet, and we are not prepared to abandon our boat.'

A pensive look came over Tricks's face, then he reached into a drawer and brought out a notebook. 'You'd better tell me about this, Miss McGuinness, starting from the beginning.'

His official role was to record all facts accurately and, although unsaid, to evaluate my credibility. He interrupted his notetaking from time to time to pose obvious questions. After being told of the *Hetty Mitchell* he asked, 'Is it so unusual for a ship to call at Cochin? It is, I believe, the second-busiest port in India.'

Very carefully I detailed what I knew of the *Hetty Mitchell* and its movements, and what I had learned of the smuggling operations. I explained to the Consul that there were seldom more than half a dozen foreigners staying in Cochin, but when the *Hetty Mitchell* was due, several foreign men suddenly appeared at the Bolghatty Hotel for a meeting. It seemed obvious to us at the time that they were not known to each other and had only one common associate – Jim Howard. When he had arrived on the ship they had been very active, then almost at once they had all left, but in different directions.

I told Tricks that customs officers, investigating the Australian nationals Jim Howard and Jyl Gocher, as well as other foreigners, for their involvement in drug smuggling, had searched Jim Howard's yacht and his Bolghatty Hotel room, and what they found there led them to suspect that he was also a spy.

To an official in a foreign consulate a drug story is a drug story, but the suggestion that an Australian passport holder was suspected of involvement in espionage is a far more serious matter.

'Oh. Well, hmmm. Would you like some coffee, Miss, er, Alison?'

After Tricks had spoken his orders into a telephone, he swung round in his chair until he faced the window. 'And you're certain about what you've told me?'

I assured him that I was.

A young Indian woman entered, carrying a tray. Cups and saucers were distributed, coffee pot and milk jug were set out, and then she withdrew.

'And what has become of Miss Gocher and Mr Howard?' Tricks asked.

I answered that when I left Cochin, Jyl Gocher was with Jim Howard at the Bolghatty Hotel. A week earlier she had turned up at our boatyard, saying that she needed help to get away from Howard, whom she had apparently left in Singapore. She had cried and pleaded with us to help her, telling us about Jim Howard's criminal and high political connections. A day later, Howard had returned to Cochin.

'Did she name the political connections?' interrupted the consul.

'Her confession did contain many details and several names, Mr Tricks, but I didn't come here to create a scandal. I came here to expose a major drug network. Anyway, Howard may have lied about these politicians to Gocher, and she in turn to us.'

Consul Tricks tactfully chose not to pursue the issue.

To finish my story I related the events of two days later when we had attended the Hindu village festival and almost been ambushed by Howard's thugs at the boatyard. I repeated that the customs chief and the police commissioner, for whatever reason, now weren't prepared to acknowledge that a drug network could be operating from Cochin. 'So here I am. Here to ask if you can help,' I concluded.

Tricks explained that his role as consul did not permit him to become involved in drug matters. But he would do what he could, he told me. He would pass the relevant details to the Australian Federal Police Drug Liaison Unit's overseas headquarters in Bangkok, who would take the appropriate action. 'What will you do now, Miss McGuiness?'

'Go back to Cochin,' I replied, 'to help Brian get *Tiger Rag* out of there before the monsoon season begins. And be very cautious until this matter can be investigated.'

It was early afternoon when I emerged from the consulate building and into the premonsoon furnacelike temperature. The sun was beating down steadily on the city. The *dabbawallahs* pushed their lunchbox trolleys through the crowded streets, and all around people seemed to be trying to stamp the heat back into the betel-stained pavements. Those who could had abandoned the seething streets for the cool of concrete buildings, or disappeared into doorways, displaying signs: MEALS READY. I hailed a taxi and hung on while its driver, a Sikh with a death wish and the glint of battle in his eye, raced through the tangled traffic to the Indian Airlines office at Naraman Point. A letter of request, a kind gesture from the Australian consul, helped me to cut through the 'fittest shall survive' ethic that pervades all Indian travel offices and I booked a seat on the first available plane to Cochin.

Apprehension and fears for Brian returned, though now I felt relieved to have delivered the information I had carried in fear from Cochin. Ian Tricks had not spoken many words, but his manner suggested that my journey had not been in vain.

*

In Canberra, Australia, far removed from the intensity of Bombay, are the air-conditioned offices of the Department of Foreign Affairs, overlooking the artificial Lake Burley Griffin.

That Thursday afternoon, deep within the Foreign Affairs offices, a telex machine came to line with a message from Bombay: . . .

O. BM218   21.4.83 UNC
to CANBERRA fm BOMBAY.
ALISON MCGUINNESS . . . HOLDER OF AUSTRALIAN PASSPORT ISSUED SYDNEY CAME TO OFFICE THIS MORNING IN VERY CONCERNED STATE . . . LIFE THREATENED BY DRUG INTERESTS. SHE WANTED STORY PASSED TO INTERNATIONAL POLICE. IT IS A LONG AND COMPLEX ONE . . . DETAILS TO NLO NEW DELHI FOR TRANSMISSION . . . BANGKOK. NECESSARY ACTION. MCGUINNESS RETURNING COCHIN ASAP. ACTION: FOREIGN AFFAIRS.

*

Bombay's domestic airport seemed arranged to attack all the senses at once. Concrete was visible everywhere, the seating in the waiting room was made of unyielding plastic and the lighting might have been installed by a conspiracy of opticians. Modern popular Indian music shrieked through the air and the pungent smells of tobacco smoke, spices and sweaty bodies fought each other for the licence to linger longest. The Indian Airlines staff manned their counters in an attitude of great calm, while all round them the stirring and pushing became more urgent and vigorous with the approach of each scheduled departure.

The accommodation I had dreamed of finding at the airport terminal had long since been taken. A kind lady supervisor instead directed me to a women's retreat room; a sanctuary for the exhausted on an upper floor of the building. There, in the clean and simple room, I settled down on a wooden bench for the long and uncomfortable interval till 4 a.m. when the Indian Airlines check-in counter reopened and the colourful pandemonium resumed.

Apprehension filled me as I stepped out from the terminal building at Cochin airport. I made my way past the touts, hustlers and restless taxi drivers who had been waiting since dawn for this first plane of the day to arrive, and went instead to the head of a long file of autorickshaws, pushed my bag into the cabin and followed it in. With only three wheels and a feeble two-stroke engine, these small vehicles provide an adequate, inexpensive and usually bumpy service, but comfortable enough to take me from the airport on Willingdon Island to my destination.

When the little auto reached the main road I gestured to the driver to stop. I waited until the vehicles following had passed down the long bitumen road before I directed him to make a right turn, rather than the left turn he would usually make to go to the city. Fifteen minutes later, when the auto jolted to a stop at my instructions, I paid the fare and set off down the village path to find *Tiger Rag* and Brian. As I hastened along I recalled the night five days earlier when Jim Howard had been hiding in the boatyard. I had faltered onward, as if in a weird complement to the final throes of the temple drummers, but today the morning sun filtered through the trees, shining on a peaceful scene of rural activity. Happy greetings from familiar village women comforted me as I strode on towards the riverfront.

The boatyard gate yielded to my push and I hurried into

the yard and called Brian. I was answered by silence and the area appeared to be deserted. Where was Brian? With a feeling of dread I found the timber ladder and apprehensively climbed aboard the yacht. It was open, its contents in disarray. The boat had been ransacked.

My travel bag dropped from my hand to the cockpit floor and I stared through the hatchway into the mess that was our home. Who had been here? Who had intruded? The small amount of reassurance I had brought back from Bombay had evaporated, and the nightmare had returned.

Foremost in my mind were fears for Brian's safety. Someone must know what had happened? I climbed hurriedly down from the ladder and ran to a nearby house where I knew that some English was spoken, but the neighbours could only give me the barest details. Brian had been here, two days ago, and there had been a fight very early in the morning. Brian had chased away two men who had gone onto *Tiger Rag*. When he came back he had looked frightened. Later the police had come.

Back on the yacht I looked for any message or clue to what had happened. After sifting through the mess I could not say what if anything, was missing, not even Brian's bag or spare clothing. Wherever he had gone, he had taken only the clothes he was wearing. As I walked, almost ran, back along the paths of the village on my way to Cochin, distress must have shown on my face because the conversation of the villagers hushed. I stopped to question two ladies, but learned no more. I felt chilled with panic.

The constable who manned the desk at Cochin police headquarters managed only two words, 'No English', before beckoning me into an inside office. Then he went off to find his senior officer.

'What?' The single word came as a challenge from the thickset police officer as he entered the room. I explained that I had come to report a missing person.

'Who?' The officer was as rude as the power of his senior position allowed him.

'Brian Milgate,' I replied. Rudeness was replaced by

rancour as the officer turned abruptly to stare, examining me with an obvious display of distaste, then spat out a dismissal. 'Go away and do not come again. He is not here.' I weathered the hostility, anxious for news of Brian, whose name the officer had clearly recognized. I asked if he could tell me anything at all.

'No. Now remove yourself.'

I was insistent, saying that the police had come to Edacochin after there had been trouble there. As I spoke, the officer approached and stood over me, scowling, impatient for me to leave. 'Will you please tell me what has happened?' I pleaded. The belligerent officer reached out and pushed me so that I stumbled in the direction of the door, grabbing it for support. Two big hands shoved me towards the exit. I was forced through the doorway and fell sprawled out on the dusty street. 'Bastard!' I muttered beneath my breath, full of rage. Then came feelings of humiliation, disgust and finally tears. In a state of outrage I picked myself up, dusted myself off and walked away, still not knowing whether Brian was dead or alive.

I headed along the seafront and in the direction of the Ernakulam bazaar. Perhaps Brian had been seen there. I picked up my shaky step, trying hard to tell myself not to be frightened. For my own safety, I had to keep myself together. Turning off Shanmughan Road I was again in the area I knew – the merchants' bazaar. Here we had transacted regular business with several shopkeepers and one of them might know something about Brian.

At Krishna Bhat Hardware I found our reliable acquaintance Shridar Bhat who each day sat in his chair at the entrance to his store. The bright-eyed trader missed little of the daily bazaar life.

'We haven't seen his good self in recent days. Two days, three days, four days.' Shridar's response to my second enquiry was the quaint Indian head wobble that looks like a vehement no, but is a mannerism to indicate yes – permission granted to use his office telephone.

'Consul Ian Tricks . . . Hello, it's Alison McGuinness.

Yes, I'm all right, thank you, but Brian is missing. When I got here I went straight to the yacht. Brian was not there and the boat had been ransacked. The local people told me there had been a fight. Nobody has seen Brian since. Yes, I went to the police this morning, but they won't help. I don't know why but they were very hostile and threw me out of the police station. Yes, I'll do that and call you as soon as I find out what has happened. Thank you. Goodbye.'

*

Ian Tricks sent a further telex to Canberra: . . .

O. BM2188   22.4.83 UNC
to CANBERRA fm BOMBAY.
MCGUINNESS RETURNED TO COCHIN THIS MORN-
ING AND RANG US THIS AFTERNOON TO SAY THAT
MILGATE HAD BEEN MISSING FOR TWO DAYS . . .
SHE IS MOST CONCERNED FOR HIS SAFETY. SHE
SAYS SHE HAS REPORTED HIS DISAPPEARANCE TO
POLICE BUT THEY HAVE SHOWN NO INTEREST . . . AT
SUGGESTION OF POLICE COMMISSIONER BOMBAY WE
ARE TELEPHONING DIRECTOR–GENERAL OF POLICE
FOR KERALA STATE TO DIRECT COCHIN AUTHORI-
TIES TO INVESTIGATE MATTER AND REPORT TO US
ASAP. ANY INFORMATION RECEIVED WILL BE
PASSED TO NEW DELHI AND A DECISION WILL BE
MADE AS TO WHETHER A CONSULAR OFFICER GOES
TO COCHIN . . . MCGUINNESS WHEN REPORTING DIS-
APPEARANCE OF MILGATE ALSO SAID THEIR YACHT
'TIGER RAG' HAD BEEN RANSACKED . . . YACHT AT
KOCHUVEETIL BOATYARD EDACOCHIN ABOUT SIX
KILOMETRES SOUTH OF THOPPUMPADY JUNCTION.
ACTION: FOREIGN AFFAIRS
RP. NEW DELHI BANGKOK.

*

The ferry to Willingdon Island was ready to leave the wharf as I boarded. The old timber vessel scudded and shuddered its way along the city's wharves where foreign ships, mostly from Communist-bloc countries, loaded and unloaded the usual array of crates. Further out in the harbour, primitive cargo lighters made of coconut logs lashed together sailed majestically to and from their destinations, some only just stemming the tide which ran against them. Many sails billowed in the sea breeze now blowing through the harbour entrance. When the ferry engine slowed, the port office with its prominent clock tower came into view; slightly behind was the customs house. I was anxious to speak to the customs chief who had turned his back on us, but at the same time I was very much afraid to do so. After my last encounter with the man I didn't know what to expect from him.

Additional Collector Venugopalan agreed to see me. 'Come in, my dear. Please sit down. What is it I can do for you?'

His office was large and comfortable, with regional and state maps on the walls. Overhead a fan slowly turned. I settled into a chair and watched his expression as I told him that Brian was missing.

'Missing?' He listened with patience to my account of the events that had been seen by the villagers and of my visit to police headquarters, biding his time before asking the question which I thought would have been foremost in his mind. 'And have you been away, my dear?'

I hesitated. It would be better for me to have the assurance of some cooperation from the man before telling him what he was most anxious to hear. Rather than satisfy his curiosity, I got back to the point of my visit, explaining that *Tiger Rag* had been open when I reached the boatyard, which had made me fear for Brian's safety all the more. I choked the words out through the despair that gnawed at me, but held back my tears. I needed to show all the strength I could, even if I didn't feel it.

'Is there anyone who can help you?'

His question sounded to me more like a probe, and again I felt suspicious of this man who so recently had not been forthright and truthful to us. I answered that I had come to him for help.

'Yes, my dear. Of course I will help you.' Having been put on the spot Venugopalan had committed himself to assisting.

'Have you been to see your Australian government officials here?' The additional collector was no longer able to mask his anxiety to know where I had been when I too must have been posted as missing. I told him that I had telephoned them, that they were very concerned to hear that there had been foul play at the boatyard, and that they suggested a consular official might be sent to Cochin.

My answer must have hit home, because the customs chief lost some of his composure. 'Brian may have gone for a rest, my dear. He was looking very tired when I last saw him. He will turn up safe and well, and back in Cochin before very long.'

Venugopalan's words seemed to have a ring of conviction in them, or was that just my wishful thinking? Chattering voices could be heard somewhere in the building, someone in Indian slippers shuffled up the corridor, outside the window ubiquitous Kerala crows cawed, and a tugboat whistle tooted out its commands – but in the office there was silence. We had reached an impasse.

Finally Venugopalan smiled at me, sat up in his chair and said, with veiled concern, 'Tomorrow, my dear. If your Brian is still missing tomorrow, you come and see me and we will do what we can do.'

Out in the street again I felt more at ease. But I did not trust the customs chief, who knew more than the little he was prepared to tell. Somehow I knew that he held a clue to the mystery.

The Malabar Hotel was my next call. Today the telephone was working and the conversation I had with Maxwell Fernandez, the journalist, was brief and to the point. He agreed to come to the boatyard at five o'clock.

It was three in the afternoon when the gateman saluted my exit from the Malabar Hotel, and a two-minute walk took me to the commuters' wharf at the end of the island. A public boatman rowed me across the narrow harbour channel to Fort Cochin, which stands on the southern side of the entrance to Cochin harbour, where I hailed an autorickshaw for the five-minute ride to my next destination – Fort Cochin post office. Today the old quarter of the town, where I had often walked with Brian, brought me no joy. The nightmare I was living in was all too real.

The little auto whined on past the ancient Portuguese church and stopped at the adjacent post-office building. A letter was there from my mother with a date stamp that revealed it had arrived four days earlier. But no message from Brian. I felt shattered by this disappointment, and was running out of places to look. Brian could not have known exactly when I was coming back from Bombay, but he would surely have left a message for me if he had decided to leave Cochin.

The afternoon shadows were beginning to creep away from the sun when the door of the bus swung open at the Edacochin stop, and as the bus sped away I set off down the village path towards the boatyard to await my visitor. If anybody could help me solve the mystery of Brian's absence, it was Maxwell Fernandez. He knew more of certain covert activities than we did; apart from his role as informer to Venugopalan, Fernandez had struck up an association with Jim Howard. But could we trust him? Fernandez had been seen too many times in the company of Jim Howard and various foreigners who we knew were Howard's inner circle. But now I needed to know what Fernandez knew, what he may have heard whispered by those people who stood beyond the middle ground.

I was not tired, though I had had only little sleep. All day I had not eaten, yet there was no hunger in me. As I strode on down the path to the boatyard I had only one consuming need; I needed to find the man I loved.

8

On the Run

There wasn't enough time for me to leave a message for Alison explaining my absence from Cochin, as it turned out, but there was plenty of time that day, 20 April, to reflect on the early-morning boatyard incident that had brought about my sudden decision to run for Madras, to inform senior officials there just what was happening in Cochin.

Shortly before dawn that Wednesday I was dozing in the cockpit of *Tiger Rag* when something disturbed me. In the murky light I could just see two men on the yacht's foredeck, one of whom seemed to be reaching inside the hatch. I jumped up and rushed forward, shrieking an involuntary battle cry. I crashed into one Indian and sent him reeling backwards with a squeal, over the side of the yacht and down the nine feet to the ground. Like a madman I grabbed the second as he was recoiling from the forehatch and to-gether we toppled off the yacht's deck.

The two Indians must have been as startled by the ferocity of my attack as I was; the first one was running hard for the boatyard gate by the time I had picked myself up from the ground and the second was scrambling after the first. I leaped after him, grabbing his shirt and twisting him round, but it wasn't enough to hold him. I chased the two through the village, sending hens, dogs and ducks scattering. When they reached the main road I was still in hot pursuit, but tiring, and I realized that both must have been startled enough to run all the way to Ernakulam.

I returned to the boatyard feeling shaken and full of apprehension at why the two men had come. Back on board *Tiger Rag* a possible explanation occurred to me and I began a frantic search. I found the little plastic bag filled with a white powdery substance within reach of the forehatch. Its contents weighed about half a kilo and tasted bitter – I suspected it was heroin. The two men had been sent to plant drugs aboard, and I guessed that the Customs Department were to receive an anonymous tip-off and the Rummage Squad would be on their way, so I threw the evil package as far out into the river as possible.

To plant *Tiger Rag* with drugs seemed an obvious plan when I gave it more consideration. There was something in it for everybody, except us – Venugopalan's reputation would be enhanced by the bust, the pressure to silence us would be off the drug network, and *Tiger Rag* would be confiscated, later to be sold cheaply and perhaps used for a drug run back to Australia. I decided to go to the village's only telephone, in a house further along the riverfront, to phone Venugopalan myself and invite him to come with his customs officers and search *Tiger Rag*.

After stopping to assure the boatyard neighbours I wasn't hurt, I walked along the twisting riverfront path to the telephone. When the phone at Venugopalan's residence was answered I introduced myself and asked to speak to him, but was told that he didn't intend to speak to me.

I started to make my way back to the boatyard, uncertain about what I should do next, when I saw two heavy-looking Indians coming towards me along the path. I couldn't remember having ever seen either in the village, and to avoid them I turned down a path which led away from the riverfront. The two men turned in the same direction. I jumped down to a dry earth field and began to run. They broke into a run, too. As I was being chased, I made the sudden decision to go to Madras for help.

I didn't know exactly who was following me when I left Cochin, but when I was on a bus 40 miles to the north I saw four or five men in a Mahindra jeep. I saw the same men when I got on a northbound train around midday, and I found out later that those men weren't the only ones who followed me out of Cochin.

I changed to a Madras train at a midsouthern Indian

junction and started to recognize the men trailing me. They weren't hard to pick out. The official-looking group of four or five, wearing government-issue working boots, had discreetly taken positions in the next carriage. Another two, with the tough look of thugs, were in the same carriage as I was, but at the opposite end.

An hour later, when the slow regional train stopped at an important station, I had thought of a way to outsmart them. I joined the crowd of passengers getting down to go to the toilet or for a glass of hot tea. My idea was to show to those following me a routine at every stop. Late in the night, when they were napping, I would make my move. When I boarded the train again I noticed one of the official group lurking midway down my carriage.

The long hours of Indian twilight made most of the passengers drowsy. Someone asked me the time. I looked up and recognized the man as the official type who had joined the car several stations back. He had chosen his time well and had worked his way through the passengers and their baggage to the end where I sat on the corner of a wooden bench. He stood hunched over, wanting to give the appearance that he was just another traveller. A minute or so after I had told him the time he again looked at me and smiled, wanting to communicate with me. His clothes were rumpled but surprisingly still clean, although the polish on his boots had been scuffed. The ends of his teeth were tinged black and red, a sign that at one time in his youth he had been an avid chewer of betel nut. 'Cochin?' he asked.

I answered yes in Malayalam, the language of Kerala State, now lying far to the south. He nodded his head without looking at me.

I didn't think he would speak much English, though I was certain that he had come to talk to me about something. He asked me if I knew Mr Howard, but seemed unable to understand my answer. He mentioned the name Gordon Gold. Confusion must have shown on my face. He indicated the two thugs, just visible standing asleep together at the end of the car.

I asked him if he was a customs officer from Cochin, but then his English conveniently failed him, and he slipped away.

The train stopped close to midnight at a district junction. I got off the train and watched the station come to life. The now familiar faces of my followers were never far away as I stretched my tired body. I walked briskly up and down the narrow strip of concrete beside the carriage in which I had been travelling, until all my muscles began to liven up. When the whistle blew I joined the carriage immediately and regained my seat. As the last stray passenger crowded onto the train and a second whistle blew, I felt the train jolt forward. Then I stood up and leaped quickly towards the door. The passengers hadn't settled as yet and there was still confusion. The train was moving off slowly when I swung out onto a rung and jumped the two steps down. I hit the platform running and swerved towards a staircase under an exit sign. I didn't hear any footsteps running down the stairs, nor did I wait to discover if the emergency stop on the train had been pulled.

The attendant at the barrier looked at my almost half used Madras ticket and shrugged. I took off through the gateway to the street. The usual *chi* stalls with their open fires lit the sleepy junction. I slid off into the darkness down the first street I could find, without turning to see if anybody was still tailing me.

Two miles from the station I came to a main road. I took a left turn that would lead me to Bangalore City where I could turn east for Madras. After dawn a concrete delivery truck gave me a lift, and a few hours' relief from walking the road made me feel easier, but at noon I was walking again. I stopped for a meal at a small group of cafés beyond a rural town, a place where truck drivers also stopped for their meals. Ahead, farther into the countryside, was the Karnataka border revenue checkpoint, and to the east and running parallel to my northerly route were the Ghats — mountain ranges that divide the subcontinent east to west. On the other side of the Ghats were the plains of Tamil

Nadu State. Madras, its capital city, was my destination, but no roads crossed the high ranges that I could see rising out of the plains about 25 miles away.

I put word out at the cafés that I was looking for a ride to Bangalore and had a few rupees to pay, and an hour later I had a taker. The driver spoke no English but with the help of an interpreter we settled on a fare. The truck was a big one, transporting a large machine. In the cabin I joined three other passengers and I started to feel more at ease as we pulled out from the truck stop. Then suddenly I went cold. Parked on the fringe was a green van and sitting in the driver's seat was a man I recognized as one of the thugs.

Late at night the truck stopped again and I woke up. I had drifted off into an exhausted doze from the miles of lonely winding road. The driver was a sullen man and my fellow passengers had found it difficult to make themselves heard above the noise of the crude diesel engine.

We had driven into an open area where a number of similar vehicles were parked. Another revenue checkpoint, I decided, as the driver climbed down with a clipboard and shuffled off towards a small, well-lit building that dominated the clearing. I looked about warily for the green van but the night was too dark to see into the shadows. When the driver returned he called to the other three passengers to get out and there followed a serious conversation with much head-shaking before the trio returned and resumed their positions. Bangalore City was still hours away and I felt I should continue on.

In the early hours of the morning the truck pulled over on a deserted stretch of road and the headlamps were extinguished. We had just passed through what I guessed to be a forest and all about was quiet. The driver spoke to the other passengers, who climbed down from the cabin and disappeared in different directions into the darkness. Something about their unified action made me feel uneasy, and leaning across, I looked into the truck's wing mirror. I could see the lights of a vehicle which had stopped at a distance of

200 feet behind. Sliding over to the passenger's side I dropped to the ground and in a crouch moved forward to a huge tree, the branches of which crowned the roadway. I crossed to the far side of the road and hid in a cluster of young trees. My breathing was rapid as I watched the black form of the truck and waited.

A minute later a dark figure approached from behind the vehicle, moved down its right-hand side, climbed onto the small step below the driver's door and peered into the cab. When the figure dropped back to the ground he let out a call which pierced the silence. An answer came from far off in the bush to my left. Two, then three more replies followed from the trees on the other side of the road. From the rear of the truck a torch beam flashed on.

That made too many people. I turned into the bushes and scrambled off in panic. A bullet whistled through the air somewhere above my head an instant before I heard the crack of the gun that fired it. A second crack came but I didn't hear the bullet pass – I was 30 feet from the road and running fast over broken ground. Behind me there was shouting, but I had got away.

When the sun rose above the Ghats I was miles to the northeast, having found a rutted track that must have been used by oxen and carts only. The terrain I was passing through was in stark contrast to the fertile, well-watered landscape of Kerala. The fields were fallow and the scattered huts bore stark witness to the extreme poverty of the inhabitants. There appeared to be no roads, only well-trodden paths and tracks like the one on which I walked. I was obviously an intruder and it was impossible not to be openly observed, and I felt relief that there were no roads between me and the mountain range, which rose sharply out of the plateau. Anyone following me would have to do so on foot, and I was setting a steady pace towards the pass in the ranges that I could see ahead.

By the afternoon I was climbing a winding trail between rocky outcrops. Hours later it was a little-used goat track and near the top of the pass I had to force my aching body step by step onward. As I descended into Tamil Nadu State I started to come across scattered communities of goat herders and small farms. At one humble dwelling I stopped to ask for water, and the kindness I received from the family there was overwhelming. I rested for a little while, and they fed me and gave me water to bathe in. They offered me a bed, but I had to keep moving.

I came to a small village in the early evening, and soon after I was on a bus heading for a junction town of regional importance, a place where I had been told I could catch a train to Madras.

The railway station was deserted except for the station master. The train was due at midnight and not until shortly before would the ticket office open. I left the platform, thinking that it would be the obvious place for my pursuers to look if they hadn't lost my scent. But not 100 yards from the station I faltered. Drawn up together were the buses that serviced the local area, and the man questioning the driver saw me and recognized me as I saw him. Across the fifty paces of distance between us, the remarkable bald head of Archutha Menon was unmistakable.

In terror I took flight. I feared the worst, especially as the superintendent's mission must be unofficial, his jurisdiction having ended two states behind.

That night I slept in a tiny temple high up on a barren hill. Many miles away across the open plain were the lights of the regional town. My muscles ached with cramp and my limbs were scratched and bruised, but nevertheless I slept deeply on the cold stone floor.

The next morning I could see the extent of my predicament. I was a captive of the terrain I had walked into. It was a valley with high ranges and cliffs on three sides, and the town, in the direction I had to go, was on the fourth.

I caught a bus about midday and thought I was in the clear, but having blond hair, blue eyes, white skin and torn clothes I was totally conspicuous. When a jeep I thought I recognized passed at speed I wasn't so sure I had escaped. Then later, when two unsavoury characters boarded the bus as it moved off and then ordered an old woman who sat behind me to change to another seat, I had no doubts. I moved fast. In four bounds I was on the bottom step of the rear door, and the fifth bound took me into midair. The commotion of the passengers brought the bus to a halt about 100 yards further on, but by then I had picked myself up from the embankment down which I had sprawled and was heading towards the centre of town.

As I walked into the town's police station, the conversation of the duty policemen stopped at the sight of my bleeding body. Inside the Harur District police headquarters I waited for the inspector to be brought back from his lunch. Blood from the grazes on my body dripped on the floor but I did my best not to leave a mess.

When several young constables stood to attention I sensed the arrival of the inspector. He was younger than I had expected and looked smart in his khaki uniform. There were no formalities when I was ushered into his office; he came right to the point and asked me what I wanted from him. 'Police protection,' I answered, and explained the events of the preceding forty-eight hours. He listened in silence before speaking to an aide standing near his desk. An old man was called into the office and stood before the inspector's desk. It was the bus driver, and I assumed he was relating the events on his bus, turning cautiously to look at me. After he had been dismissed, a young man entered the office, snapped a salute, then spoke. Another man, a little out of breath, appeared at the door, and after he had spoken the inspector again turned his attention to me, satisfied that I had told him the truth about what had happened in his town.

I told the inspector that I wanted a police escort to Madras since I had important information to pass along to the Directorate of Revenue Intelligence (DRI). A discussion started about my drug information and of reasons why the Cochin customs chief might have closed the case. No DRI office had been established in Cochin, despite its importance as a major seaport. The DRI was a federal body, the Customs Department in Cochin only a state organization. I hoped that the DRI would urge their masters in the central Indian government to order a more thorough investigation.

The inspector heard me out before telling me that while he couldn't be sure of me, he was sure that today a number of Kerala State customs officials had unexpectedly arrived in town. He needed time to sort the matter out. He asked for my passport and ordered his aide, a burly sergeant, to take me to a Christian missionary hostel nearby where they would see to my wounds. Tomorrow he would either provide a policeman to escort me safely to Madras, or arrest me.

I spent the night at the Catholic mission and orphanage on the outskirts of the small town of Harur. In the morning the young orphan boys took me to church to listen to them sing. As we walked along the town's dusty main street towards the bell ringing from their small stone church, I recognized two government jeeps parked alongside the Public Works Department travellers' bungalow. They belonged to the Cochin Customs Department.

It wasn't till much later, however, that I learned that Superintendent Menon was resting inside. The strain of the chase, hundreds of miles out of his jurisdiction, had been too much for his old body and he had suffered a heart attack. His squad had frantically telephoned Additional Collector Venugopalan in Cochin, who had acted immediately to get his men out of Tamil Nadu State. Past favours were returned that Sunday morning when a Navy helicopter lifted off from the airstrip at the Willingdon Island military base for an unofficial mission into the Melagiri Hills to evacuate the stricken Superintendent Menon.

For the Customs Department the chase was over, and their attempt to restrain me from alerting federal officials outside Cochin had failed. But I didn't find out what became of the other two men who had chased me halfway across southern India.

The Tamil Nadu policeman who was to accompany me as bodyguard for the journey to Madras was an uncommonly big fellow for a southern Indian. With him he carried a small bag containing his uniform, cleaned and pressed. He explained that when the bus arrived in Madras he intended to present himself in his best apparel to his headquarters before delivering me to the DRI offices.

From the window of the long-distance coach I could see the huge tiered sacred temples of Kanchipuram rising above the parched earth. Tamil Nadu State had been without monsoon rains for the previous two years and the unbroken drought had resulted in huge cracks in the earth, far worse than anything I had ever seen in the desert in Australia. Where there were taps with running water I had seen long lines of people, often as many as one hundred, waiting patiently with buckets and containers. Madras itself was also in the grip of an acute water shortage. The large ornate public buildings built in Victorian times lay unwashed beneath a veil of dust. The trees were lifeless and withered.

After we had been formally received the police bodyguard and I shared a meal of tiffins together and on the doorstep of the DRI building he shook my hand and wished me good luck.

It was a public holiday in Madras but the duty clerk at the Directorate of Revenue Intelligence was able to contact a senior officer who was prepared to come and talk to me. All through the long afternoon the patient high-ranking officer took down my information, methodically cross-referencing and meticulously checking for errors. When the scorching sun had dropped below the dusty Madras skyline a junior security officer brought sandwiches and *chi* and the windows were opened.

The officer told me that before his promotion to Madras he had been an assistant collector of customs in Tuticorin, a small port much further to the south, and that he was familiar with southern Indian harbours. He explained the structure of the regulatory body in India and together we discussed the circumstances that had made Cochin such an ideal venue for an international drug-smuggling syndicate. Not only was there no DRI office in Cochin, but even its Customs Department was broken into two bodies, with the excise section located on the mainland, far removed from shipping activity. And unlike other major ports in India, Cochin was not a state capital and did not have the intense police community found in Madras, Bombay or Calcutta. Isolated opium-poppy fields had been found and destroyed in the neighbouring regions in recent years, and the easy availability of almost pure heroin on the streets of Cochin attested to its being an unrestrained distribution centre. But no discovery of international drug trafficking had been made at the port, so the world remained oblivious to its role.

When darkness came I was left in the care of the young security officer, who would find a place for me to sleep in his residence a few miles from the building. His transportation was a sturdy Indian bicycle and I sat on the carry rack as he pedalled his usual route home. Crowds were gathering for their festival to Jagannath, eighth avatar of Vishnu, god of the universe. As we navigated between the many buildings of the sacred Hindu temple I hung on, spellbound with fascination at what I saw. Mammoth wooden structures, 70 feet or more in height, were being pulled and pushed by an abundance of willing manpower. As the huge timber wheels turned, the whole assemblage progressed along the ancient byway towards the heart of the temple complex where religious men were chanting, and others held burning tapers.

Later that night, after a generous meal of dhals, rice and vegetables, I slept soundly and securely on the open rooftop of one of the countless overcrowded tenement blocks that are a feature of all Indian cities.

The most senior officer of the Madras DRI eyed me with disdain when I was taken into his office the following morning. He had read the report prepared on the previous day, and although no conclusions were drawn in it, aspersions had been cast on the integrity of the Cochin customs chief Venugopalan. The DRI chief told me that he knew Venugopalan personally and had phoned him in Cochin after reading the information report. Venugopalan had said, 'Milgate is suffering from delusions and cannot be believed.

He should be sent back to Cochin without delay.' However, the Tamil Nadu police had verified my version of the happenings in Harur, and his own DRI officer, who had spent most of the previous day with me, had suggested that the information I had given him could not be ignored. The DRI chief's perplexity was evident. He told me that something would be done to look into my allegations about the Cochin drug network, but stressed that if I had lied about any one thing I would face a long prison sentence for giving false information.

Later I was handed a train ticket to Cochin, and money enough to see me through the journey, and driven to the central railway station. The train west was due to depart at 5 p.m. so I wandered restlessly in the bazaar and then explored the huge railway station before settling into a seat in the waiting area.

I was completely lost in thought and did not immediately notice that the young DRI officer had slipped into a seat next to me. He had come to bring me a message, and although he did not say so I suspected that his duty was unofficial. Miss Alison was in Cochin, he told me; she had spoken on the telephone and knew that I was safe. He waited until my pleasure at hearing this news subsided, before concluding the message. 'You must protect yourself and your family. In India, there is now great danger for you.'

9

Diplomatic Dilemma

Relief flooded through me when I hurried into the Eda-cochin boatyard on Tuesday 26 April and found Alison safe on board *Tiger Rag*. We were overjoyed at seeing each other, although both of us were shocked by the other's gaunt appearance. The stress and worry of our recent ordeals showed on our faces, and my body still bore grazes and lumps. The boatyard at Edacochin was not the place for us to discuss what had happened during the preceding week. Before long word would be out that we were together on *Tiger Rag*, and together we were an easier target, especially at the secluded riverfront boatyard. So we decided to take a few things we needed and go into hiding, and then plan what we should do next.

From the privacy of the Seagull Hotel later that day we made a telephone call to Bombay to inform Consul Tricks that I had returned to Cochin. Tricks informed us that the relaying of our drug information had been taken out of his hands. Instead we should call a Mr Trenery, Narcotics Liaison Officer at the Australian high commission in New Delhi.

Anxious to find out what was being done with our information, we telephoned New Delhi. But while we were told Mr Trenery was in his office, he wouldn't take our call. After considerable delay by embassy officials we were put through to a vice consul, John Woods, who told us very bluntly that since our information related to a drug matter he could not help us. He told us to go to a local police station or leave Cochin.

We were shocked. It was clearly evident that Vice Consul Woods knew exactly who we were, and knew the seriousness of our situation. We tried to explain the urgent need to act on our information – some of the smuggling vessels that had left Cochin in March would still be at sea, and the trails of those that had reached port might still be fresh. But Woods dismissed us arrogantly, saying that if we had anything urgent to tell him we should put it in a letter to his office. Then the line went dead.

For many hours that night we talked, unable to understand why it was proving so difficult to find somebody who would act on our information. Despite our individual efforts to alert authorities we had been given no assurance that an investigation would be undertaken. And we couldn't satisfy ourselves that the Australian government was committed to busting major drug networks, especially those with connections in Asia and Australia. The words that Jyl Gocher had spoken with such conviction still echoed in our minds – that Jim Howard was well-known in Australian government circles.

At that time, however, we didn't know what had been going on in diplomatic circles. At the Australian consulate in Bombay the telex machine had been busy since Alison visited Ian Tricks less than one week before. The Bombay folder on her held eight telexes sent through that office, and more telex messages about her visit, which were not repeated to the Bombay office, had passed between other offices. But the messages to Bombay didn't all relate directly to the information Alison had given. One telex, sent from Canberra, contained a reprimand to Tricks from his superiors for passing those first details to the Australian Federal Police Drug Liaison Unit stationed in Bangkok. Tricks was a skilled consular officer, and he had been chosen for the Bombay appointment because of his broad experience in sorting out all manner of difficulties that Australian citizens got caught up in when travelling abroad. He had advised his superiors that McGuinness had spoken 'coherently and convincingly' and what she had told him was 'worth following up'. Tricks had even suggested that the Australian Federal Police might wish to interview her, and that they should telephone him as soon as possible so that he could give them further briefing in the case, but it seemed that those responsible weren't interested. Telex message CH106695, from Canberra, which had rattled off the Bombay consulate machine, spelled out the point of Canberra's instructions to Tricks. Part of the text read:

... WE SEE THE NECESSITY FOR YOU TO USE DIS-CRETION IN WHAT IS PASSED TO THE AUSTRALIAN FEDERAL POLICE AND THAT YOU WOULD ONLY PASS THAT INFORMATION WHICH WOULD NOT JEOP-ARDIZE THE LEGAL OR CONSULAR STANDING OF THE AUSTRALIAN [Jim Howard] INVOLVED IN THE CASE. K.J. McMAHON 27.4.83 CP.

That telex raised many questions. Just who was Jim Howard that he should receive this preferential protection? If there had been laws broken in India, why shouldn't there be an investigation, even if those involved were Australians? Was it the consul's duty to protect a criminal alleged to be a drug trafficker, especially at the sacrifice of other Australian citizens?

Although Tricks had been ordered to have no further involvement in the drug aspect, and thus it was not necessary for him to communicate further with Canberra on the matter, he nevertheless sent one final telex message. Telex BM2199 was cloaked in diplomacy, though it still clearly reflected his attitude:

... MCGUINNESS APPEARED TO US TO BE A LEVEL-HEADED RATIONAL PERSON AND HER ALLEGATIONS NOT TO BE IGNORED. WE CONSIDER THAT ANY DELAY ON OUR PART IN ALERTING AUSTRALIAN FEDERAL POLICE LIAISON OFFICER, PARTICULARLY AT A TIME WHEN IT APPEARED SOMETHING UNPLEASANT MAY HAVE HAPPENED TO MILGATE, WOULD HAVE BEEN RED TAPE OF THE MOST REPREHENSIBLE KIND.

We were thankful for the security of Fort Cochin's Seagull

Hotel where we spent that first night together again. The next morning, refreshed from a few hours' sleep, we talked more about the plan which we decided might be our best course of action.

In the early afternoon we came out of our hiding place, went to the city and took the remaining funds from our bank deposit box. Alison stowed the money and her passport into her big cane basket and I walked with her to the bus stop from where a service ran south to Edacochin.

We had moved about Cochin cautiously, not knowing who might be following us, and although it was only my second day back we soon found that messages had been left that morning for us by Jim Howard with two of the merchants in the bazaar where we often called. Both read that we should contact Jim immediately, or suffer dire consequences.

When the Edacochin bus stopped Alison climbed aboard. As the bus pulled away I saw her turn her lovely blonde head and wave a sad farewell. Nobody was to know where she was heading, or why.

10

A Cowardly Confrontation

As I walked down the long concrete driveway of Cochin Marine Corporation my thoughts were of Alison. By now the bus she had caught would have reached the Edacochin stop and perhaps she had crossed the bridge at the end of the island. I hoped the diversion I was about to create would take all attention off her whereabouts until she was safely away.

My purpose in coming to Cochin Marine Corporation was to leave a message for Jim Howard. Mr Jacobs, the manager of the dry dock, would also be interested in what I had to say. Jacobs had been interviewed in connection with the drug network, along with Howard and Gold, and Cochin Marine Corporation had been searched for evidence that it had been used to conceal narcotics in machinery which had been brought there from ships and yachts. But that was before Additional Collector Venugopalan had suddenly closed the case, now one week ago. Cochin Marine Corporation had also been investigated; the dry dock was thought to have been used to conceal narcotics in machinery which had been brought there from ships and yachts.

Mr Jacobs was in his office, and I could hear words of bewilderment coming from inside when an old clerk announced that I was waiting in the outer office to see him. Through the big doorway I could see the ketch *Steppenwolf* lying in the mud beyond the dry dock, languishing and uncared for. As I studied the yacht I became sure that Jim Howard had no intention of doing what he had told me back in January he would do – sail *Steppenwolf* from Cochin before the harbour officially closed in five weeks' time.

When Mr Jacobs came to the door of his office, he noticed my interest in the ketch. He wanted it out of his dry dock, he told me, but Jim Howard was still causing problems. I shrugged my shoulders, letting his complaints about Howard's unreasonableness come forth.

When we went into his office he closed the door and waited for me to begin. I told him that I had come to leave a message for Howard, and Jacobs listened while I explained that we wanted to have no further communication with Howard, all we wanted was to finish our work on *Tiger Rag*, launch it and be gone from Cochin and India before the monsoon season began. 'We want no more trouble,' I said. 'We'll cool our allegations about the drug network if Howard will agree to leave us alone.' Quick to appreciate the beneficial implications for him in my message, Jacobs agreed to pass it on, and complimented me on my sensible decision.

As I walked back through the dockyard I felt someone watching me. Perhaps Georgie, Jacobs's right-hand man, was lurking about the dry dock playing his watchdog role. However, I considered my visit to Cochin Marine Corporation had been worth the risk.

There was shouting from somewhere behind me when I approached the uptown ferry wharf in the Ernakulam District. As I turned round to see what the fuss was, a lathi struck me violently on the shoulder. The baton had been aimed at my head but in turning I had avoided the policeman's swing. From twenty paces away I heard the voice of Jim Howard start to yell, 'Stop, thief! Stop, thief!' With a painful movement I narrowly ducked under a second vicious swing, then with my arm deflected a lunge made at my groin. I stood my ground, facing the policeman who was now poised to strike me again, and looking into his cold cruel eyes. Neither of us moved. A fat figure in a khaki uniform pushed through the gathering crowd, lathi in hand. Howard moved ten paces closer, to the fringe of the crowd, still trying to make them believe that I was a dangerous man.

Ten minutes later a small police van arrived; reinforcements had come. I was pushed from behind into the van, a bolt was slid to lock me in, then the policeman and Howard climbed into the front and we lurched away. Instead of stopping at central police headquarters, the van drove on until it reached a small out-of-the-way police station near Power House Road. This station was under the control of Police Commissioner C. T. Antony. I remembered walking past it once in our first weeks in India when looking for Joseph Vellapally's office, which was just around the corner.

From the van I was roughly directed into an interview room at the rear of the station. A young constable stood outside the doorway, loosely at attention, an Enfield service rifle with bayonet fixed at his side. Behind its steel door the room was bare, except for two benches and two chairs at opposite sides of an old table. Howard pulled a chair up to the table and sat down. We were alone in the room.

I first noticed that Howard had his attaché case with him when he lifted it to the table. From it he took a cigar and a small tape recorder. He had come well prepared for this 'spontaneous' arrest, I thought angrily. He lit his cigar, flicked a switch on his machine, and a red light came on. He sat back arrogantly and asked, 'How did you find out about me?'

I didn't answer. There were too many reasons for me to hold my tongue, even though I fully expected this to enrage him. Somewhere, miles to the south, Alison was on a bus. Until she had had time enough to get safely out of Kerala State I would refuse to answer.

An hour passed in which I said nothing. Nobody came into the room. Howard obviously had unofficial licence to use the police station. He puffed his cigars and repeated his questions, all the time blowing smoke at me, knowing that I didn't smoke. He tried to provoke me with perverse statements – 'Alison is also being held' and 'If you don't cooperate with me I'll have her raped by as many Indian men as I can find.' He told me he would take *Tiger Rag* from us, in fact it was as good as his. But I didn't believe him, and though I was often tempted to answer him, I held back.

An officer entered the room and nodded to Howard. Together they went out, closing the steel door behind them, and left me to my thoughts. Alison should be 100 miles to the south now, at Quilon Junction railway station. At midnight a train would take her east.

I was not released that night. Instead, my hands were pulled behind my back and handcuffed together and I was taken into the night air to a group of cells in an enclosure behind the police station. A raucous shouting of what I presumed were Indian profanities was being directed at the guard who had brought me. I was shoved heavily into the cell, and the door was slammed closed and padlocked.

It was a small concrete cell about 12 feet square. Bars and a steel door made up one side. A small bundle was in one corner and a hole for the toilet bucket was in another. The guard paused long enough to spit at his insulter through the bars, but the agile prisoner sidestepped, then launched himself back to the bars to retaliate. Under the eaves of the police-station building was a naked electric blub, but the concrete walls were black with grime and little light penetrated into the cell. In the dimness I could just see three ragged and dirty men. The voluble prisoner was in his twenties and stood with his back to the door, eyeing me with curiosity. Two older men sat against the wall together near the bars, docile and resigned to their fate.

I moved to the corner opposite the toilet bucket, as far away from its stench as possible, and sat down. My hands, handcuffed behind my back, didn't help the pain in my shoulder that was now a deep ache, but I tried to put it out of my mind. I raised my head and noticed that the young prisoner was still looking at me. He smiled and in very poor English welcomed me. It was oddly amusing to be welcomed to such a place, and I smiled. We had a conversation of sorts and I was grateful when I understood that the guard would be changed at midnight and the incoming fellow, a Tamil like himself, might remove the handcuffs. He told me his crime had not been so bad, only selling stolen goods. The other two were in for murder.

Time passed slowly. My cellmate wanted to know about me and my circumstances. I told him a little of myself but he seemed more interested to hear of Australia and life beyond the shores of India, where he thought everybody was a rich man.

A torch beam flashing at the faces of the prisoners announced that the new guard was making his checks. I was surprised when the bundle in the corner stirred and sat up. It was a small boy, maybe eleven years old, and in the light of the torch I could see streaks on his cheeks where tears had washed away a layer of dirt on his face. Words passed between the Tamil prisoner and the guard and the jingle of keys brought me to my feet. After the handcuffs had been removed I headed straight for the bucket; for hours I had been bursting for a pee.

The prisoners' day began early when buckets of water were thrown into the cell. A full bucket and a metal cup were left against the bar on the outside for drinking and washing. The Tamil prisoner told me that no food was provided, but the old woman who came to sweep up would fetch what I wanted if I had money to pay. In prison meals were organized, I was told, but police cells were for temporary detention and any allowance paid to the station to provide sustenance for detainees was pilfered. He had been there for two days, as had the murderers, all waiting for an order for their transfer to prison. The young boy was a juvenile who had yet to face the court. Today I would be either charged or released; under Indian law a person cannot be held in custody longer than twenty-four hours without being formally charged. I had yet to be questioned and wondered what possible charge could be made against me.

The cleaning woman was a pleasant old thing and for 15 rupees she willingly brought three large rice, dhal and vegetable meals wrapped neatly in banana leaves and tied with coir string. One meal was far too much for me; the Tamil also was unable to finish his and the remains of both were devoured by the murderers. The small boy ate a whole meal, and the wretched sight of him and the welts from a whipping he had recently received made me ashamed to be a human being in a world that allowed brutality and inhumanity to exist in the lives of children. The old cleaning woman explained that the boy had been caught stealing pipes from a building site. His father was dead and the boy and his mother had nothing to eat.

The guard came for me in midmorning. I was again handcuffed and taken to the same interview room. Howard was waiting and when we were left alone his questioning resumed. But I maintained my silence. I expected that Alison would by now have made a train connection at Madurai that would take her to Rameswaram. There a regular local ferry service ran the short distance across the Palk Strait to Sri Lanka, and out of India.

Frustrated by my silence, Howard summoned the help of the same policeman who had struck me so painfully with his lathi the day before. The policeman now stood ready to hit me again, a look of contempt on his face. I told Howard that I was now prepared to answer his questions. He smiled. First he wanted to know where Alison was.

I lied, saying that we had had a fight and that she had gone off to a tourist resort, a beach in the south called Kovalam. I said that I didn't know where she would stay or for how long she would be gone. For a long moment he looked questioningly at me, weighing up what I had said, then he left the room for as long as it might take to make a telephone call.

When Howard returned, his mood had changed. Instead of turning on the tape recorder and continuing his previous pattern of questioning, he told me that my life was in danger and that I should trust him because only he could protect me from powerful persons in Cochin who wanted to see me dead. If I would confide in him then he would help me, just as he was helping Jyl Gocher. I told him that if he left us alone we would cause no more trouble, but Howard wasn't interested. He repeated his earlier threat that powerful people in Cochin wanted me 'out of the way'. I sensed truth in his words, and asked him to let me think it over for ten minutes, then perhaps we could make a deal. He left the room.

My guess, correct as it turned out, was that Howard was the front man in the network and more exposed than those who stood in the background to the blame for any actions meant to silence or intimidate me – such as my illegal imprisonment here, or even my murder. And I guessed it was for those other people that he needed some answers on his tape recorder, people that maybe even he feared.

That afternoon I filled two tapes with conversation. It was a tall story that I told, and one which certainly implicated the Cochin authorities, but also gave a clear message of warning. As I told it, there were enough people now aware of the drug-smuggling activities for me to have had the confidence to return to Cochin. But I had provided only circumstantial evidence and there might be doubts about my story – unless my disappearance came to their attention. I told Howard that I had made arrangements to make sure that it definitely would. My warning could not be ignored. Howard heard me out, then packed up his case and told me he would return in the morning.

The handcuffs still held my arms stiffly behind me as the police guard pushed me back towards the outside cell block. But before we left the building the policeman struck me from behind with his lathi, again on the injured shoulder. I shrieked in pain and half collapsed to the floor. He kicked me in the back as I tried to stagger on to the door; where his cruelty would be witnessed by others. As I lurched forward I heard the loud thud of his steel-banded lathi strike the wall. He cursed. Outside the cell block he caught up with me. His body crashed into me and I was pinioned face first against the concrete wall, my hands unable to break the impact. This time I went down to the ground, doubled up in pain.

An old police guard later threw a bucket of water over me and shouted, 'Cell! Cell!' All night I shivered with cold and pain, now alone in the cell, stirring only at midnight to the jingle of keys that mercifully meant release from the handcuffs and relief for my aching arms.

In the morning I washed my bruised body and my torn

shirt, and decided that today I must try to escape. Sometime later the steel door of the cell was opened and I was marched without explanation through the street exit. Howard was waiting there, and loitering near a car behind him were the two thugs I had seen a week before on the train to Madras. I turned round to walk back into the police station but the policeman on guard duty lowered his rifle until it was aimed right at me, the point of its bayonet not a foot from my stomach. Reluctantly I turned back to Howard, who walked ahead of me to the car and opened the door.

Howard sat up front, I sat in the back, a thug on each side of me. The car pulled up in front of an expensive four-star hotel on the Ernakulam seafront. The commissionaire looked distraught at the sight of me, but a 10-rupee note from Howard removed his reluctance to admit me. The first-floor bar was attached to a restaurant and I guessed Howard was a regular, because the barman knew his order. He thirstily gulped down a glass of beer and nodded for a second. 'I told you I'd protect you,' he said.

Howard settled down to his third beer. The thugs moved out of earshot. He pulled a cigar from his attaché case. 'Havana,' he drawled. 'Buy'em by the case.' Then to impress me, or to pass a little time, maybe both, Howard pulled an odd assortment of items one by one from his attaché case and explained their purpose. The first was a rubber suction cap about two inches in diameter with two wires extending from it to a small jack plug. Inside was a microphone, he explained, and when the rubber cap was pressed onto the telephone receiver and the other end plugged into a tape recorder, calls could be taped. There was also a lapel badge with a concealed microphone, a multidirectional microphone which looked almost undetectable from a photographic flash cube, and the 35-mm reflex camera he produced was half the size of a cigarette packet. This must have been part of the 'sophisticated electronic equipment' that Menon's Rummage Squad had seized from room 44 of the Bolghatty Hotel. The rumours which had run about Cochin Marine Corporation had been accurate. Howard claimed that he needed these items for his work. But what kind of work? I wondered. It had been more than ten years since he worked as a photographer.

'Are you some sort of spy?' I asked bluntly, knowing that Howard liked any opportunity to talk about himself. He just laughed, before draining his glass and ordering another beer.

A carved wooden partition screened the bar from the restaurant and the two of us were the only bar customers. In the dining area three tables were occupied, two at the far end alongside the window that overlooked the harbour and its islands, while the third held a lone diner who sat with his back to us on the other side of the partition, not more than four feet away. It was his position rather than his proximity that first caused me to wonder. Howard had had a definite change of mood when the dinner arrived some thirty minutes before, and I had heard a faint but familiar American accent over the piped Indian bar music. All three things combined to give me the notion that the diner might be Gordon Gold.

More beer came. Howard's repetitive threats continued, but his manner had dissolved into weariness and he reminded me of an old lion. Perhaps he had been a roaring beast in his youth, but now, at sixty, his vitality was easily drained. I had eaten my way through half a dozen dishes of table nuts and drunk two beers, and the terror of the police cells had begun to leave me when Howard rallied into a final bout of threats. He reminded me that it would be easy for him to dispose of me. He also gave me a ten-minute speech on how highly connected Gordon Gold was, flashing documents at me and giving me barely enough time to read the names and positions of high-ranking naval, military and political persons who had written to Gold. Then Howard told me that I could go.

The thugs were nowhere in sight when I left the bar and cautiously descended the stairs. At the bottom I turned towards a tourist shop, expecting to get a view of the street from inside, but before opening the shop's door I saw another opportunity. I ducked through a service door and found a hallway, then a staff room, a kitchen, an exit door and an alleyway. Twenty steps led me to the congestion of the bazaar.

By sunset I had cautiously made my way to the boatyard at Edacochin. The last of the sun filtering through the coconut trees brought tranquillity. Then at the sight of *Tiger Rag* I knew I was home.

But that glimpse of happiness vanished when I climbed aboard the yacht – everything was a shambles. An hour later I knew the worst. The intruders hadn't been common thieves; our stereo tape player and many sought-after Western tapes lay untouched. The interest of the intruders had been focused on our personal papers and files. Some of these had been taken, but I suspected that what they had hoped to find hadn't been there. Weeks earlier we had realized the value of certain documents and notebooks and had rented a security box at the State Bank of India in the city.

Then I discovered that something much more crucial had been taken. Items that had been specially cast and machined for *Tiger Rag*'s steering had been stolen. The intrusion had also been calculated to immobolize the yacht, and now any hope of getting *Tiger Rag* out of Cochin before the monsoon season was gone.

When night came a black feeling of despair enveloped me, the depths of which I had never felt before.

11

Two Faces of Canberra

After I left Brian at the city bus stop in Cochin it took me two days to reach Rameswaram, on the southeastern tip of India. There a regular passenger ferry made the short crossing of the Palk Strait to Sri Lanka. The need to keep my whereabouts secret until I was out of India was foremost in my mind; and the cross-country route by bus, train and ferry was almost untraceable. I had put my long hair up and covered it with a scarf, and wore sunglasses. The thought of being pursued, as Brian had been a week earlier when he had gone to Madras for help, added to my caution.

I was on my way to the Australian high commission in Colombo, Sri Lanka, to try once more to persuade Australian officials of the importance of our information about drug smuggling from Cochin, as well as of our urgent need for protection until we could get *Tiger Rag* out of India. The help we had hoped to get after my trip to see Australian officials in Bombay hadn't come, and the tone of the phone conversation with John Woods of the Australian high commission in New Delhi left us with the realization that help would not be coming. If necessary, I was prepared to go all the way back to Australia to get help.

During the long and often tedious hours of travel and uncomfortable waiting rooms, I made extensive notes on what we knew about the Cochin drug network. I wanted to be sure that when I again related the complex details about people and movements, nothing would be confused and nothing omitted. After a Sri Lankan bus had taken me from the ferry terminal at Talaimannar south during the night and dropped me into the morning peak-hour traffic of Colombo, I made my way directly to the offices of the Australian high commission.

The consul, Trevor Spring, had his office on the ground floor of the expensively converted suburban mansion. It was an hour before the receptionist showed me into his comfortable office. Consul Spring was a young man, smartly dressed and confident. Although I had only just walked into his office, he knew who I was, and he knew about the situation in Cochin. During the forty minutes of our first meeting I carefully explained the method the drug network had used to conceal narcotics aboard ships and yachts, and the circumstantial evidence which suggested that this Cochin connection had been established for a long time. Consul Spring took notes.

In a longer, second meeting held that afternoon, Spring questioned me at length about our movements before we had arrived at Cochin on *Tiger Rag*, and about Jim Howard and the other people whom the Customs Department had investigated. He told me he would draft a detailed message to be telexed the following day. I left his office feeling confident that he had understood the information I had come to Colombo to relate. Exhausted from the long day I went off to a room at the Colombo YWCA to wait till the morning, when I could return to the high commission and check the draft message.

At ten o'clock on my second day in Colombo I was waiting at the offices of the Australian high commission, expecting to read the draft of the telex. However, Spring had seen no urgency and hadn't prepared the draft, even though I had told him that ships which had taken drugs from Cochin must still be at sea. I waited till the offices closed at two o'clock and, very disappointed, made my way back to the YWCA.

When I spoke to Spring that day I asked him if Jim Howard was indeed known to officials at the Colombo high commission, as Jyl Gocher had told us. Spring replied that while he didn't know Howard personally, others in the high commission did. Consul Spring was unwilling to be drawn further.

Between sessions at the high commission I telephoned

Sydney and spoke with my parents, relating what was happening to us and assuring them that if I couldn't arrange positive help for us in India, as well as a further investigation into the Cochin network, then I would fly back to Australia. I arranged for almost $1000 to be sent to me from home as our funds in India were nearly exhausted. I also tried to phone Cochin for news of Brian. Unable to get a message to him through the contact we had arranged for communication, I sent a telegram asking him to ring me in Colombo..

Consul Spring eventually sent off restricted telex CLI 3957 relaying the information on the drug network in Cochin three days after my arrival in Colombo. However, Consul Spring denied me any opportunity to check it. Six months later I finally read the seven-page telex, but only after I had arranged for it to be released to us under the Australian Freedom of Information Act.

Under the Freedom of Information Act 1982, Australian citizens are entitled to have access to their files held by government departments. By using the Act Brian and I later learned that Kevin McMahon, an officer of the Department of Foreign Affairs in Canberra, was at the centre of events. McMahon became involved after my visit to the Australian consulate in Bombay when I had first attempted to pass along the drug information. It was McMahon who had instructed Consul Tricks in Bombay 'to use discretion in what is passed to the Australian Federal Police', and also advised that the 'standing of the Australian involved in the case', Jim Howard, should not be 'jeopardized'. When Brian and I telephoned the high commission in New Delhi to follow up on what was being done, McMahon had again become involved. From Canberra he had sent telex CHI06695 to New Delhi, in which he agreed that the Australian government's formal response to the Milgate/McGuinness request for assistance should be to write a letter to us. That letter, signed by John Woods and dated 27 April 1983, reads:

It is not clear to us that you [Milgate] are not receiving the same benefits of the laws, administration and protection that an Indian citizen is entitled to in this country. Therefore, there is no ground for representation by us on your behalf. As I suggested to you, if you are concerned about your welfare, you should either contact the police or leave Cochin.

So Brian and I had been correct to think that while we remained in Cochin, the Australian government intended to do nothing further about our situation. However, my unexpected arrival on the doorstep of the high commission in Colombo changed all that.

Having access to our file also revealed Consul Spring's telex CL13957, which was found to contain critical misrepresentations, errors and omissions. The telex had no reference to *any* established drug network in Cochin with links to Australia, it did not mention that the Cochin Customs Department had conducted *any* investigation; Howard was described as a wealthy and influential businessman, with no mention of his alleged involvement in drug trafficking, his past criminal record, or the second passport he held, or that in India a summons had been issued for his arrest for smuggling, or that the customs chief had been convinced that Howard was a spy. The telex also failed to mention that the *Hetty Mitchell* had been the subject of two customs rummages as well as a Customs Tribunal, or the rummages of Jim Howard's Bolghatty Hotel room and of his ketch *Steppenwolf*. Furthermore, instead of presenting the alleged drug smugglers as suspects, Spring instead cast aspersions on our credibility, portraying us as being suspicious of almost every foreigner we had met in Cochin, without offering any explanation.

In May 1983, as I had not seen the telex, I had no reason to suspect that it contained anything other than my explicit details of the drug network in Cochin. At the time Consul Spring was trying hard to assure me that the Australian government were very concerned, in fact so concerned that

Canberra had issued instructions for a consular officer to be sent to look into the situation in Cochin. The news brought me great relief, and mistakenly I thought that at last help would be on its way.

But was the Australian government more interested in the way their handling of the Cochin matter might be seen than in helping us? Their motives would have been clearer to me if I had been able to read their telex CH108369 sent by Canberra to New Delhi on 4 May:

. . . WE HAVE RE-EXAMINED OUR DECISION AND NOW CONSIDER IT ADVISABLE THAT A CONSULAR OFFICER PROCEED TO COCHIN TO INTERVIEW ABOVE NAMED [Milgate and McGuinness]. WE ARE CONCERNED THAT IF ANYTHING UNTOWARD HAPPENS TO EITHER OF THEM THEN WE SHOULD BE IN A POSITION TO DEMON-STRATE THAT THEIR REQUEST FOR ASSISTANCE WAS ADEQUATELY HANDLED.

12

An Ambiguous Ambassador

Only a few days had passed since my release from enforced detention in a Cochin police cell. My body still ached from the beating I had been given, but I had once again started on the work needed to get *Tiger Rag* repaired and out of India.

At ten o'clock on the morning of 6 May I saw a foreign man approaching the boatyard gate, followed closely by a smartly dressed police officer. In a broad Australian accent the man was cursing loudly, and when he came into the yard one look at his muddy shoes indicated that he had slipped off the narrow earthen embankment across the tidal canal that led to the gate.

The man gave me his card and introduced himself – John Woods, vice consul of the Australian high commission, New Delhi. He had written me a letter, he told me, but now his superiors had re-examined the matter and sent him to Cochin. I looked him over. He was a short man with a large square face, eyes set close to a broad nose below wiry dark hair, and had a habit of not looking at the person he was speaking to. I noticed it particularly when he told me that the district inspector general of police had been kind enough to send along the officer to accompany him. It was necessary for me to go with him to the police headquarters and talk to the DIG about my welfare. A car was waiting, he added.

On the way to the city I expressed surprise that a consular officer had been sent to Cochin. Why hadn't a narcotics officer been sent? After all, I explained, the primary concern was to stop at its source a drug route for hard narcotics that reached to Australia. But Woods wouldn't be drawn, saying only that he was unable in his consular position even to discuss the drug matter. I knew that stationed at the Australian high commission in New Delhi was a narcotics liaison officer, but Woods had nothing to say on this point. He remained silent during the journey to Ernakulam, so I lost myself in thoughts of what the police officer's reaction would be when I arrived there.

District Inspector General of Police Krishnan Nair was a well-spoken, handsome man without the brusque arrogance of his immediate subordinate, City Police Commissioner Antony. Krishnan Nair's office was simple and uncluttered. He told us that he constantly travelled over a large territory and hadn't been briefed about why we had come, so we had to explain ourselves thoroughly.

In diplomatically couched phrases Vice Consul Woods conveyed that he had come to this meeting with Brian Milgate, an Australian citizen who thought that he needed police protection. Milgate felt that the Cochin authorities had not provided him 'adequate protection' and had made a complaint. The Australian government had sent him to look into the matter, Woods concluded.

Krishnan Nair nodded his head and looked at me. He picked up a pencil from his desk, prepared to make notes. 'I've heard rumours, of course,' he said, 'but has there been any violence towards you?'

I told him of the attempted ambush at Edacochin and of the fight I had had there with Indian intruders. I described the events on my journey to Madras, and told him that earlier in the week I had been illegally imprisoned for three days at a local Cochin police station.

'No!' he shouted, slamming his fist on the desk, breaking his pencil in two and sending a wave of shock through the office that made John Woods jump. The officer who had escorted us from the boatyard rushed into the office. Krishnan Nair shouted at him in a shrill voice, his blood pressure high, his composure lost. When he had finished, the officer went out.

'Are you injured?' The district inspector general's concern seemed genuine. I stood and slipped off my shirt, the extensive bruising visible on my shoulder and back being more forceful a testimony than words. Again Krishnan Nair thumped his desk, an almost crude reaction for a man whose eloquent style showed him to have been highly educated. He looked across at John Woods who was now reticent, almost cringing in his chair, then turned his attention to me as if to dismiss the diplomat. 'Have you written a statement?' Before I could answer we were interrupted by the return of the police officer. Krishnan Nair listened to the officer's brisk report. Again his temper soared, and I realized that his anger was brought on by the actions of his city police commissioner Antony, and not by me.

John Woods remained taciturn for the rest of the meeting, even when the DIG told him that it had been confirmed that I had been illegally jailed for three days. To my surprise, Woods raised no objections on my behalf. I promised Krishnan Nair that I would write out a statement for him that day, and would call on him in the future if I considered my circumstances should warrant it. In the meantime he said he would order a routine police patrol to be made on the boatyard at Edacochin.

On my way out of the building I borrowed pen and paper, and on the veranda of the police headquarters I wrote out a brief statement. John Woods insisted that a copy be made for his office. Thirty minutes later I handed the original to Krishnan Nair's bearer and a copy to the vice consul.

At the Grand Hotel on M.G. Road John Woods and I had lunch together. He said very little and was reluctant to discuss the meeting we had just come from. Before I left him at the hotel, Woods instructed me to call on him the next afternoon at the Malabar Hotel where he was staying. I was to prepare a further statement for him – 'something about drug smuggling to send back to Australia'.

The following afternoon I met John Woods as arranged. I was courteous and cooperative, not wanting to offend the representative of the Australian government, which we expected to help us. To establish our credibility I took with me personal documents and references, and also gave him the statements he had asked me to prepare – complaints about my illegal detention in the police station, together with yet another about the operations of the Cochin drug network. I explained every aspect of them, including our allegations about Jim Howard. Woods shrugged his shoulders when Howard's name was mentioned. 'Never met the man,' he commented. I asked if he planned to meet Jim Howard while he was in Cochin, but he didn't answer my question.

Woods was not a good communicator, and throughout the meeting at the Malabar Hotel he sat, listened, and drank beer with a passion that astonished me. It was late in the night by the time he had satisfied his thirst and left the table to retire for the night. His last words to me were that I should return to the hotel at nine o'clock the following morning.

All bus and ferry services on Willingdon Island had long since been finished for the night, forcing me to walk the five miles to Thoppumpady Junction where I could find an autorickshaw for the remainder of my journey south to Edacochin. It was a warm night and the long walk cleared my head. It troubled me that Woods had dismissed my complaints about the police, warning me that to make such complaints would only bring me further trouble. But hadn't these complaints been his reason for coming to Cochin?

The next day I went to the customs house with Woods for an appointment with Additional Collector Venugopalan. It was only a five-minute meeting. There wasn't much to say since the two men had already spoken in private by phone about the issues concerning them. Venugopalan so played up his diligence to law and order that I knew it was just a show put on for the benefit of John Woods and myself, though I could see that he wasn't pleased when he showed me a letter he had received from the Madras DRI indicating that they had begun their own inquiries into the case, and strongly suggesting that Venugopalan should reopen his investigation. I was very coolly told that Customs Intelligence Unit Superintendent Shreedharan had been appointed to further investigate the drug network, since Superintendent Menon was still in hospital convalescing from his heart attack. We could be assured, Venugopalan went on, that he had done everything possible to ensure that no evidence would be suppressed. He even told John Woods that he expected to make an arrest soon. However, I couldn't believe that he had any intention of carrying this out; his words were just a further attempt to cover up what was really going on in Cochin.

When Woods walked away from the customs house after the meeting I went in the opposite direction, and never saw the man again.

I felt encouraged that as a result of my trip to see Directorate of Revenue Intelligence officials in Madras, further inquiries into the drug network had been initiated. And although I didn't know it then, Additional Collector Venugopalan had not been the only one to get a letter from the Madras DRI. At the time of John Woods's visit to Cochin, the Australian high commission in New Delhi was already aware that the Madras DRI had begun to gather intelligence through their own network of agents. The text of one DRI letter, dated 5 May 1983, on file in the high commission in New Delhi, reads:

. . . Howard, aged about sixty, weatherbeaten, tough build, permanent scar on left temple, first came to Cochin on 28.9.82 as skipper on yacht *Steppenwolf* (ex *Timshel*), British colours, owned by M/S Voyages Maldives, 2 Fardhedhee, Magu, Male. The vessel *Steppenwolf* is reported to be undergoing repairs from September 1982 onwards. Howard had gone to the UK and Germany to arrange spares which included highly sophisticated diving equipment, microcomputers, cameras etc. Howard was found to be receiving heavy remittances from Hong Kong, Singapore and London . . .

The initial DRI investigation had extended to other foreigners in Cochin: 'a female named Miss Jyl Gocher arrived on board a luxury yacht', it was also known that 'the female had been making contact with other yachts visiting

Cochin'. The DRI 5 May letter to the Australian high commission ended its intelligence, 'Nothing adverse known to DRI re Milgate/McGuinness.'

Keen to make myself known to Superintendent Shreedharan, the CIU officer appointed to look into aspects of the drug network, I went to introduce myself. His office was not in the customs house on Willingdon Island as I had expected, but in an Excise and Revenue building on the Ernakulam mainland. The CIU which Superintendent Shreedharan headed was not affiliated to the main body of the customs maritime activity, and Venugopalan had shrewdly permitted the CIU to look only for new evidence; further inquiry into the *Hetty Mitchell* or other alleged drug vessels was out of bounds. So, in effect, the original case remained closed. However, right from the beginning Shreedharan was committed to finding contradictions in Jim Howard's and Jyl Gocher's alibis, and to say that they ended up by feeling anything less than seething hatred for Shreedharan would be to understate their feelings. Perhaps the only reason why he was unable to topple the Cochin network was that Venugopalan had imposed such limitations on his authority to investigate.

I soon found that Shreedharan was a man given to few words. He always appeared calm. In his office in the downtown Ernakulam District I noticed his staff were close to him, their loyalty quite obvious. His subordinate, Inspector Sampson, in contrast to the large-framed Shreedharan, was very small and jovial. They seemed a most unlikely pair, but together they worked well. Sampson was always out and about asking questions and gathering facts, while Shreedharan sat at his desk. My independent knowledge concerning the people the CIU were to investigate was a much welcomed contribution.

Shreedharan began his inquiries with a large pile of papers, some of which had been taken from the bottom of Jyl Gocher's camera case, others seized during a rummage of the Bolghatty Hotel room. Gocher, who had been keeping her head low at the Bolghatty Hotel, was brought to the C I U office for questioning. She came with the lawyer Joseph Vellapally, and Inspector Sampson recalled that she had walked in with a confident swagger. He imitated her wobble and laughed. Later I was given permission to read some of the documents that Gocher was questioned about during her first session with Shreedharan. One was from Jim Howard and stated that the *Steppenwolf* was now in her name, and on another a reference was made to a number of emeralds. Jyl Gocher explained that Jim had left the gemstones in question with the U K Customs Department for safekeeping when he was on his last trip to England, but they had 'lost' them. Very careless, she said. In correspondence with persons in Australia a large property with many acres of marijuana was discussed, but Gocher assured her questioners that this wasn't at all unusual – 'Marijuana is grown everywhere in Australia.' She denied that she had gone to Idikki District in February to meet two foreigners, Alice and Christie, who were known to the authorities as narcotics traffickers. However, she had not been able to give a satisfactory explanation of why she had remained in Cochin for so long. Inspector Sampson told me that when she had left the office it had been without her wobble, and instead she had looked profoundly shaken.

Maxwell Fernandez came to visit me at the boatyard on Saturday 8 May. He was surprised to find two uniformed constables there, sitting down at a game of cards. He had heard a story that I had been in prison, and had heard also that Alison was missing. Jim Howard had first told him that Alison was in danger, and had sent someone to Kovalam Beach to look for her, but since then Jim had discovered that she was in Sri Lanka. Somewhat curious, Fernandez had come to find out for himself what was going on.

I wasn't too sure how far I could trust Maxwell Fernandez. He was still on good terms with Howard, now a regular at Maxwell's press club, and a New Zealander named Neil Parry, who had come to Cochin to meet Jim Howard was staying as a guest in Maxwell's house. But the journalist's association with Venugopalan was the corner-stone of my doubts about him. Fernandez had admitted to snooping on Venugopalan's behalf, but now he was confused by Venugopalan's sudden closing of the case. Maxwell thought that Howard's hostility towards me seemed unwarranted, unless Howard had something to hide. He also told me with a laugh that he wasn't sure if I was really as mad as Venugopalan had suggested to him recently, or indeed if I was as jealous of Jim as Jim had claimed. Maxwell just didn't know what was happening in Cochin, he told me, but he was determined to find out.

On 10 May I received the telegram Alison had sent from Sri Lanka asking me to telephone her there.

In Cochin there was no ISD facility; the telecommunications exchange was an incredible place, forgotten by time and technology. In a large open room dozens of clerks sat in drab booths hunched over Morse-key senders, tapping out telegrams. Communications to exchanges with more modern machinery were sent through battered and weary telex machines of ancient vintage. Everywhere loose wiring ran untidily across floor and walls, converging at unspecified intervals into mass disorganization. Joins in the wire were exposed, pieces of sticky tape hung unravelled by the tropical heat, and here and there wires suddenly emerged from the core to hang free, their identity long since untraceable. Making a telephone call at any time in India we expected crossed lines, but whenever I made a call from the Cochin exchange it was my fingers that were crossed.

Alison sounded relieved when the operator put me through. Both of us were heartened to hear each other's voice again. She told me about the delays and disappointments at the Australian high commission offices, and said she would be returning to India as soon as it could be arranged. Her family in Sydney had agreed to keep in touch with the Australian Foreign Affairs Department. I told Alison that I was reluctant for her to return to Cochin; it might be premature and expose her to further danger. The situation was still unsettled, though the boatyard was now being patrolled by uniformed officers, and the Madras DRI as well as a local superintendent had begun to investigate the drug network. I also told her briefly of my imprisonment and the theft from *Tiger Rag*.

She was amazed, having been given an entirely different story by Austalian officials. 'John Woods telephoned Colombo on his return from Cochin. But I wasn't told about your imprisonment, or that anything like that had happened there. It was even reported that Howard would be leaving Cochin by May 15th.'

It was my turn to be amazed.

Alison continued over the crackling line, 'I'm coming back, Brian. I worry about you, and I'd rather stand with you and face whatever lies ahead than agonize here or in Australia, not knowing what's happening. I'll see you in a couple of days' time. Be very careful, my darling. Goodbye.'

13

From Pillar to Post

The Cochin police Special Branch is a body independent from the mainstream of routine police work, and its operations are extremely confidential. Its offices on the Ernakulam mainland are separate from those of the state police force, and its staff, who don't wear uniforms, drive civilian vehicles. So we were dismayed when an officer of the Special Branch approached us on 13 May, only hours after Alison's return from Sri Lanka, and told us we were required without delay for questioning.

The officer interested in us was Deputy Superintendent of Police (DYSP) Burushotaman Pullai. He demanded to see our papers for *Tiger Rag*, and wanted to know all details about our source of income, including our arrangement with Mr Howard, and what papers we had to support it. But beneath the thin veneer of excuse, 'police routine for all foreigners', lay what we soon suspected were the DYSP's probes to assess our legal vulnerability, and we realized that a secondary purpose of the meeting was for the DYSP to obtain copies of our documents. Perhaps these same documents had been partly what intruders had recently broken into *Tiger Rag* to find. If so, this could explain why they had waited till Alison had returned to make their next move, assuming that she must have the missing papers with her.

DYSP Pullai was a man in his forties with a full build, large feet and a long bristling moustache, the fashion at that time among Indian police officers of middle rank. There was a ruthlessness in his manner and although he tried to be pleasant, we both agreed later that affability didn't come naturally to him. He also laughed excessively at his own attempts at humour.

1. Brian and Alison

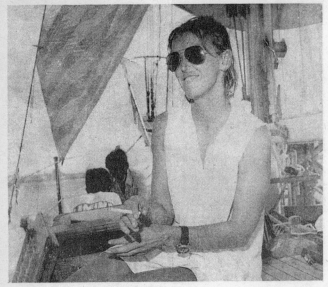

2. James Charles Howard: 'You can smuggle anything if you have the brains' (*Photo: Malayalam Manorama, Kerala*)

3. Jyl Gocher aboard the ketch *Steppenwolf* (*Photo: Malayalam Manorama, Kerala*)

4. The ketch *Steppenwolf* lying outside the Cochin Marine Corporation drydock, March 1983 (*Photo: Malayalam Manorama, Kerala*)
5. Jim Howard and Jyl Gocher taking coconut cocktails together at the Malabar Hotel, May 1983 (*Photo: Malayalam Manorama, Kerala*)

6. Brian Milgate in the Edacochin boatyard, December 1983 (*Photo: Barrie Penrose*)

7. Alison on the verandah of the Bolghatty Hotel, February 1983.

8. The *Hetty* (*Photo: United States Customs Service, Office of Enforcement, Philadelphia*)

9. US Customs take custody of the *Hetty*: Cape May, New Jersey, November 1983. (*Photo: United States Customs Service*)

10. Part of the drugs concealment hidden on the *Hetty* (*Photo: United States Customs Service*)

11. The *Hetty* crew being led away after their arrest by law enforcement officers, November 1983 (*Photo: United States Customs Service*)

a Donald Dickinson

b Stephen Marriott

c Peter Jackson

d William Charlesworth

12. The crew of the *Hetty* (*Photos: United States Customs Service*)

13. Consul General Ian Tricks talking to Brian and Alison Milgate outside the Chief Judicial Magistrate's court in Ernakulam, March 1984 (*Photo: Indian Express, Cochin*)
14. The authors' yacht, *Tiger Rag*

Our session in his office amounted to nothing short of harassment. Finally he told us that we were not permitted to leave Cochin. This had something to do with a civil case being taken against us, the DYSP explained, expressing the view that Mr Howard certainly had it in for us. A private fight between Milgate and Howard was how he saw it, between the *Steppenwolf* and the *Tiger Rag*. 'The wolf versus the tiger. Who will win between the wolf and the tiger?' He laughed heartily at his own wit, bouncing up and down in his chair like a puppet on a string. We were not amused, and afraid that something deeper than harassment lay behind the policeman's intent.

That afternoon we tracked Maxwell Fernandez down to where he worked in the publication office at Gandhi Nagar. A few minutes of time in the newspaper's library was all we asked of him. But when he heard a little about our morning with the DYSP, he packed up his desk and we all went out for coffee at a local café.

Maxwell, with his knowledge of Jim Howard, his skills as an investigative journalist and his familiarity with Cochin, turned out to be the right person to have sought out. Howard's lawyer, Maxwell told us, was Joseph Vellapally, but recently Howard had been meeting a lawyer named Sukumaran Nair who was Vellapally's friend. Nair headed a firm of well-known criminal lawyers who were feared by their advocate colleagues. A junior partner in the firm was one B. Raman Pillai, who just happened to be a close relative of the DYSP we had seen that morning – a convenient connection.

Like us, Maxwell wondered what civil case Howard could take out against us. He said he could help us and went off to call on a friend, a lawyer who might know of any gossip among the barristers and the court staff. He returned after five o'clock to tell us that no rumours had been heard in legal circles.

When we arrived that night at the Edacochin boatyard we found it in darkness. The light hadn't been turned on at day's end as usual. Instead the local caretaker had waited to tell us that the proprietors from whom we rented the yard had come and turned off the electricity and padlocked the gate shut. The following morning the two Indian carpenters I had hired to help me with *Tiger Rag* came to tell me that they could no longer come to work. Both had been threatened by the proprietors of the yard that they would be beaten up if they came again.

We went to the customs house to check the special licence the proprietors of the yard were required to have for foreign vessels. They passed us from office to office and eventually told us that we were no longer permitted to remain at the boatyard. The proprietors had no licence, nor had they met the bond requirements of the Customs Department.

The Port Authority were more helpful. They had been sceptical about the Edacochin boatyard when the proprietors had first applied for permission to haul out a foreign vessel, and had asked them for a reference. Port Authority's records showed the name of the proprietor's referee as Joseph Vellapally.

We were incensed. *Tiger Rag* was under siege, having been manipulated into a vulnerable position, and we could see how similar our circumstances were to those of the German welder who had eventually lost his yacht to Gordon Gold back in 1981.

On Friday night, 20 May, we watched Maxwell Fernandez climb through the back entrance gate of the boatyard and step nervously across the distance to *Tiger Rag*. He looked pale with fear. His trembling hands fumbled to unfasten the chin strap of the big red helmet he had worn all the way down the path to the boatyard, afraid that he might be struck from behind. Someone had been following him recently, he told us in a whisper, and he had received a threatening telephone call.

Forbidden by his chief editor to become further involved in the investigation, he had then traced the interference to the publication's owner, whose lawyer neighbour had warned him off the story. Maxwell was certain the Cochin under-world were behind the threats against him, which confirmed the local roots of the drug network. He had let himself be drawn into the conflict without caution, fraternizing openly with both sides, but the seriousness of the situation had caught up with him. 'Fools rush in where angels fear to tread' was how he chose to see it, though Maxwell was university-educated and clearly not a fool. He felt disgusted with himself for having put so much faith in the convincing Jim Howard, and his feeling that he had been deceived had led to his commitment to help us now. At last we had an ally.

Maxwell explained that the Cochin underworld was part of the 'Indian mafia', organized crime of a kind that has permeated most societies. Cochin was the crime centre of Kerala State and it was common knowledge that the Erna-kulam police aided and abetted its growth. So entrenched had corruption become in Cochin that senior state officials could do little to relieve its powerful stranglehold. But high political dignitaries should be able to bring the influence which could ensure us a fair passage through this storm, Maxwell reasoned, and the most effective way to reach these men was through the press.

Maxwell had good connections in the media. At one time he had been a reporter on the *Indian Express* newspaper, the leading English-language daily syndicated in India's major cities, which included an edition in Cochin. The resident editor was a spiritual father to Maxwell and he praised the man – eminent, above reproach and unafraid, he had even continued to fight Indira Gandhi throughout the 'Emer-gency' despite duress and risk of imprisonment. Maxwell would contact him for us. Tomorrow was the resident editor's day off, but on Sunday he would be at his office preparing Monday's edition.

After we had seen Maxwell safely back to his scooter and arranged a time to telephone him the next day, we returned down the path and through the trees. The sounds of a religious festival were coming from across the river and we recalled the time we had walked to the boatyard and overheard Jim Howard's threatening words. A month and a day had passed since then, a month of living in fear.

A large ochre building on the foreshore of Fort Cochin housed the Cochin offices of the *Indian Express*. A gateman directed us to an outside timber staircase to the first floor. The large upper level was partitioned from floor to ceiling, the top half of each partition being of glass, enabling us to see inside. Compositors sat amid banks of blocks, typesetters wearing eyeshades and cuff guards bent over their work in concentration, and printers in leather aprons laboured on their machines in a room smudged black from printer's ink. The smell of ink and newsprint was strong. The last area contained rows of desks topped with typewriters and telephones.

S. K. Anantaramin, an old man and a high-caste Brahmin, sat in a simple office behind a massive desk. When we entered he rose and shook our hands, speaking softly in greeting. There was an ethereal look about him. He was clean-shaven with white hair, and wore a simple white homespun khadi shirt and *mundu*, and the ritual Brahmin chest string was visible across a tall and slender body that glowed with inner vitality. He sat pressing his hands together as he listened to what we had to say, before suggesting that we join him for a cup of tea. From a Thermos flask he poured the hot liquid into chipped English china teacups and we drank while he spoke of how he could help us. First we needed to make a statement of what we wanted to reveal, which would be passed to a lawyer who could check for possible defamation. Tomorrow we should return.

In the privacy of the Seagull Hotel we wrote out the detailed statement. The next morning in the *Indian Express* office a photograph was taken of us together, after which we left the editor, lawyer and all the skilled workers to their task of putting the newspaper together.

The 24 May edition carried the story and photograph in a prominent position on the front page. The account was brief and unsensational:

An Australian couple, now stranded in Cochin, are going from pillar to post seeking security for themselves. Mr Brian Milgate and his fiancée, Miss Alison McGuinness, believe Cochin is the base of operations of a gang of international smugglers and it is from them the two fear the worst. Twice before attempts were made on Milgate's life but he managed to escape . . .

The account went on to describe the gang – 'some foreigners with a woman and a couple of Cochinites' – but no name or physical description by which the alleged drug traffickers could be identified was given. The main emphasis of the text was on local authorities. 'Milgate and his fiancée approached the customs, the local police and even the Australian high commission but they feel they are not getting a fair hearing . . . local authorities are said to be lukewarm . . . it was hard to understand why . . .'

Reaction was immediate, but it didn't come from the authorities. That afternoon three foreigners began a systematic search to locate us. Robert Fisher, a young New Zealander who had recently arrived in Cochin, caught up with us the next day at Edacochin. He had come as Jim Howard's spokesman, he told us. Jim had seen the newspaper report and he was furious. He demanded to see us at once. His lawyer was preparing a document and we must go to the Bolghatty Hotel and sign it. We asked what the document contained. 'A statement attesting to the fact that Jim is not one of the alleged traffickers,' Fisher said seriously, 'and I want my name put on that document as well.' We argued that no names had been printed in the newspaper story, but the tall New Zealander only glared at us, his face distorted with rage, his fists clenched. 'Jim's got the police in Australia looking into your backgrounds. He's out to get you, and he swears he'll get *Tiger Rag* too!'

On Friday we anxiously travelled with Maxwell Fernandez to Panampilly Nagar, a well-to-do residential suburb to the east of the city where the lawyer Vincent Panikulangara had his office and residence. As well as having a law degree, Vincent was a doctor of philosophy, a highly respected man who often became involved in public-interest cases. On his own initiative and at his own expense he was fighting a lengthy legal battle all the way to the supreme court to have the list of drugs available to the public in India reduced. Certain drugs which long ago had been proved to have dangerous side-effects and were banned in developed countries were still being pushed into the Third World by unscrupulous multinational pill pedlars. Vincent was on a crusade against them. At various times he had worked in Europe and America, but though there might have been many opportunities for him overseas, Kerala was his home.

The lawyer, who had a noble appearance and an honest and intelligent face, gave us much of his valuable time in explaining some of the intricacies of Indian legal procedure. He was interested in our allegations, and S. K. Anantaramin, his close friend and neighbour, had given our statement to him in confidence to check for defamation. More of our case had come to him from Maxwell Fernandez. But they were journalists, he told us, whereas he was a lawyer, and if, or rather when, our fight with this drug network moved into his arena through a civil or criminal case being brought against us, then he promised he would see us through whatever happened. Although he would be going overseas for a time, we were not to worry about his absence. In India legal matters moved very slowly and the courts had an enormous backlog. He would be back in time to see that justice was done.

14

A Timely Objection

31 May was just another day for the Cochin journalist who covered the proceedings of the chief judicial magistrate's court for the *Indian Express*. Murder, rape or robbery were usual topics in the journalist's day because the magistrate's court's jurisdiction was over criminal rather than civil matters, which were handled by another court. There were two reasons why that journalist was later able clearly to recall the court proceedings on the morning of 31 May: firstly because of the unusual nature of the charge brought in the court, and secondly because the charge was, in part, brought against his newspaper, the *Indian Express*. The charge was defamation, and what made it unusual was that it had been brought as a criminal complaint instead of a civil complaint.

The story he had to describe was this. The criminal lawyer Sukumaran Nair had just stepped onto the veranda from the magistrate's private chambers, wearing a look of smug assurance, while further along the wide timber veranda of the two-storeyed court complex the usher had started to ring the bell. The clerk of the court, looking like a drum major in his braids and sashes, hurried between the sheriff's rooms and his honour's bench to place the last legal papers on a pile for that morning's session. Perched on the courtroom's front benches in their black cloaks, like crows at a picnic, were the advocates who practised daily in the court of the chief judicial magistrate. Further behind, two sleepy legal journalists perused the day's lists, while outside on the veranda stragglers lingered to chat, or coach anxious defendants and witnesses with last-minute instructions about their testimony. Lurking there with the advocates, felons and legal clerks was Jim Howard, slouched against a wall and puffing smoke rings into the air. Among the last to be ushered in was

Sukumaran Nair, to the surprise of the junior barristers already seated there. The senior lawyer swished back his cloak and took a seat. The usher cried, 'All stand, please. The court is now in session.' Mr Mathew, chief judicial magistrate, entered through a side door and climbed to his chair at the bench.

Sukumaran Nair sat idle, waiting for his case to be called. Alongside the other advocates he looked out of place. His black courtroom cloak was of silk, and he wore expensive clothes and gold jewellery to display his success. His modern spectacles had slightly tinted glass and fine metal frames, helping to make him look very smooth indeed. Casually he surveyed the courtroom, casting an eye down the row of barristers to see who might be there to object to the final petition he would try to push through the court. When he turned back to face the bench he was satisfied that nobody present would have the nerve to object to him.

All attention was on Sukumaran Nair when his case was announced and he stood and opened his address to the court. 'Criminal defamation is a serious matter.' Barristers sat up and paid attention, as did the newspaper journalists, who began scribbling on their notepads. The first petition was read:

Complainant: James Charles Howard, now residing at the Bolghatty Palace Hotel, Cochin.
Accused1 : Brian Milgate, now residing in yacht *Tiger Rag*, Edacochin.
Accused2 : Miss Alison McGuinness, now residing in yacht *Tiger Rag*, Edacochin.
Accused3 : P. Krishnaswamy, printer and publisher, *Indian Express*, Calvarty, Fort Cochin.
Accused4 : S. K. Anantaramin, resident editor, *Indian Express*, Calvarty, Fort Cochin.

The chief judicial magistrate, Mr Mathew, from his bench high above the court, looked down on Nair giving the arguments for his honour's acceptance of the petition and supporting affidavits as a prima facie case for criminal defamation. 'Four solid and respectable citizens read the *Indian Express* edition of 24 May and in an instant identified the complainant.'

Mr Mathew looked down at his own copy and noted the names of the four citizens cited as witnesses – Mr K. T. Jacobs, Cochin Marine Corporation; Mr George Thomas, also of Cochin Marine Corporation and a relative of the first witness; Mr Robert John Fisher, a foreigner residing at Bolghatty Island; and Shri Shaheed, a local journalist who worked with a newspaper that was in opposition to the *Indian Express*. There had originally been five names on the petition given to the magistrate in his chambers before the morning's session, but the fifth name had been inked over – that of Maxwell Fernandez.

Mr Mathew's attention turned back to the courtroom where Sukumaran Nair read out the last affidavit. It referred to accused number one and accused number two, Milgate and McGuinness, and their yacht *Tiger Rag*.

'I reliably learn that the above yacht is now under repair and that accused number one and number two will be leaving the jurisdiction of this honourable court within three or four days. They are making preparations to do so in order to evade the process of this honourable court. The cause of justice will suffer and the purpose of the above complaint will be defeated if accused numbers one and two are allowed to leave the country.'

Sukumaran Nair paused. Nobody had interrupted so far. It was a lie that accused number one and two were about to sail from India, and if challenged he could not substantiate the claim, but to his relief no challenge came. He continued his address. 'For reasons stated in the accompanying affidavit, it is most humbly prayed that this honourable court may be pleased to issue non-bailable warrants for the arrest and apprehension of accused one and accused two.'

Nair saw one of the barristers stand in objection, but he continued to lean forward with his hands splayed on the table until he finished reading his address. The chief judicial magistrate looked up from the notes he was making to acknowledge with a nod the barrister who had just risen. The courtroom was silent while Mr Mathew finished his notes.

Nair looked over the seated barristers to the advocate standing. Though he didn't know his name, he knew the old barrister regularly practised in this court, mostly taking the cases of the poor. On this occasion, even though he hadn't met those involved, the old barrister saw there was a need to raise an objection – arrest and detention without opportunity for bail was an extreme imposition in a matter of defamation.

Mathew nodded to the old barrister to begin his objection, but Sukumaran Nair loudly challenged what authority he had to represent the accused. A murmur went through the courtroom. The old barrister looked down at his sandals, his simple clothes and his carefully patched black cotton cloak, and when he lifted his head to speak there was a hint of irony in his faint smile. 'I am authorized to represent all people, your honour.'

Nair remained standing, glaring at the old barrister. The magistrate looked hard at the objecting barrister for a long moment before giving a flick of his hand that the old barrister knew was his permission to continue. Another murmur went through the courtroom as he waited for Nair to sit down before beginning his objection.

His words were softly spoken and his reasoning simple. He had read the newspaper in question. It was a respectable publication, no doubt his honour read it himself. He glanced expectantly up at the bench. The magistrate gave an impatient groan, and the old barrister had to wait for his colleagues to finish tittering. It was for the court to decide this matter, he went on, a matter of foreigner against foreigner that unfortunately implicated Cochin's own citizens. But it was, in his stated opinion, necessary to speak out against the issue of non-bailable warrants for the arrest of the accused. 'Why should they be denied the right to bail? Surely moderation is necessary here.'

There was a babble of agreement from those in the

courtroom. The old barrister glanced up again at the magistrate, but Mathew appeared unmoved. The faint smile returned to the old man's face as he told the court that even if his objection here today was overruled, he would at least be able to retire a happy man, proud to have been a part of his honour's honourable court which today would create legal history and make them all famous. Mathew was getting impatient now, and those below were puzzled. Sukumaran Nair again got to his feet, but the old barrister went on to explain himself. The issue of non-bailable warrants would be recorded as a precedent, since in 'all of India' it had never been done before in a defamation case. Mathew's face reddened and he slapped down his gavel to restore order to his court.

Nair glowered sourly at the old barrister, who had resumed his seat, but the criminal lawyer knew that Mathew must now refuse his final petition for the issue of non-bailable warrants. Mathew again slapped down his gavel.

'I direct that bailable warrants be issued for all four accused. They are to be summonsed to present themselves to this court for the matter of bail before the first date for the hearing of the trial set down for 14 June. Next case.'

When Sukumaran Nair left the courtroom, Jim Howard was still waiting on the veranda. Deep in conversation they walked together to a cool-drink stall set beneath a huge tree in the court's grounds. The criminal lawyer ordered lime sodas. Their conversation continued while the vendor cut a green lime in two and put the halves into a small hand press. As he shook the last drops of juice into the glasses, his other hand reached into his coolbox and pulled out a bottle of soda water which he deftly opened by popping the marble seal at the top. While he poured the soda he added liquid sugar and salt and stirred briskly. Looking up from his work, the vendor saw he had another customer, the *Indian Express* journalist who came here each day to report for the newspaper.

While Howard sipped his cool drink and listened intently to his lawyer, the journalist standing nearby listened carefully too. He heard the lawyer tell Howard that while the two accused couldn't be immediately arrested and imprisoned, their original plan could still succeed. The two accused now had to face the court within fourteen days and take bail, and he would see to it that a very substantial sum for bail was set. Mathew could be persuaded.

15

A Verdict of Suicide

During May 1983 we had been under considerable strain, even though we were not yet aware of the legal nightmare that lay ahead for us.

Huge and heavy storm clouds blew in each day from the Arabian Sea to hang threateningly over the coastal lands, but no rain had fallen in May to relieve the clammy premonsoon swelter. Both of us felt despondent about our predicament, frightened and appalled by the thought that the Australian government had forsaken us. At the Edacochin boatyard the siege of *Tiger Rag* continued. With the electricity disconnected, work was difficult, though we didn't lose hope of finding a way out when in August the rains would end. At a workshop many miles south of Cochin we had secretly begun to rebuild the rudder and steering mechanism for *Tiger Rag* as a replacement for the one stolen at the beginning of May. Little of our time was spent at the boatyard, and instead we chose to hide in various hotels. Our movements around town were discreet, though not discreet enough: on two occasions we realized we were being followed.

Elsewhere in Cochin pressure was beginning to mount. Our allegation about the existence of the drug-smuggling syndicate was now a public affair which divided the growing number of people who knew of it into opposing camps. Jim Howard's foreign visitors were becoming nervous about their association with him and he worked hard at drawing them closer to him, and Jyl Gocher had been near to breaking point after the methodical questioning she had been subjected to by Customs Superintendent Shreedharan. From the state capital, Trivandrum, word was sent by DRI officials to inform us that our allegations were being looked into, while at the local district police station near Edacochin, where the subinspector had interviewed the boatyard proprietors about the thefts from *Tiger Rag* and harassment of our workers, rumour had it that the policeman had been very heavy-handed. But from the Australian government we had heard nothing.

On 1 June when we checked the boatyard we found a notice attached to the hull of *Tiger Rag*. It was from the boatyard proprietors – two typed pages of legally worded demands for the removal of the yacht within twenty-four hours and the payment of 7000 rupees within seven days. Failure to act in compliance with the demands, the notice stated, would bring further claims for compensation. These outrageous demands, made through Joseph Vellapally, angered and distressed us. More than just harassment, they were a blatant attempt to bleed us of funds. It was impossible for us to launch *Tiger Rag* with the hole still in her bottom where the damaged rudder had been cut away.

We tore down the notice and were just leaving the boatyard to get legal advice when we encountered Maxwell Fernandez hurrying down the path from the opposite direction. The news he brought us was horrifying. For the first time we heard that Jim Howard had taken out the defamation case against us, even though neither Howard's name nor description had been printed. Howard's sole intention was to have us imprisoned, Maxwell explained, and warrants had been issued for our arrest. We would have to post bail within the next thirteen days, or be imprisoned. Howard planned to have us out of the way in prison awaiting trial for defamation, so that his lawyers could proceed unchallenged with his other scheme – to take *Tiger Rag* from us.

The shock of this news hit us hard. In response to our despair Maxwell's eyes narrowed and he raised a fist to the heavens and vowed to fight. He offered to contact the lawyer Vincent Panikulangara for us, and suggested that in the meantime we should find a discreet place to stay until the details of our bail requirements were known and additional funds arrived from Australia. The police had orders to arrest us, but it would look better if we could go voluntarily to the court.

Late that night Maxwell came to the Geo Hotel, where we had ensconced ourselves. His sources had so far failed to establish the proposed sum for bail. In itself that was strange. Those Maxwell spoke to thought Howard's chances of winning the case were remote, and even if the judge, for whatever reason, saw it in Howard's favour, appeals could be made to a higher court. Maxwell had also spoken to the other accused, S. K. Anantaramin and P. Krishnaswamy of the *Indian Express*, and established they had no intention of printing an apology – they wanted to fight the case. However, we were distressed to learn that Dr Panikulangara had left only days before on his overseas trip. Maxwell thought it a dirty move that the two separate actions against us – the defamation case and claims against *Tiger Rag* – had been launched on the same day, and had been delayed until after our lawyer had left India.

The following day we sent off two telegrams. One was to Alison's family in Australia with a request that money be transferred to our bank account in Cochin; we were anticipating being required to post a substantial sum for bail. The second telegram was to the Australian high commission in New Delhi, saying that we were facing arrest and requesting that the Indian central government be informed.

Then work to prepare our defence against the defamation charge began in earnest. As our lawyer, Dr Panikulangara, employed no junior staff who could step in during his absence, Maxwell introduced us to a junior lawyer, Rajan Babu, from a firm of established solicitors who agreed to take our case. A senior lawyer would take over the brief when the preparation was in an advanced state. Our strategy was to name Jyl Gocher as our witness, thinking that under cross-examination she might break. A subpoena to ensure that she remained in Cochin was prepared and given to the Ernakulam police to be served.

We made an appointment to see District Inspector General of Police Krishnan Nair early on Sunday morning at his residential quarters at Gandhi Nagar. While we knew that in doing this we would face possible arrest, we decided to take the chance. We wanted to establish an understanding with this senior official who could ensure fair play towards us on the part of the police.

The DIG received us cordially. We explained what we had done to get our bail money, though the amount was still undisclosed. Krishnan Nair listened sympathetically to what we had to say before assuring us that he would ask his officers to delay serving the arrest warrants. But understandably, he could no longer justify the police patrols of the boatyard as this would be a conflict of interest. About the claims against *Tiger Rag*, we should write a detailed statement for him, setting out the circumstances, and he promised to look into it.

The next day Maxwell discovered that Jyl Gocher had suddenly left Cochin. Jim Howard had announced that she was on a photographic holiday of north India, but Maxwell was sure she was off to the Australian high commission in New Delhi. He had learned this from a contact who worked the switchboard at the Bolghatty Hotel. Our subpoena to confine Gocher to Cochin had not been served – it had ended up two days before on the desk of Deputy Superintendent Burushotaman Pullai at the Special Branch.

Determined to keep up our spirits, on Tuesday morning we went to meet Isher Iyer, the senior lawyer who would represent us. His office was a busy and important place and while waiting we studied the textbook defamation cases. Although Maxwell had warned us about the senior advocate's obesity we were astonished at the freakish sight of a 26-stone man dressed in white singlet and *mundu*. When he spoke, ripples reverberated down many chins. If our money had not come through by the end of the week he would arrange for two persons who owned property to stand surety for us in place of bail, he told us, and we weren't to worry, he didn't lose cases. After a few unsubtle hints had been dropped about his fee, our appointment was over. Neither of us had taken to the man, who had told us he was a leading Cochin lawyer.

Our next call was to our bank to see if either of the two

transfers of money we expected had arrived. The head clerk from the foreign-exchange section tried to convince us that the money could not have been sent, until we showed him a telegram confirming the earlier transfer. 'Then it must have been credited to the wrong account,' he said, and shrugged with indifference. I felt like thumping him but Alison led me to the manager's office. He wasn't able to help either, he said, adding that the auditors would sort it out when they came for the bank audit in July.

The stress of living with the fear of impending arrest increased as our time ran out. The first hearing was set for 14 June, the following Tuesday, and we had to post bail before then. We were thoroughly fed up with playing hide and seek with the police, who were now under considerable pressure from Howard's lawyers to arrest us.

On Friday we went to see our advocates to arrange the sureties necessary for us to take bail. They confirmed that it would be arranged by Monday and we were instructed to be in their offices by 10 a.m. dressed for court, bringing the money to pay the sureties. Accompanied by a lawyer we would surrender ourselves to the court.

Over the weekend we changed hotels again. We had prepared the best defence we could, though we could not understand why the Australian government hadn't responded to our call for help. We had not yet heard one word from them. Had it to do with Jim Howard? Maybe Jyl Gocher was indeed visiting them in New Delhi. We didn't know, and could only speculate on what was happening outside Cochin while we waited out the anxious days until facing the court.

*

An armed maritime police boat on patrol of the waters of Singapore paid scant attention to the small British freighter *Hetty Mitchell* as it chugged slowly into the designated shipping channel south of the island on 14 June 1983. The lights of Singapore's tall skyscrapers became more pronounced when seen from the ship as it took its place to the side of the eastbound lane where low-powered vessels must navigate. Beyond the anchor lights of hundreds of idle ships offshore, the airport on Changi Point was visible. Huge aircraft with landing lights flashing taxied along the tarmac, and in the sky at the end of the northwestern approach more planes were on holding patterns until their turn to touch down on Singapore earth. The airport was built on reclaimed land, and further to the east dredgers were still working around the clock, reclaiming more land to provide the overcrowded Singapore Island with room to breathe. Visible ahead of the freighter at the tip of a dense black mass was the blinking lighthouse which marked the lower end of the Malaysian peninsula. A similar distance south of the ship were lights that dotted the tangle of islands that make up Indonesia's northern frontier.

For the young New Zealand captain, Donald Dickinson, and his three crew, the day had been a tiring one, but now they resumed their shipboard duties. At dawn that day they had brought the *Hetty Mitchell* in towards Singapore for a second time. For three days previously they had chugged aimlessly around the South China Sea, a welcome break from the many weeks of preparation necessary to set up the ship's run. But his crew – the Englishmen Stephen Marriott and Peter Jackson, and the Canadian Willie Charlesworth – had had very little to do with planning this next run; that was Richard Merkley's role.

When the *Hetty Mitchell* had completed its dry-docking and moved to an offshore anchorage, Merkley sacked the ship's agents. A month later another agent was appointed, but Merkley's agreement with Marathone United Agency Pte Ltd stipulated that there was to be no physical attendance to the ship by the agents. Merkley then flew abroad. From Hong Kong he had organized finance for the next run, and also bought and had corrected the nautical charts the ship would need on its route. Using the alias of 'Mr Anson', Merkley had approached Jordan & Sons (Isle of Man) Ltd and purchased from them an 'off the shelf' company – Millsden Limited, General Merchants, Importers/ Exporters, with a registered office at 5 Upper Street, Isle of Man. On his return to Singapore, Merkley had made official calls to shipping agencies to arrange the ship's next voyage. Then, on the morning of 10 June, the agents Marathone United had filed a clearance for the *Hetty Mitchell*. Merkley paid the agent's fees in cash and later in the day the ship had sailed east and into the South China Sea.

After the entry recording the departure of the *Hetty Mitchell* had been punched into the Singapore Port Authority's computer, Merkley approached the British high commission, situated off the end of Orchard Road, where, on behalf of Primrose Investments, the name of the *Hetty Mitchell* was officially changed to just *Hetty*. Merkley had then remained in Singapore to wait the ship's return.

In the meantime he turned his attention to a new ship he had recently bought – the *Elysee Maru*, an attractive blue-hulled vessel for which US$175,000 was paid in cash. Earlier in the year Richard Merkley and Jim Howard had inspected the ship together. She was a sister ship to *Calypso*, Jacques Cousteau's famous ocean-research ship, though the newly acquired vessel would be used for an entirely different purpose.

Three days after leaving, and right on schedule, the *Hetty* motored back along Singapore Island and dropped her anchor in the roads. Merkley watched discreetly from the shore, while onboard the *Hetty* the crew knew what was expected of them. Singapore Port Authority records show that when the boarding officer arrived, Captain Dickinson told him that the ship's compass was broken and they would be remaining only that one day in Singapore waters.

Early in the afternoon an American, like Merkley of medium build with dark hair and a bushy moustache, boarded the ship with the explanation that he had come to repair the compass. Carrying a small satchel he walked straight to the bridge where he spoke to the *Hetty*'s young captain. However, nobody could later recall whether or not the ship's visitor was still carrying the small satchel when the service launch took him ashore. In the evening the service launch brought the ship's clearance papers for Port Moresby,

Papua New Guinea, and the anchor was winched aboard.

Richard Merkley must have been deeply concerned when news first reached him from India that the *Hetty Mitchell* had been named as a drug runner. So he had sent the ship away from Singapore, then changed its name and details before ordering the ship to return to Singapore. He knew that the Port of Singapore's computer would not cross-reference *Hetty* with *Hetty Mitchell*; instead, the records would show two separate ships, their unassociated movements lost in the hundreds recorded each day for Singapore waters. As the small freighter passed the lighthouse close to the east of Singapore with its four young crew members aboard, it was now known officially as *Hetty*, on charter to Millsden Ltd of the Isle of Man, owned by a Mr Anson and paid for from the Chartered Bank in Hong Kong. And so Merkley would have fully expected that if anything regarding the ship went wrong again, the records could not be traced back to his name, nor to that of Jim Howard.

*

Monday 13 June had begun in Cochin with a torrential downpour of rain. We lay in bed in the hotel room listening to its drumming on the roof and making our plans for the important day ahead.

At nine o'clock we gingerly stepped out into a street full of puddles and people clinging to large black umbrellas. We made our way carefully to an autorickshaw stand, trying to avoid speeding autos that drove through puddles spraying water, not wanting to soil our best clothes which we wore for our appearance in court that day, or the folders and notebooks which contained the essence of our defence. On the road passing the Naval Command Headquarters there was the usual monsoon flooding and traffic was down to a crawl, buses and trucks sounding their pitched airhorns as they joined the great push. From the height of the Thoppumpady bridge we could see the vehicles stretched out in line right across Willingdon Island and were relieved to have made an early enough start.

When we reached our lawyer's office we expected to meet Isher Iyer, but he was not available. There had been a change of plan, a fat junior advocate told us brusquely, and Isher Iyer had decided not to take the case after all.

I reached out and picked up the chubby little advocate by the collar, demanding an explanation. Had they realized what it would mean to back out on the last day that remained for us to take bail? There was fright in the advocate's eyes and he couldn't speak to answer my questions, but just whimpered. I dumped him unceremoniously into a corner to cringe. A second advocate confirmed what the first had said – that the lawyers were withdrawing their representation. But we didn't know then what had influenced their decision.

The bazaar was bright and busy and the world was going about its business around us as we walked with fear and worry towards the bank. No money had arrived from Australia, but the clerk told us that a Maxwell Fernandez had left a message for us to contact him urgently.

The *Malayalam Manorama*, a daily local-language newspaper which also published the current affairs magazine for which Maxwell worked, has an impressive office close to the railway bridge at Gandhi Nagar. When we walked into the reception area an obviously nervous Maxwell looked up from his desk and without a word to the others busy in the office stole towards the reception area, passing by us, and went out of the door. We slowly followed him outside.

Over coffee at a nearby café we talked with Maxwell. Anguish showed on his face and his fist lightly hit the top of the table as Alison told him that we still intended to go to court today, without a lawyer, and do the best possible to plead with the judge to set bail requirements within our capabilities. Maxwell thought it would be a brave act, but it was an act that should definitely not be taken. All morning he had been leaving urgent messages in every place where he thought we might go, he told us. Very early in the morning his telephone had rung, and he had been tipped off. On his way to the office he called on a law student he knew to check the source of the tip-off. But it had taken calls to two more of his contacts before the pieces had started to fall into place and he could be certain that what he now had to tell us was true. Even though the drug network had failed to get non-bailable warrants for our arrest and imprisonment, they had continued with their plan to get us in prison, because they had arranged for us to be murdered there. A verdict of suicide would be given.

Maxwell's revelation stunned us and he could see that we understood. He was taking a big risk in helping us, he went on, and if the underworld knew what he had told us they would kill him for sure. Shaking our hands and saying that he would be praying for us, he slipped nervously across the café and disappeared in the busy street.

At Fort Cochin we quickly checked the post office for mail delivery but nothing had come from Australia or from the Australian high commission in New Delhi. Before returning to the city we changed our clothes at the hotel, Alison tied a scarf around her long blonde hair and I tried to make myself look like a tourist. But our attempts at disguise seemed to have failed when a big blue police bus rolled slowly towards us down Shanmughan Road. With dread we heard our names being called. But it was our friend from the hardware store, Shridar Bhat, leaning halfway out of the police bus to call to us while two irritable policemen tried to pull the big man back inside the window frame. He and his friends had been arrested during a melee with the police at their local Hindu temple, Shridar called out jovially. We weren't sure whether to wave or try to look discreet as the riotous police bus rolled on down the road.

At the bank we locked our documents, evidence and notebooks inside our rented security box. One day we would need these papers to fight the court case. After hiding the key in the lining of a wallet, we returned by ferry to Fort Cochin.

Walking through our favourite streets of the old quarter, we made our way to the Mattancherry police station. There we gave a fourteen-page statement of every detail of the extortion attempt on *Tiger Rag* to Shri Moni, a senior police officer who DIG of Police Krishnan Nair had told us could be trusted to look into the fraudulent claims. The Mattancherry police station didn't come under the direct influence of Commissioner Antony's police headquarters on the Ernakulam mainland, where both of us had been treated with marked hostility, and our conversation with the Mattancherry officer was short and to the point. With a quiet hope that *Tiger Rag* would now be protected from further extortion attempts, we returned to the hotel to wait until dark.

Late in the night we checked out of the hotel and caught the last bus south. Before the Edacochin stop we got down and made our way cautiously to the boatyard. *Tiger Rag* was as we had left her, and nobody appeared to be about. Today had been our last day to take bail and we knew that the police would soon come to arrest us. Our time had run out. Despite our telegrams to the Australian government for help, they had not even tried to contact us. We couldn't understand why, nor did we know what had become of the money for bail we were sure would have been sent from Australia.

By candlelight inside the cabin Alison packed what she could into two bags. I was barely able to control my emotions. *Tiger Rag* was our home, all our familiar possessions were there, and now we had to leave her behind. Would we ever be able to return? And if we did, would we find the yacht safely here in this yard? When we left the boatyard by the back gate I dared not look back for fear my heart would break.

At midnight on 14 June, the day of our court case, we began the four-mile walk south to the Aroor Bridge. We would follow the same escape route Alison had taken when she had gone to Sri Lanka. Heavy clouds now rolled in over the moon, making it an eerie night. Our hearts were heavy with grief at leaving, but we were not defeated. One day we would return to Cochin for *Tiger Rag*.

16

The Rae Memorandum

'Hello, Mum,' I shouted into the telephone, 'I'm calling from Sri Lanka.' My voice carried from the telephone booth to where Brian sat on a broken chair in the rundown Colombo telephone exchange. Noise from heavy machinery on a nearby building site penetrated the telephone room, making it difficult to be heard. 'I'm coming back to Australia,' I continued. 'Can you send money for the fares?' I cupped one hand over my ear to block out the noise while we made arrangements for the bank transfer. 'And Mum, did you get my telegram about the bail money?' I listened to my mother explaining why the money hadn't been sent, and telling me about the communications she had had with the government in Canberra and the Australian Federal Police in Sydney who had been investigating our backgrounds. I was shocked at what she told me.

Brian and I walked back onto the streets of Colombo to join the Sunday-afternoon strollers, and I related the phone conversation with my mother in Sydney. 'Mum told me she has kept constantly in contact with the Foreign Affairs Department in Canberra, who have been telling her that we didn't face arrest, but were "safe and well". They also told her that "the situation in Cochin was calm". She wrote down the exact words for Dad. So when our telegram asking for bail money was delivered she phoned Canberra for advice. The official who returned her call insisted that "no money should be sent to India".'

Brian was stunned. Could there have been confusion, or a bureaucratic mistake? 'That occurred to me too,' I replied, 'so I asked if she was sure. But there was no mistake. Mum was told not to send the money. Last week she wrote about it in a letter to us. She said it was written right after Canberra had telephoned, and she kept a copy.'

Our aimless meandering had taken us to the seafront, where we sat and talked. The news about the actions of the Australian government official made us wonder if there was a conspiracy against us. We determined that once back in Australia we would seek out the appropriate authority and try to get to the bottom of it all.

We discussed the reason why, as my mother had told me on the telephone, the Australian Federal Police should mount an investigation into our backgrounds, when it was Jim Howard who was under investigation by the Indian authorities. We remembered Jim Howard's messenger in Cochin telling us that Howard had got the police in Australia looking into our backgrounds, and we concluded now that Howard did indeed have 'good connections' in Australian government circles as Jyl Gocher had insisted. But we had nothing to hide: neither of us had ever been in trouble with any authority.

The sun had fallen below the horizon of the Indian Ocean before we turned back down the city streets. A bus would take us the few miles to where we had taken a room in a private house next door to the YWCA, a place to recover from our four-day journey of escape across India. While we remained waiting in Colombo to arrange our flights to Australia we knew we had to be careful. In the previous two months both Jyl Gocher and Jim Howard had come to Colombo to deliver things or do business, and Consul Spring had admitted that Howard was known to officials of the Australian high commission here.

Back in Australia we would still be at risk from the drug network. We knew that couriers, ships and yachts had left from Cochin for many destinations in Australia, Europe and America, and we couldn't ignore Jim Howard's claim back in January that an Australian, a powerful man with endless wealth, was backing them.

While we wondered if elements within Australian government circles were either conspiring against us or simply inept, we didn't have any idea about what was going on between the various government offices involved. Many months later we used the Freedom of Information Act to obtain the information given in the following account.

On 21 June, a week after Brian and I had unexpectedly disappeared from Cochin, the high commission in New Delhi had still not formally reported to Canberra that we had gone missing, although at the time New Delhi were sending out official word that they were monitoring our situation in Cochin. Within twenty-four hours of my mother's telephone call to Canberra telling the Foreign Affairs Department that she had received a phone call from me in Colombo, the Canberra office sent telex CH118812 to the high commissions in New Delhi and Colombo.

Receiving that telex at the New Delhi high commission was the first secretary, Mr Bruce Rae, who had a personal interest in the file. The information which the Canberra telex relayed to him was that I had asked my mother to send A$2000 to me in Colombo to cover the costs of returning to Australia, and that Canberra had suggested that my mother not send any money but instead a one-way prepaid ticket for one person only, a ticket that could not be cashed in. But my mother had already made up her mind, she trusted me and had done as I had asked. The Canberra telex went on to give, for Consul Spring of the high commission in Colombo, further details like the name of the bank where the money from my mother would be sent, and the place where I was thought to be staying in Colombo. Canberra suggested to Consul Spring that he locate me in Colombo.

The Colombo high commission replied to Canberra in telex CL 14213. From the copy sent to New Delhi, Bruce Rae read that so far attempts to locate me in Colombo had failed, but contact had been made with the Chartered Bank where the A$2000 was being sent. Further developments would be advised to Canberra and New Delhi offices.

Two other files of interest were active in New Delhi at that time. One related to Jyl Gocher, who had walked into Bruce Rae's office earlier in the month, as Maxwell Fernandez had correctly informed us she would. Bruce Rae was later to admit that they had gone for drinks together and he had warmed to the young lady. The other active file of interest in New Delhi concerned Jim Howard, and that file showed that Howard had been making regular contact with Vice Consul John Woods.

While Brian and I had remained in Cochin, in great danger, the Australian government had advised my mother not to send money to us in India for bail. This would have resulted in our imprisonment in Cochin, had we not unexpectedly fled to Sri Lanka.

The Chartered Bank of Colombo has its head office in a prominent city location across the road from the parliament buildings. The principal banking floor is an enormous area with massive marble-clad columns. The counters are high and broad, and it gives the impression of a solid and secure institution.

The clerk in the inward-remittance section looked down his list of uncleared receipts until he found the name McGuinness. He went to a folder of papers on his desk and flicked through till he found the supporting documents. Two thousand Australian dollars had come in, he told us, but he required my passport for identification and told me that it would take thirty minutes or so before he would return with the completed paperwork. While waiting, Brian and I remained at the counter, adding up the expected cost of our airfares, accommodation and other expenses against the incoming remittance. I leaned across the counter to see if I could read the exchange rate on the papers that lay open on the clerk's desk, only to see on the top document, marked in bold red writing, an instruction that the remittance clerk was to notify the Australian high commission immediately when McGuinness arrived to collect her money.

Ten minutes later we were still wondering why Australian government officials might want to keep surveillance on us when I noticed a man who had just entered the bank. The short foreigner of average build had stopped inside to scan the floor until his eyes settled on us and he boldly approached. 'Here comes Trevor Spring of the Australian high commission,' I said slowly to Brian. Trevor Spring was gussied up like a magazine advertisement – monogrammed shirt, brand-name sunglasses, permanent-press slacks, handmade shoes with shiny brass buckles and matching leather attaché case.

'What a coincidence!' he said with an air of self-satisfaction. 'How are you, Alison?' He said that he would like us to accompany him to his office at the Australian high commission for a chat, his manner of authority suggesting we were obliged to do so. We said we might come later, after we'd talked it over first. After a prolonged silence Spring shrugged his shoulders and diplomatically withdrew into the banking chamber.

In the afternoon we caught a taxi for the short ride to the Australian high commission offices. Our conversation with Spring was cool, and got off to a bad start when I put him on the spot by asking him to reconfirm, this time in Brian's presence, whether or not Jim Howard was known to Australian diplomats in Colombo. He hesitated, then said Howard was known. We tried to press him for details, but Spring became tense and changed the subject.

The questions Spring anxiously asked us could not be disguised as bearing any relationship to his official interest in our welfare. Why were we suspicious of the Foreign Affairs Department and their consular officers? Where were we staying in Colombo? How much did we know of Howard's activities in Cochin? We wrote down Spring's questions in our notebook, and we told him that we would answer relevant questions in writing. Before coming to the Australian high commission we had purchased a notebook after Brian had reminded me that on my earlier visit to Sri Lanka in May I had not been allowed to see what Spring had written on his detailed telex to Canberra – an aspect of that meeting which still concerned us both very much.

We told Spring that the reason we had come wasn't because he had invited us for a 'chat', but there was one thing we wanted him to do for us. We explained that our knowledge of the drug connections had continued to grow, and much less than 50 per cent of our information had ever been passed along, and even less than that about connections to Australia. Therefore, could a telex be sent to Australia asking for an appointment with an official of the Australian police who could take this information from us? Consul Spring noted our request and asked us to return at the same time the following day for an answer.

In the afternoon that remained and late into the night we drafted a list of some of the foreign couriers, including Australians, who we were sure were involved in drug trafficking. We wrote two letters of complaint to the Australian government, in addition to drafting a statement which clearly set out the situation of *Tiger Rag*.

Our final visit to Consul Spring the next day was brief and formal. He told us that he had received a telex from Canberra stating that the Australian Federal Police had no wish to communicate with us. Telex CE584404 of 22 June read:

... THERE APPEARS TO BE NO ACTION WHICH THE AUSTRALIAN FEDERAL POLICE CAN TAKE IN RELATION TO THE ALLEGATIONS. IN VIEW OF THE FACT THAT MILGATE/MCGUINNESS HAVE ALREADY ADVISED THE INDIAN AUTHORITIES OF THEIR SUSPICIONS THERE SEEMS LITTLE POINT IN AUSTRALIAN FEDERAL POLICE CONTACTING THEM ...

We were astonished by this reply. While the Australian police had been prepared to conduct an investigation into our backgrounds, they weren't prepared even to consider looking into serious allegations that a drug ring involving Australian nationals was smuggling narcotics into Australia.

We asked Spring to witness our signatures on a letter of complaint, mentioning that it was only one of a number we would be writing about consular officers of the Foreign Affairs Department. As he read our words of complaint he

looked most distressed. The complaint also related to an
intrusive and unnecessary investigation into our private
affairs which had been carried out in Sydney at the request
of the Narcotics Liaison Officer of the high commission in
New Delhi. The information gathered had been leaked back
to Jim Howard, and although we knew that there could be
nothing against us in it, we were objecting to this invasion of
our privacy.

When the sun rose the next day we were still working
fervently at a borrowed typewriter in our rented accommodation. Determination overcame exhaustion as we added the
finishing touches to what had become five extensive folders
of information. After an early breakfast we made our way to
the Australian high commission offices to leave a copy for
Consul Spring in the care of an out-of-hours security attendant. In the city we posted others to Australia, including one
to the Honourable R. J. Hawke, prime minister of Australia.

It was nearing the end of June 1983 and our campaign,
which we hoped would result in our repossession of *Tiger
Rag*, had been set in motion.

News travels fast in diplomatic circles. Within hours of the
delivery to the Australian high commission in Colombo of
the dossier we had prepared, Mr Bruce Rae, first secretary
of the Australian high commission in New Delhi, was preparing a memorandum about the situation for Canberra.
From the telexes on his file Rae could see that there was to
be no investigation by Federal Police in Australia into the
allegations of drug smuggling, and so the memorandum he
was writing could close the Milgate/McGuinness file 550/2
for ever. This memorandum, M9356, contained false value
judgements, omitted certain facts, and cast aspersions on the
credibility of Brian Milgate and Alison McGuinness.

The memorandum ran to three pages, the comments made
in it left no doubts in the mind of any reader of how they
should view the situation. Rae referred to Milgate as 'reckless', a person who had gone against the best advice of his
own consular officers. Other comments Rae made misre-

presented the facts, for instance, 'We are not aware that Milgate was in any physical danger from Indian authorities, nor for that matter from any other source.' No mention was made of the attacks on Brian Milgate and a later imprisonment when Brian had been physically abused, although these facts had been confirmed to Vice Consul John Woods in May by Indian police authorities. Instead Rae chose to state that Milgate had a 'preoccupation' with an 'apparent crusade', and Miss Jyl Gocher had 'confirmed the problems she and Howard were experiencing' due to Milgate's 'totally false allegations'. The memorandum depicted Jyl Gocher as an innocent victim and failed to mention that Jim Howard had phoned the Australian high commission on the same day as the memo was written, to ask that a message be passed to Jyl Gocher alerting her that Cochin authorities were still looking for her. (She had earlier fled from an unserved subpoena in Cochin, as well as unfinished interviews with Superintendent Shreedharan.)

On the topic of the defamation case Rae continued to be elusive. Details of the case had first been revealed to him three weeks earlier when Maxwell Fernandez had rung the high commission, and our telegram from Cochin reached him a few days later. In addition Jyl Gocher had filled in the missing points a week later when she had arrived at his office. But Rae blamed poor Indian communications for his 'inability' to report the matter to Canberra.

Having completed his memorandum, Rae included it in the diplomatic mailbag to Canberra on 24 June. Our complaints against certain consular officers would now be dismissed, as our attempts to pass information to the Australian Federal Police had been.

17

The Blinds are Down

The British Airways jumbo jet banked high above the capital city of Western Australia. Looking down, Brian and I could see the lights and neon signs contrasted against the blackness of the Indian Ocean. It was 4 a.m. and most of the city's 750,000 inhabitants were asleep. Built on the western edge of Australia's vast interior desert, Perth is truly remote. Our home city of Sydney lay 3000 miles to the east, but we had decided that it would be better to hide from the drug-smuggling syndicate's Australian connections in a place where we weren't known.

The jumbo touched down and taxied to the terminal building. We disembarked and walked huddled close together across the tarmac to the immigration building. The air temperature was seven degrees Celsius and a chilling wind was blowing; winter had come to the southern hemisphere. Our winter clothes were locked in a storeroom at Edacochin. With one travel bag apiece and enough money only for a humble start, our prospects seemed bleak.

However, by the end of our first week in Perth we had started to find our feet. A kind divorcee had given us temporary accommodation in her comfortable suburban home, and both of us had legally changed our surnames, an action we decided was necessary for our security. Under my new name I had applied at local high schools for relief teaching positions, and early on two mornings I had been called to take the classes of absent teachers. We had rented a private mailbox at the city's central post office as an anonymous address, and Brian, having been given the loan of an old typewriter, had turned his attention to getting *Tiger Rag* back.

The first of our official calls was made on the day after

our return to Australia. Mr Frank Hedges, a deputy commonwealth ombudsman representing the state of Western Australia, was at first curious about us. We looked drawn, displaced and tinged blue from the cold. Our nightmarish tale of intrigue in faraway India seemed quite out of place on the eighteenth floor of the prestigious concrete and glass City Centre Tower complex overlooking Perth's picturesque Swan River. An affable and helpful man, Mr Hedges explained that we had done the right thing in coming to his office. The Commonwealth ombudsman functioned to investigate complaints against federal public servants, though our case might be considered in a different light as its events had mostly occurred beyond Australian shores. He would find out what he could from Canberra and promised not to divulge our whereabouts or new identities.

When we next called to see Mr Hedges he told us that the Foreign Affairs Department had been very negative to his first approach. He couldn't understand the reason for their uncooperative response, nor could he see why the Federal Police were unwilling to interview us. After our meeting, Mr Hedges's secretary suggested that we make an appointment to see Senator Fred Chaney, leader of the opposition in the Australian senate, who also kept an office in the City Centre Tower.

Our appointment with Senator Chaney was fixed for 8.30 a.m. on the sixth day after our return to Australia. It was a very cold morning so to keep warm we dressed in layer upon layer of summer clothing. On the ground floor of the City Centre Tower we waited for the elevator and the ride up to the twenty-third floor. A neatly dressed man of distinguished appearance joined us in the lift, and a short time later he saw us being shown into his office.

Senator Chaney was an approachable man with the common touch, and the intelligence and skill he showed in getting to the heart of our problems impressed us. He questioned us to gauge the strength of our story and, satisfied, offered to write a letter on our behalf to the prime minister. The letter would ask what assistance could be provided to recover our property from India and who was the appropriate body or person in Australia to whom we could give information.

The last thing we did during this first week back in Australia was to write a long and detailed letter to the Honourable Mr Justice D. G. Stewart, the eminent man who had previously presided over a royal commission into the notorious Terrance Clark and the 'Mr Asia' drug syndicate. Support from a royal commissioner could be helpful in getting an investigation into our drug-trafficking allegations. There was also the possibility that a link existed between the smugglers we thought were bringing drugs into Australia and the sinister Nugan Hand group whose activities Mr Justice Stewart had recently been appointed to inquire into. Brian recalled Jim Howard having boasted of knowing the now deceased Mr Frank Nugan during his menacing interrogation when Brian had been held prisoner in Cochin.

My teaching work became more regular and Brian found casual work. We sold our camera and bought bicycles with the money, and when our first wage cheques came in we started to look for a more permanent and private place to live. Frustrated that we had received no reply or acknowledgement to the many letters we had written to various departments of the Australian government, we wrote a second letter to the prime minister, suggesting in it that information on organized crime links to Australia had been suppressed by government officers.

Two days later the Commonwealth ombudsman's office phoned to ask us to call in, but the news Mr Hedges gave us was grave. The Foreign Affairs Department had decided to dismiss our allegations and were not prepared in the slightest way to assist with the recovery of *Tiger Rag*. Nor was it interested to discover whether *Tiger Rag* was going to be used by the network as a courier vessel for one drug run, only to be scuttled afterwards, as we explained was common practice among drug smugglers. Mr Hedges assured us that the ombudsman's office were willing to fight the Foreign Affairs Department decision on our behalf.

The disappointment hit me hard, and when we emerged onto the city streets I broke into a flood of tears. The faith I had maintained in the Australian government system had been finally destroyed. We walked solemnly along St George's Terrace in the direction of our pushbikes, but when we passed the offices of the *West Australian* newspaper Brian decided the time had come to try the press once more. If pressure was applied to those in authority, we might be given a hearing.

The *West Australian* is Perth's long-established morning daily. Its traditional layout and large format reflect conservative views. When we entered at six o'clock the building was still a scene of activity, though the deadline for the following day's first edition had passed.

Norm Aisbett, the journalist sent to speak with us, was a big fellow who still had the spring of youth in his step. He led us through the editorial office to a disarray of desks and dragged up extra chairs. His own desk was in a state of confusion but he quickly found pen and pad and settled into his chair. However, his shorthand notes soon stopped and he just listened as we went through the bones of our complicated story. The newspaper's reputation was considerable and we must be thoroughly checked out, he told us as he leaned back precariously in his small chair. He wanted first to photocopy our passports and documents and do some independent checking, and if his editor thought the story was a possibility he would get in touch with us. Norm Aisbett therefore became the third person who knew our identity, trust being necessary from our side as well as his.

The next day Norm came to see us. The smile on his boyish face was broad as he told us he had phoned a contact who had confirmed that one person we had named was an Australian drug courier and two Australian-registered vessels we had mentioned had been subject to past surveillance, suspected of smuggling narcotics by sea into northern Australia. Norm's editor, normally a sceptical man, had privately phoned his own confidential sources in Canberra and found another of our alleged traffickers who was known to be involved in the drug trade. That was enough to satisfy the chief editor. But Norm told us that so far nothing had come back about the *Hetty Mitchell*.

The edition of the *West Australian* for 16 July carried a front-page story written by Norman Aisbett and headed TWO FLED DRUG TERROR. It told our account simply and accurately, and we hoped it would bring a reply from Canberra. Three days later a follow-up entitled CHANEY TAKES UP COUPLE'S CHARGE was published, along with a picture of the popular local senator.

Apart from a tersely worded telegram from the Department of Foreign Affairs stating that it had no intention of assisting us with the recovery of *Tiger Rag* and detailing the limits of consular repsonsibility in a foreign country, no other response came from Canberra. No spokesman could be found in Canberra who was willing to make a specific public comment on our case. At the Foreign Affairs Department the blinds had been pulled down.

Later we were able to learn that during the last two weeks of July the number of people in Canberra who opened and closed the Milgate/McGuinness file increased from just a few to many. Word spread among the public servants who knew about the case that since our return to Australia we had gathered influential backing. Latest to add his support was Royal Commissioner Mr Justice Stewart who had offered to pass our information to Major General Grey, head of the Australian Federal Police. Senior public servants were beginning to ask the question of those of lower rank – were Milgate and McGuinness liars, or were their own consular boys at fault?

After our allegations that the Australian Federal Police had dismissed our information about the way organized crime was smuggling drugs into Australia, the ball was passed around the full circle of police and consular collaborators in Canberra, Columbo, Bangkok and India (even Jim Howard got into the game), but the Narcotics Liaison Officer in New Delhi sent the ball out of play with his telex ND 38912 to Canberra: WE ARE RELUCTANT TO ASK THE DRI ABOUT ITS [INDIAN] INVESTIGATION UNTIL WE HAVE PROVIDED THEM WITH THE INFORMATION THEY HAVE REQUESTED. However, nobody in Canberra asked *why* the information requested by the Indian DRI and gathered in Australia some months before was still being withheld.

Some of our complaints about the actions of its own consular officers were eventually recognized by the Australian high commission in New Delhi. In telex ND 39021 of 4 August 1983, it was acknowledged that Brian Milgate had indeed been illegally imprisoned as he had claimed, and that the imprisonment had been revealed to Vice Consul John Woods when he had visited Cochin's DIG of police, Krishnan Nair, in May. In New Delhi's words, on telex ND 39021 ... HE [MILGATE] DID NOT RAISE THE MATTER AGAIN DURING WOODS' STAY IN COCHIN WHICH LED WOODS TO BELIEVE THAT MILGATE WAS SATISFIED NOT TO PRESS THE MATTER FURTHER WITH POLICE. New Delhi gave no explanation of how Woods made this assessment, or why the imprisonment had not been reported to Canberra, or why the copy of Brian's statement of complaint to the DIG of police, given to John Woods, had never been put on the New Delhi file.

Facts about other claims we had made began to gather in Canberra. On 5 August, Kevin McMahon, executive officer of the consular operations section of the Foreign Affairs Department, considered his legal position in the light of our letters of complaint sent from Sri Lanka and the conflicting letter sent on the same day from India by Bruce Rae. (McMahon's name became known to us in Colombo when we read it on the cover of our file in Consul Spring's office. On our return to Australia, Deputy Ombudsman Frank Hedges informed us that McMahon was the contact officer in our case. It was from McMahon's department that Alison's mother in Sydney had been telephoned about the bail money, and Perth-based journalists had learned of McMahon's involvement from their Canberra contacts.)

Kevin McMahon began the opening paragraph of the internal memo he wrote that day, 'The purpose of this minute is to forewarn you that I may require Commonwealth Legal Assistance if civil proceedings are instituted against me by Mr Brian Milgate and Ms Alison McGuinness.'

Our complaints eventually came to the attention of senior consular public servants who reported to the foreign minister. The public servants decided to exercise their initiative and order an inquiry, perhaps thinking it would pre-empt the minister's decision. Somebody from the security and intelligence section was chosen to conduct the investigation.

*

Donald Dickinson, the young New Zealand captain of the *Hetty*, had gone up to the bridge to begin his regular watch. Low on the horizon to the northwest he could see a smudge of dark grey. The far-off cliffs of Oman hadn't moved since he was last on the bridge, when the *Hetty*'s engine had been shut down. The regular sightings of other ships bound to or from the Persian Gulf confirmed their position close to the shipping lane. Dirty fuel had caused the ship's diesel engine's injectors to become clogged and inefficient, and to effect repairs it had been necessary to shut down all power except the ship's generator. As the ship wallowed on the gentle ocean swell, Dickinson wrote up the logbook.

Far below the bridge where Dickinson sat, Stephen Marriott was on duty in the engine-room, with his friend Willie Charlesworth helping him. Both men had been recruited by Richard Merkley and flown from the Virgin Islands nine months before to join the ship in London. Marriott by now knew the repair procedure well. This run was important and since the ship still had a long way to go he would need to work patiently to ensure there would be no further complications.

Elsewhere on board was the *Hetty*'s fourth crewman. Peter Jackson was a 34-year-old Englishman from Lancashire whom Richard Merkley had also recruited from the Virgin Islands, and in April he had been flown to Singapore to join the ship. Unlike Marriott and Charlesworth, Jackson was not a roughneck. His American wife and their two daughters were waiting for him back in her home town of Liberty, Missouri.

Captain Dickinson had started the logbook he was writing up on 14 June when the *Hetty* had sailed from Singapore for Port Moresby. But the ship hadn't made for New Guinea, as Richard Merkley had told the Singapore authorities, instead it had steamed directly to Surabaya, an Indonesian port on the eastern end of the long island of Java, where the four passports belonging to the crew had been stamped on 30 June.

For six weeks after their arrival in Surabaya there was no entry in the logbook. While the *Hetty* remained at anchor, Marriott and Charlesworth had wasted no time in taking a holiday. However, before they caught the local passenger ferry for the approximately 150-mile voyage southeast to the tourist island of Bali, they had an important operation to carry out.

Carefully cutting lengthways through the sole of a thick rubber thong, they sliced out a square cavity from the inside. Heroin in white powder form was inserted into the cavity and rubber compound was used to glue the thong back together. The two were so pleased with themselves that they took photographs of their ingenious idea of concealment. The narcotics were part of their cut from the *Hetty*'s Cochin-to-Singapore run, and sold on the street in Bali it would give them plenty of money for a luxury holiday.

On 14 August the *Hetty* was moved from its outside mooring to a loading berth alongside the Surabaya wharf. The next step in Richard Merkley's plan to disguise the movements of the ship was for Captain Dickinson to misreport to Lloyd's Shipping Intelligence Unit that the ship had arrived in Surabaya that day, after sailing empty from Port Moresby. A cargo of cheap muranti timber was loaded into the hold and, with extra fuel aboard, the *Hetty* cleared Surabaya port on 15 August bound for Philadelphia, USA.

Logbook entries recorded the ship's route along the northern side of Java Island, and leaving Sumatra to starboard, the ship entered the Indian Ocean through the Sunda Strait and set course for Sri Lanka. The logbook records that on 23 August the *Hetty* received a radio message from Mr Merkley of Singapore, 'Ship proceed to Dubai.'

On its route northwest towards the Persian Gulf port of Dubai, the ship steamed close along the coast of southwestern India, and late on the night of 27 August the lights on the coast of Kerala State were clearly visible. When the *Hetty* was in a more or less central position in the Indian Ocean the engine was stopped. For twenty-two hours the ship remained in position, close to a fishing bank sometimes worked by large deep-ocean trawlers that ran out of ports with fish-canning and frozen-packaging facilities – Karachi to the north, Bombay to the northeast and Cochin to the southeast.

When the *Hetty* officially arrived in Dubai harbour on 7 September, their agent Mubarak Shipping reported that part of the ship's cargo of timber had to be unloaded. However, during the *Hetty*'s three days in Dubai, the ship's holds remained closed and padlocked. Apart from entry and clearance paperwork and getting extra fuel for the vessel, the ship's agent performed only one other task. They arranged two boarding passes, one for the man they knew only as Mr Anson, and one for his business colleague. The men had come to inspect the cargo in the ship's holds. Their access was by way of a small deck hatch forward of the captain's dayroom and the two men took torches before disappearing together down the steel-runged ladder into the darkness of the hold.

Young Captain Dickinson was aware that this inspection was the real reason for the *Hetty* having been ordered to Dubai. The man who went aboard with Richard Merkley, alias Mr Anson, would have insisted on seeing the merchandise in the hold before his organization would put up front the huge cash deposit which Merkley would have demanded before the shipment could be delivered.

From Dubai the *Hetty* had recommenced its voyage to Philadelphia. But off the coast of Oman the trouble with the dirty fuel injectors had come. Captain Dickinson finished his entry in the logbook. Soon the ship would be underway once more and their passage would take them into the Gulf of Aden, up the Red Sea and in convoy through the Suez Canal. After steaming west across the Mediterranean Sea a stop for fuel would be made in Gibraltar, necessary before the long haul to the other side of the Atlantic Ocean. By Christmas the run would be over. The precious cargo the ship carried would have been halfway round the world and delivered, and Dickinson expected to be safely back in the Virgin Islands, a very wealthy young man.

*

Throughout August we kept up our struggle to get the Australian government to look into our two main complaints – against certain consular officers, and against the Australian Federal Police who had disregarded information about a drug syndicate with operations extending into Australia.

Also in August Brian and I moved into a discreetly located suburban apartment. When the unusual accommodation was offered to us we had some reservations, but Eric Kenny, the manager of the establishment, immediately put us at ease. Downstairs was a funeral parlour, while upstairs were two modern apartments which were offered rent-free in exchange for out-of-hours telephone answering shared between tenants. This suited us because it was an extremely good place for us to hide out, and convenient as well; I had accepted a temporary teaching appointment at a nearby high school until the end of the 1983 school year. Three of the four telephone lines installed into the building's switchboard had unlisted numbers as a precaution against hoax callers.

A small portable typewriter had been among the many items we bought to re-establish ourselves. Late into the night we typed out the pages of letters and statements, and the copies in our Australian files began to number in the hundreds. The benefit of having an unlisted telephone number was appreciated as our enquiries began into the movements of couriers who came and went from Cochin to Australia. Twice our telephone budget enabled us to speak to Cochin. From Superintendent Shreedharan we discovered that Jim Howard was still in the Bolghatty Hotel and foreigners still came to visit him. The *Steppenwolf* was ready to leave and had been moved to the anchorage off the island, but the superintendent thought that Howard had been waiting for something else. Nobody had gone out to Edacochin, however, so we could get no news about *Tiger Rag*.

At the very end of August a message came from the ombudsman's office that the local division of the Federal Police were willing to interview us, so we took a day off work and rode our pushbikes into the city to meet two detectives. The interview lasted two hours in which we briefly outlined what we knew concerning drug connections into Australia. We explained the drug network's original plan of bringing the *Hetty* into the port of Townsville in Queensland loaded with a cargo of explosives destined for the mines of Mount Isa. The idea of setting up the route as a permanent run had been passed to the *Hetty*'s former mate, Robert Turnbull, by the crew that had been recruited by Merkley, and then in turn by him to us. But no mention was made to Turnbull of what may have been concealed in the boxes marked EXPLOSIVES. In one of our first meetings with Howard we could remember him questioning Brian after he had learned that *Tiger Rag* had once put into the port of Townsville. Howard had been anxious to know what we knew of the security layout of the port and how strictly customs procedures were enforced. Later Jyl Gocher had also mentioned the same 'run to Townsville'.

We told the Federal Police detectives that apart from the *Hetty*, the drug network used other vessels – at least two other ships and several yachts. We gave details of a New Zealander who had brought a Vietnamese-built fishing boat to Cochin in March 1983, with at least one convicted heroin trafficker among his crew. A large plywood catamaran with an Australian captain had also arrived in March 1983, from Bali. It was then already under suspicion of smuggling drugs into Australia, and a young female member of the crew had an Australian drug conviction. A yacht whose ownership was traced to a Melbourne laywer, had likewise been sailed to India, but its departure from Australia had not been reported to the Australian authorities. Once in India the crew had made their way directly to the Bolghatty Hotel to meet Jim Howard. We also told the detectives that the port of Darwin in Australia's vast north was preferred by one particular cell of couriers who were acquainted with each other. Darwin is a relatively small city, and the people we met in Cochin who regularly commuted there by aircraft or yacht became obvious to us soon after we had met Jim Howard. These couriers were recruited mostly from the young and un-employed.

Throughout the interview with the Federal Police not one detail was taken down, and the officers said they were unaware of who Jim Howard was or even that he had a criminal record in Australia. We came away feeling that it had been a waste of our time, that the interview had only been an attempt by Canberra to placate us and to allow the police to be seen to have interviewed us. But our de-termination to get *Tiger Rag* back didn't falter, and neither, it seemed, had the regular flow of drugs from Cochin. Almost every other day we read reports in the media of drug-related crime and drug addiction, all confirming the evils of the drug world. So why was our information ignored by the Australian police? We didn't know.

In September, to spread our information even further, we wrote long detailed letters to international police forces – the Police Department of the Home Office in London, the Sous-direction d'Affaires Criminelles in Paris, and the Drug Enforcement Administration in Washington – naming people, ships and yachts we thought might come up on their computers, including the *Hetty Mitchell* and mentioning its use for running drugs.

18

Intelligence at Work

A phone call on the last day of September led us to a most unorthodox meeting. The cloak-and-dagger style of the man who interviewed us caused us to contemplate one possible aspect of Jim Howard's 'association' with the Australian government which we had been reluctant to pursue.

The scenario began when a message came from the ombudsman's office – we were to telephone a number in Canberra and ask for 'Mr Sever of the Foreign Affairs Department'. When we called we expected to be connected through a switchboard, but it was a private line. Mr Sever told us he would be coming to Perth to talk to us and it would only suit him to fly the 3000 miles the following Sunday, 2 October. We were to meet him in the Foreign Affairs Department offices in the city at 1300 hours sharp. A guard would be expecting us then and would let us into the building.

Having been given such short notice of the meeting we began immediately to prepare our paperwork. A seven-page typed statement, finished on the Sunday morning of our appointment, detailed every meeting and phone call that had taken place between consular officers and ourselves. The document was comprehensive, its contents irrefutable.

Perth's streets were all but deserted when we cycled through them to the Department of Foreign Affairs office in St George's Terrace. The following day was also a public holiday and a good many of the city's inhabitants had fled for the three-day weekend to holiday venues along the coast. All the car parks were empty. It seemed strange that on a Sunday holiday we should be going to an official meeting in the deserted city skyscraper which housed commonwealth and state public offices.

The interview took place behind the closed doors of the inner sanctum of the Foreign Affairs Department, and the security section to which we were directed had many extra precautions – specially fitted doors, alarms, red lights and key panels. We had thought a security section was meant to protect rather than to be protected itself.

Mr Adrian Sever was waiting in the office we had been directed to by one of his Perth-based colleagues. He was a chubby middle-aged man whose eyes darted about the room from person to person. His Perth colleague looked bored.

After introductions had been made we produced the statement which we had worked hard to prepare. Mr Sever gave it to his colleague to take to another section to photocopy while he explained his position as a senior officer of the security and intelligence section of the Foreign Affairs Department. He had come to Perth to review our complaints and the meeting was to be recorded on tape. But his main concern was the connection which we had discerned that Howard had with the Australian government. Sever brought up the subject of the Australian Secret Intelligence Service (ASIS), a unit of the Foreign Affairs Department he worked with, asking why we thought Howard had connections with it. We were stunned by Sever's question; neither of us had ever suggested that Jim Howard had any involvement with ASIS.

The interview lasted four hours during which Sever steered us round in circles, avoiding the real issue – our complaints against consular officers of the department. We objected that we had not been informed beforehand that this was to be the department's one and only meeting with us, and that Sever had known that more than a month before, we had applied under the Freedom of Information Act for copies of the hundreds of telexes and memos in the department's Canberra files on us. Without these documents, due to be released within days, we were severely disadvantaged in not knowing what officers had done against us. The typed statement we had prepared lay ignored and unread on the table in front of the chubby intelligence man, and he refused to be drawn into discussing what we had given as our complaints. Instead, Sever held a kangaroo court.

When we waited later at the ground-floor exit for the guard to let us out of the building, Sever emerged from the lift. He had put on a neutral-coloured gaberdine trench coat which was buckled at the waist and had the collar pulled up. Looking like a character from a Len Deighton spy novel, he peered suspiciously out at the street before emerging into the warm spring evening. His last question to us was for directions to the cinemas. He said he was a nervous man who found it hard to relax, and taking in a movie before his six-hour flight back to Canberra might help. We suggested dryly that the James Bond film showing up the road might suit him.

Our meeting with Sever left us feeling cheated and angry. His intent had been shown in his support and open praise of the New Delhi vice consul, John Woods, and in his words of total exoneration of Executive Officer Kevin McMahon of Canberra, before he had heard our side of the story. Sever was convinced that a 'Mr Elliott', a person who worked for an opposition politician, was the person who had advised Alison's mother not to send the bail money to us in India. After the meeting we put a call through to Sydney and spoke to Alison's mother. Her recollection of circumstances was clear and no 'Mr Elliott' had at any time been involved. But she had been in contact with a Hazel Elliot, a secretary in the office of Don Dobie, a local member of Federal Parliament in her constituency. Twice we wrote to Don Dobie seeking clarification on this very serious charge, but Dobie wouldn't even answer our letters.

In the days after our meeting with Sever we summarized our complaints in a letter which we addressed to the foreign minister, Bill Hayden, and posted on 4 October. However, we remained haunted by a peculiar feeling about Mr Sever and his reluctance to discuss Jim Howard. He had noticeably stirred when we told him that Howard's deportation from South Africa for political reasons had been recently confirmed, as had his extensive criminal record there. Moreover, that was not the only country which we now knew had deported him. Sever must also have known that Howard's passport address, as given to the Australian high commission in Colombo, was Beirut, Lebanon.

Our suspicions about the curious Mr Sever heightened when we phoned the Department of Foreign Affairs in Canberra and were told there was no Adrian Sever listed in their directory. Sever hadn't specified his unit when sending official correspondence. A media source found that the Canberra-based man did hold a position in some unit of the Department of Foreign Affairs. From the Perth public library we found that in the 1970s the Australian Secret Intelligence Service had come under the cover of the Foreign Affairs Department. ASIS, originally established in 1952, is Australia's overseas espionage unit. It uses agents operating under diplomatic or business cover to spy on foreign governments, and such activities are widely carried out by ASIS in the Asian region. The head of ASIS was a former diplomat in the Foreign Affairs Department and ironically had held the same administrative positions as those in Canberra who were now reviewing our case.

When six months previously an investigation had first been mounted by Cochin customs into Howard's espionage connections, we had been sceptical, thinking it to have been just a red herring on the part of Additional Collector Venugopalan to make allegations about Howard seem all the more unbelievable. Many things had happened, however, in the intervening period to make us reconsider. Cochin was a sensitive port visited daily by Soviet shipping and active warships of many foreign countries, as well as being the base of India's Southern Naval Command. Howard's past had given him easy access to the intelligence community as he moved around Asian and African trouble spots taking photographs, and Jyl Gocher had been most convincing when she told us Howard 'worked for the Australian government'. Certainly he carried all the gadgets, electronic aids and darkroom photographic facilities that one would expect an agent to use. We had seen him operating the computer, whose floppy disks investigators had been unable to find and which were thought to have contained naval and military information passed to Howard from sources within Cochin. From his front room in Cochin's Bolghatty Hotel Howard was suspected of having noted the movement of shipping to and from the port and later recorded those and other details on his computer. The collected facts pointed to Howard having an espionage connection, but we didn't expect that the Australian government would ever admit that he was a spy.

In October we finally received the overdue copies of telexes and memos we had applied for in August under the Freedom of Information Act. A covering letter sent by a director of the Foreign Affairs Department claimed that 'all documents held by the department in Canberra' had been sent, and that 'nothing is deliberately being withheld and no exemptions are being claimed'. However, because the Act did not apply to Australian government offices outside Australia, documents held exclusively on file in Colombo or New Delhi were not released to us.

Despite Canberra's reassurance that we were receiving the complete file, we methodically listed and cross-referenced all numbers and codes, only to find that Canberra had tried to mislead us — a good many of the documents had been omitted. At once we sent a letter to the director of the Foreign Affairs Department listing eight reference numbers of telexes known to be missing from our Canberra file, and asking that these and other missing documents be sent or explanation given of why they were being withheld, this being our right under Australian law.

While we waited for Canberra to respond, we pored carefully through the documents we had been given. Confirmation of the attitude shown towards us by certain consular officers was evident in the text, and we found enough damaging facts about Jim Howard for us to decide that, added to what we already had, it was now worth the risk of returning to India to face Howard in court. Our faint hopes that we would be able to return one day for our *Tiger Rag* were burning brighter.

It was what *had not* been said in the telex reports that worried us most. When Alison had gone to Sri Lanka from Cochin and spoken to Consul Trevor Spring, she had not been permitted to check the telex Spring had sent to Canberra which related Alison's information. We now read it and were aghast at its failure to even convey Jim Howard's alleged involvement in drug-smuggling. We also read for the first time about First Secretary Bruce Rae's memorandum discrediting us, about John Woods's failure to report the situation in Cochin correctly, and about the reprimand given to the Bombay consul, Ian Tricks, for passing our information directly to the Australian police. There were other staggering revelations in the telexes. For what reason, we asked, had Adrian Sever rushed through the Foreign Affairs Department inquiry into our complaints before we were given access to these documents?

The documents confirmed our impression that Jim Howard was in regular communication with the Australian government, though we were still uncertain of the nature of this communication. We wondered if the missing telexes would bring an answer, because the sequence of the file made it appear that most of them must contain references to Jim Howard. However, the Foreign Affairs Department refused us access to them. The reason given was the closest answer to the Howard mystery that we could expect the government would ever issue ... 'REFUSED BECAUSE TELEX ... CONTAINS DIRECTIONS WHOSE DISCLOSURE COULD REASONABLY BE EXPECTED TO HAVE AN ADVERSE EFFECT ON THE DEPARTMENT'S INTELLIGENCE GATHERING FUNCTION.'

19

Bahamas or Bust

The pilot of the small jet was pleased with the late autumn weather. The sun was dipping behind the low flat countryside of New Jersey, more than 100 miles away on the United States' East Coast. It was 5.30 p.m. on Tuesday 1 November 1983 and soon he would complete his routine patrol, turning to the northeast for the flight to the Coast Guard base in Cape Cod, Massachusetts. His attention turned to the small freighter on the ocean below him. From the wash it was making, he could tell that the freighter was moving very slowly through the water, going nowhere. The pilot reached for his radio transmitter to raise the base operator and report his suspicions.

At the Coast Guard base the information was passed to a duty officer who read the brief detail, then coded himself into the computer. Sitting in front of the terminal, he keyed in the name that the pilot had read on the freighter's stern – *Hetty*. The display came up negative, and the computer requested further instructions. The duty officer keyed in the signal for display of similar names or names using the same letters. When it came up, the duty officer read down the list of vessels recorded in the computer, vessels that were known by the authorities or that the authorities had been informed were being used for drug smuggling. He noted down the code numbers of those he thought could be a possible match for the suspicious freighter, and keyed in a further request for information on those numbers. One by one the details of each ship were displayed. He read one entry twice, then he knew he had it and pushed a button on the keyboard which set a printer alongside the terminal in motion. While it was still rattling out a repeat of the display screen, the duty officer stood and straightened his uniform, eager to present his findings to the commanding officer.

The croupiers were only beginning to set up their evening tables in New Jersey's Atlantic City casinos as the 95-foot *Cape Star* cleared the harbour breakwater and put to sea. Reaching full cruising speed she set course into the Atlantic towards the last known position of the freighter, thought to be 80 or so miles to the east. At 2.30 a.m. on 2 November the *Cape Star* radioed the Coast Guard base that they had a vessel on radar the size of the freighter, and that the ship was moving very slowly.

About 50 miles to the north-northeast the radio officer of the 210-foot Coast Guard cutter *Vigorous* heard the *Cape Star*'s call. The big cutter out of the Coast Guard's base in New London, Connecticut, altered course to intercept the two vessels. With its three-inch gun and specially trained boarding party, the *Vigorous* was better prepared for the task ahead.

As dawn came, both Coast Guard vessels were in sight of the freighter and taking up position. At 5.40 a.m. the freighter was raised on the radio.

Aboard the *Hetty*, Captain Dickinson had a feeling of dread when he looked out from the bridge at the powerful cutter outlined in the steely grey dawn. After informing the Coast Guard vessel by radio that the *Hetty*'s destination was the Bahamas and that he was not allowing them to board the ship, Dickinson ordered full speed from the ship's engine and a course set to take them away from the USA coast as quickly as possible, and he tried once more to raise the maritime radio operator for a phone connection to Richard Merkley, registered at the Ramada Hotel in Connecticut under the name of Mr Anson.

At Coast Guard headquarters the situation off the coast of New Jersey was being closely monitored. The Coast Guard was entitled to board the *Hetty* under a 1981 British-American agreement that subjects British flag ships within 150 miles of the United States coast to US laws, but protocol still had to be observed. The State Department and the British embassy in Washington were informed, and presumably a message was sent to the Foreign Office in London.

As the morning slipped away, the *Vigorous* continued to shadow the *Hetty* as it raced to clear US territorial waters. At 10.15 a.m. the Coast Guard commandant's office notified the *Vigorous* that permission was given to board the freighter, using force if necessary. The cutter drew closer to the *Hetty*, small arms were broken out and distributed, and the crew prepared the deck gun for action.

By noon the *Hetty* had surrendered and shut down its engine. She lay hove to while the armed boarding party came aboard. Coast Guard men methodically searched the ship; others kept a close watch over the four crewmen, who were unwilling to answer questions. The seal of the inspection hatch to the hold was broken open and trained searchers climbed down. Long planks of timber, loaded aboard in Indonesia, filled the hold. The searchers moved forward, systematically checking the cargo, and below the forward hatch one of the men saw the corner of a burlap sack that was just visible under a thin covering of timber planks. The searcher called his partner to help move away some of the lumber. Approximately 500 burlap sacks were eventually revealed and it appeared that this cargo had been loaded some time after the timber. One of the sacks, which was pulled clear of the rest, was thought to weigh about 70 pounds. When the searcher opened the sack he let out a long whistle that brought his partner to take a closer look.

On the bridge of the *Hetty* a Coast Guard officer opened the freighter's logbook and began to write:

The MV *Hetty*, UK, has this day been seized for a violation of United States Smuggling Laws by Ens. E. Q. Kahler. This vessel was noted in violation upon positive THC test for a controlled substance in position 38° 30.5'N 072° 57.2'W by a boarding party from USCG *Vigorous* (WMEL-627) at 22.00 – at that time this vessel has been placed in my charge for a voyage to a United States port for arraignment.

While the *Hetty* made its way under escort towards Cape

May on the southern end of New Jersey, the US Customs Department were advised to take possession of the ship and its illegal cargo, while federal agents of the Drug Enforcement Administration were advised that the Coast Guard wished to hand over the freighter's four-man crew.

A news conference was called for the following morning. The Coast Guard was very pleased – it had a record haul. The *Hetty* had in its holds an estimated 30,000 blocks of hashish, each block weighing a little over one pound. This staggering 14-ton haul of hashish would have been worth more than $100 million on the American streets.

5 November 1983 to 14 March 1984

———

Parliamentary Procedure

It was the first Saturday in November and I had stayed at home to finish marking the end-of-term school papers while Brian was competing in the Western Australian championships for 18-foot skiffs on Perth's Swan River. The three-man skiffs carry an enormous sail area and with all three crew members using trapeze wires, each race needed his total concentration and effort.

I was brimming with excitement at the prospect of telling Brian the news I had read in the paper over lunch. The news clipping I thrust at him when he came in had few words, but enough to make him as exhilarated as I was. The overseas newsbrief read, 'New York. The British freighter *Hetty* was seized off the New Jersey coast after the US Coast Guard found it had a hidden cargo of 14 tons of hashish.'

The following Monday morning the journalist Norm Aisbett phoned the US authorities from his new office at the *Western Mail* newspaper. He confirmed that the ship seized in America was the *Hetty Mitchell* that we had told him about four months before. We had also given its name to the Australian government some seven months before as part of our drug-trafficking allegations. When Norm came to see us that evening he brought a request for us to phone Lieutenant Commander Booth, the US Coast Guard chief of intelligence in New York. He also brought two beers to celebrate. His support of us had paid off and now he had a story to scoop his rival newspapers.

When we telephoned Lieutenant Commander Booth we found he was a very thorough officer. He asked us to read him the first paragraph of the letter we had written to the US Drug Enforcement Administration back in September, which had tipped them off about the drug network. Satisfied of our identity, he linked up the call to Richard Smith, a DEA case officer from Atlantic City. The three-way call lasted an hour and we described the ship, its crew and antecedents known to us. We were surprised to learn that the DEA had uncovered virtually nothing of the background of either the ship or the crew.

Over the next week our phone rang regularly a little after midnight as Richard Smith and his case chief Jerry Moore began to establish a prosecution case for the US Justice Department. We learned that the *Hetty* crew were held in prison in New York and each of the four was being visited by expensive criminal lawyers. None of the crew was co-operating with the DEA. Bail had been set, though no person had come forward with the substantial sums; Donald Dickinson, $1 million, Stephen Marriott and William Charlesworth, $200,000 each, and Peter Jackson, $100,000. To the DEA we posted fifty pages of photocopies including letters, documents relating to the *Hetty*'s background, and telexes which told of the Indian DRI inquiries. We advised that more were in a Cochin bank safety-deposit box. Richard Smith expressed his appreciation for the information we were providing. The DEA had been having difficulty in checking the ship's movements before its arrest, he told us, and none of the four crew members had yet shown any willingness to talk.

It was then that we began to understand the unique position we were in, holding a good knowledge of the diversified drug-smuggling network. We alone had contacted the US authorities after the *Hetty* had been seized; the Australian Federal Police had not contacted the DEA. Richard Smith was most surprised that our information about the drug network and their ships, given to the Australian Federal Police, had not been put on the Interpol exchange of information to which the DEA computers had access.

After the *Hetty* seizure was confirmed we hadn't delayed sending off details to S. K. Anantaramin, the editor of the *Indian Express* in Cochin. He and his publisher were, in our absence, still fighting Jim Howard's defamation case against us all. Each time the case had come up for hearing Howard had failed to attend the court, and because he was to be the first called for examination, the trial had been adjourned to a later date. However, Howard's delays now suited our defence case since we would be able to offer fresh facts.

Perth's *Western Mail* featured the *Hetty* bust on a double-page spread headed SPY AND DRUG RIDDLE in their edition of 12 November. The paper's chief editor wrote in his editorial that the question needing to be asked of the Australian government was, 'Why was this couple's information ignored?' With the publication of that article we realized that we were finally vindicated.

Our future plans no longer depended on the recognition of the Australian authorities. More than 100 pages of letters had been sent to the Australian government and the Federal Police, but they had fallen on deaf ears. Our suspicion, which had begun in Sri Lanka, that there might be a conspiracy against us by elements within the Australian government had remained constantly in our minds, as had the fear of being found by the drug network. We had made our new identity and address in Perth known to only a few trusted persons – among them the journalist Norm Aisbett, Senator Chaney and Deputy Ombudsman Hedges.

On 14 November Brian booked a single ticket Perth-Singapore-Bombay for the flight on 5 December. I planned to remain in Perth for a further month to complete my teaching contract while he followed up some new leads in Singapore before flying on to India, where I would later join him. We would leave our dispute with the Australian government behind us and centre our energy once more on getting *Tiger Rag* away from Cochin.

*

In the long white parliamentary building situated prominently on a Canberra hilltop, the Australian Senate was in session. From their positions in the tiered benches of the plush red chamber the senators sat and listened to the president of the Senate drone out the final sentences of the bill before the Upper House. 'Funds have been increased from

0.47 per cent to 0.48 per cent in terms of the ratio between overseas development aid and the gross national product.' It was almost 6.30 p.m., Tuesday 15 November, the routine session was drawing to a close, and on both sides of the House a number of senators had dozed off.

Soon after, however, the senators were roused by Senator Chaney, leader of the opposition in the Senate. Chaney said that he had sent a letter on 6 July to the prime minister, and read further from a paper in his hand:

> I had representation from a young man and a young woman who had recently returned to Australia from India and Sri Lanka. That young man and young woman put a series of bits of paper in front of me, some of which were papers which had been forwarded to the prime minister. They told me a story about their suspicions and concerns about international drug activities and other criminal activities. They told me a story about their view that Australian consular officials had not properly responded to their requests for assistance and, indeed, had behaved in a way that put them at risk. They told me that they were not satisfied with the way in which the information they were trying to provide to the government was being received, and they were also concerned about a personal matter, the recovery of a yacht in which they had sailed from Australia to the port of Cochin.

Chaney continued his ten-minute address by remarking that the Australian authorities had a poor record of investigation in drug-related matters, and that he had not been very impressed by the somewhat perfunctory reply he had received in response to his letter to the prime minister.

When Senator Chaney had finished his address, another senator rose to raise a question on a different matter.

In numerous past debates in the Senate it had indeed been established that the government's record of investigation against the masterminds behind the billion-dollar drug-trafficking industry was poor. In fact, not one major trafficker had ever been apprehended in Australia, and a number of key drug figures had been allowed to slip away. The senators who listened to Chaney's address on 15 November understood the risk to the couple if they were to name openly the superboss behind the Australian side of the drug network. Certainly just the mention in Parliament of his name or the names of other Australian drug kings would cause shock and disbelief among the senators.

Others who had persisted in trying to reveal facts about drug trafficking and corruption which they believed the Australian authorities were suppressing had met with dire fates. The anti-drug campaigner Donald McKay and the newspaper publisher Juanita Nielson, for instance, had not known when to stop broadcasting their allegations. Both had been murdered and their bodies had never been found.

Parliamentary procedure in Australia has long been established. Before raising his question in the Senate on 15 November Senator Chaney had first informed his opposite number, Senator Button, leader of the government in the Senate, of his intention. Senator Button thus was given the opportunity to make visits or telephone calls to government offices and departments before he offered his reply. However, the busy senator would not have been aware of the circumstances behind what his advisers suggested he say.

So what Senator Button heard from his undisclosed sources in Canberra he repeated in his reply, although he had not cared to verify anything first-hand. Nor could he have had any idea of the extent of truth or untruth in his statement when he rose in the morning session of 16 November. Accordingly Button read to the Senate that an 'independent officer' (Adrian Sever) of the Foreign Affairs Department had found that 'the department hadn't rendered anything less than full consular support for the couple'. Button had been also told to say that 'the couple had been given every opportunity to present their case'. In his further reply to Senator Chaney's concerns he stated, 'The matter has been investigated by the Australian Federal Police and regular reports have been made to Mr Milgate and Ms McGuinness. As late as last Thursday Australian Federal Police officers were informed by Mr Milgate that he was satisfied with the action being taken by the Australian Federal Police.'

Button finished reading and sat down. The *Hansard* reporter who records the business of Parliament entered on a keyboard, 'Question resolved in the affirmative', before turning to the next paper (which was on the Commonwealth Teaching Service Act Determinations 1983 No 9), and the matter was never raised in the Senate again.

Such is parliamentary procedure in Australia.

*

When Brian and I read the *Hansard* report of Senate proceedings on 16 November we were so incensed that we wrote the following letter to the leader of the government in the Senate – Senator Button.

Dear Senator,

The statements you made before Parliament in answer to questions by Senator Chaney were totally false and misleading. The subject concerned our humble selves.

The truth is that the Foreign Affairs Department has neither acknowledged nor replied to our many letters.

The truth is that the 'independent inquiry' was conducted by an officer within the department (Adrian Sever) and this officer is well known to consular officers involved.

The truth is that at no time did we express satisfaction that all aspects of our complaints had been looked into by the investigating officer. (The interview held in the Foreign Affairs offices in Perth on Sunday 2 October was recorded and when the tape is replayed this can be verified.)

The truth is that consular officers refused to pass along drug information (telephoned to New Delhi Vice Consul John Woods on 26 April) and told us to 'just keep quiet about this and everything will be all right'. (John Woods during his visit to Cochin in May 1983.)

The truth is that consular officers have removed documents from our files to protect themselves in this matter. (Refer our letter to Foreign Affairs Department director Mr B. G. Downing.)

The truth is that the Australian Federal Police dismissed our information.

The truth is that the Australian Federal Police have had no dealings with the US authorities in this matter. (Refer Lieutenant Commander Booth, US Coast Guard chief of intelligence. Mr Richard Smith, DEA agent.)

The question we ask you, sir, are you a person democratically elected to represent the people of Australia, or somebody who stands up obediently on cue and reads parrotlike any statement his subordinates choose to give him, regardless of the veracity of that statement?

Senator Button never answered our letter.

*

The British *Sunday Times* has a readership and correspondents in most countries. Its nucleus was the *Sunday Times* building in the centre of London. The building housed an array of colourful people who contributed to the dynamism of the newspaper. Removed only a little from the news and sports desks on the floors below, the newspaper's features section, at various times working under the banners of Sunday Review and Insight, was contained in the cluttered warren of offices on the sixth floor, and the journalists who occupied these rooms were responsible for providing the in-depth background to the news stories that readers had come to expect in their Sunday paper.

When the letter from Australia was delivered to the newspaper's busy mail desk it was passed on to Colin Simpson of the features department. It related the willingness of a young Australian couple to provide the newspaper with an interesting story in exchange for background research that the newspaper could do in England, South Africa and America. An outline of the essentials of their story was given.

Colin Simpson was a senior journalist who instantly realized that if the couple had not exaggerated what they claimed in their letter, then this could be the best inside lead his group had been given into large-scale drug smuggling.

Parin Mohammed, his research assistant, was thus set the task of verifying the essential facts while Simpson sent a telegram asking the writers to phone him.

Much of the journalist's work is done on the telephone, so by the time Colin Simpson received the collect call from Australia he had been in contact with the newspaper's USA correspondent, who had good contacts inside the Drug Enforcement Administration offices in both Washington and Philadelphia. Simpson had established that the yacht *Tiger Rag* had been accepted early in 1981 as an entrant in the 1984 *Observer* single-handed transatlantic yacht race, and that James Howard belonged to the Royal Photographic Society and had relatives in London. Old hands around the Asian newspaper scene whom Colin Simpson had been able to contact had given some very interesting recollections of the former UPI combat photographer, which fell well short of being respectable. In addition, the newspaper's source library had brought to light a most curious tale.

Research in 1981 into a story that hadn't gone to press revealed that a vessel by the name of *Boston Wasp* had been purchased in England and sailed to the Mediterranean. It was supposedly converted there, and later sailed to Bermuda carrying 27 tons of marijuana loaded in Lebanon. With the proceeds of the run a small coaster named *Able Fox* had been purchased in the Virgin Islands and sailed back to the Mediterranean, where its movements had become suspicious. But what had been of most interest in the research was that one of the persons involved in the scam had the initials RM. (Colin Simpson didn't know then that Jim Howard's address at that time was also Lebanon.)

As Colin Simpson's file, now marked THE COCHIN CONNECTION , started to expand, he sent a telegram to the newspaper's stringer in Perth, Western Australia. 'Please check if Milgate is straight up. Get evidence that he is not a nut.' The reply came from the Perth-based stringer that Milgate 'certainly has some good stuff on Howard and his operation'. The stringer was able to confirm that the US Justice Department had recently phoned Brian Milgate in

Perth and invited him to visit New York at the US government's expense in order to be their witness in the forthcoming court case against the four *Hetty* crew. Milgate had accepted the invitation, but before flying to the USA he still intended to follow up his leads in Singapore and clear a bank security box in Cochin.

Colin Simpson turned a blank memorandum sheet into his typewriter and began to tap out a note to his editors, outlining the facts of the story and making a request for a budget to be allocated for a feature article. In the memo he suggested that it would be worth sending someone to meet Milgate in Singapore and return to the UK with him, adding that 'the person should have sufficient experience to sort the wheat from the chaff and dredge him during the long flight home, and witness the evidence-collecting in Singapore and Cochin'.

21

Howard Meets the Press

As the jumbo lost altitude in its descent to Singapore's Changi International Airport, I looked across at the yachts moored at the exclusive Changi Sailing Club where fifteen months earlier Alison and I had anchored *Tiger Rag*. But now I was alone; Alison was still in Perth where she was teaching until the end of the school year in December.

The jet's engine thrust died away as the runway started to emerge from the abundant Singapore foliage. Less than an hour later I walked along the island's famous Orchard Road in the direction of the Hilton Hotel where I was expected. I wondered if the journalist sent by the *Sunday Times* to accompany me to Cochin had previously been to Asia and had the 'Asian sense' that I hoped he would. The tropical Singapore street scene in which I found myself seemed not to have changed at all since my last visit. The traffic was as chaotic as ever, and the battered taxicabs just as reckless.

The two clerks at the Hilton check-in desk were busy when I arrived so I put down my travel bag and waited. One was talking on the telephone and another was attending a man at the desk. Even before I heard the man's BBC-English speech I identified him as an Englishman – long-sleeved woollen shirt, tweed trousers, sturdy shoes and thick socks. Hot equatorial air came through the hotel's entrance door and into the air-conditioned cool, causing the stocky Englishman to appear hot and flustered as he waited for the answer to his enquiry about arrival details of the flight that had brought me to Singapore.

'Mr Barrie Penrose, I presume,' I said with a straight face.

'Yes, yes,' he replied brusquely as he turned round to look

blankly at me. A few moments later he realized who I was, and asked several questions in such rapid succession that I was unable to answer any of them. 'How was the flight? How did you know who I was? Do you feel like a beer? Would you rather go to your room first? How does the tipping system work here? Have you ever seen so many Japanese tourists?'

An hour later I had been checked in and we were getting down to business. I gave Barrie Penrose some 400 pages of documents to peruse while I began my calls. I wanted to trace Richard Merkley, whom I understood to be still in Singapore. There were also a number of vessels linked to the drug network I was interested in tracing.

At 6 p.m. we met the *Sunday Times* stringer who would help me with research. Tan Lian Choo was a tall, dignified Chinese lady who quickly grasped the story and understood what was expected of her. She made notes, promising to report back the following evening.

The next day Barrie Penrose booked himself on an afternoon flight to Bangkok. With him he took some of the reference material I had lent him, and told me that he intended to speak to the officials of the Australian Federal Police Drug Liaison Unit there.

In his absence I went to see a senior detective of the Singapore Marine Police, hoping to get information on a small community of people and vessels that both Jim Howard and Jyl Gocher had mentioned they associated with in Singapore. The senior detective, who was Chinese, was not at all surprised by my questions, nor about the alleged smuggling connections I was to reveal to him. We talked about the classic schooner *So Fong*, which at that time lay at her moorings off the old timber Singapore Swimming Club. (In 1984 the US-registered schooner was confiscated by the Vietnamese government and its crew imprisoned, after the authorities announced that it had been involved in espionage in their territorial waters.) Another yacht I had hoped to find had been away for some months, and an American yacht named *White Wings* was said to have again sailed to

Thailand. The senior detective told me, off the record, that the owner of *White Wings* was a known smuggler, but because he didn't operate in Singapore waters there was little the Singapore authorities could do to apprehend him. There was also strong suspicion by police that he was involved with the American CIA.

Tan Lian Choo proved invaluable, and accurately uncovered many of the details I was missing from our *Hetty* records. However, neither of us was able to trace the *Elysee Maru*, the 170-foot blue-hulled ship that Richard Merkley had added to his small fleet some time earlier in the year, which had since disappeared from the Port Authority's records. Many attempts to telephone Merkley at a number he had given to local shipping agents went unanswered. I next made a visit to the luxury residential complex where Jyl Gocher had told us that Merkley kept an apartment. Records kept by the management there showed Merkley had vacated his apartment two weeks earlier, leaving no forwarding address.

My last call in Singapore was to Mr Paul Fitzharris, the Police Liaison Officer at the New Zealand high commission situated near the Tiger Balm Gardens. He was grateful to get details of the New Zealand nationals who were involved in the drug network.

When Barrie Penrose returned from Bangkok, I was ready to move on to India. A phone call to Cochin's Bolghatty Palace Hotel established that Jim Howard no longer occupied a room there, but instead had recently moved aboard his yacht *Steppenwolf*, which was still anchored off Bolghatty Island. While I feared direct confrontation with Jim Howard I was anxious to visit Cochin to see first-hand what damage had been done to *Tiger Rag* during our absence of almost six months.

The starkness of the international terminal at Bombay's Santa Cruz airport was Barrie Penrose's first introduction to India. The night flight from the luxury of Singapore had left the journalist slightly disorientated, but we negotiated the formalities and left the airport by taxi for the domestic terminal where we would wait out the few hours before the flight to Cochin was scheduled to depart.

Scores of tired travellers who had returned to India on the many international night flights into Bombay had likewise made their way to the domestic terminal. They were creating confusion around the Indian Airlines desk as they endeavoured to get themselves seats on planes that would take them to their various home states. The *Sunday Times* had booked two seats for us on the 7 a.m. Cochin flight, but no confirmation had been given. After a vigil to make himself understood over the fracas at the reservation desk, an exasperated Barrie Penrose returned to where I had been left in charge of our baggage. Our names were not on the confirmed list and the flight was fully booked, as were the two later flights that day to Cochin.

I settled back into an uncomfortable plastic seat. Nothing could be achieved in the two hours until 5 a.m. and the arrival of the first of the airline's officers who could exercise any authority. I explained this, adding that there was no point in worrying; successful travel in India wasn't always easy to achieve, and often took supreme effort.

Barrie Penrose should never forget his supreme efforts to get us on that early-morning flight to Cochin. He began at the Indian Airlines reservation desk at 5 a.m. when he tried to convince the clerk that we had an urgent mission in Cochin. From behind the journalist came shouts, howls and plaintive cries as every other person waiting at the desk had his or her own urgent reason to be on a flight out of Bombay. Barrie Penrose's insistence got him an audience with the reservations manager, who had now arrived for work, and he repeated his best story for the patient officer.

'Just do one thing,' the manager told him. 'Go to the check-in counter with your baggage, and I will do what I can to have your names put on the passenger list.'

The check-in counter was in an even greater state of disorder than the reservation desk had been, with a tight bunch of perhaps sixty people pushing towards it. All had tickets for the hopelessly overbooked Cochin flight. With a look of determination on his face Barrie Penrose rolled up the sleeves of his woollen shirt an extra two turns, lowered his head and went into the pack like a rugby forward into a scrum. Occasionally his arm or head would emerge from the fray and I could see that he was making good forward progress. Such a scene might bring out the riot police to some airports, but at Bombay's domestic terminal this melee was not uncommon. I took it all in from a good position standing on a chair.

As the time for the scheduled flight drew nearer Barrie Penrose got closer to the check-in counter, and the ruckus he was in became more excited. My travel bag, which he was attempting to put down on the scales, was being held suspended in midair with Penrose's strong arms pushing it forwards while other hands pulled at straps and corners to prevent its arrival at the scales. As the tug of war continued I could see Barrie Penrose vigorously working his elbows and my travel bag progressed inch by inch towards the scales. An announcement of the final check-in call for the Cochin flight echoed over the noise of the frenzied crowd as a uniformed Indian Airlines officer laid his hand on the bag and reached for the two tickets held by the hand emerging from a very rolled woollen sleeve. Barrie Penrose had triumphed.

The airport scramble and a serving of chilli-flavoured eggs for breakfast on our flight to Cochin had been quite an introduction for the *Sunday Times* journalist. Barrie Penrose now looked down with fascination as the plane approached Cochin airport. Seen from the air, Kerala State is a blanket of coconut trees interspersed by a network of waterways. The red-tiled roofs that occasionally appeared between the treetops and the wash behind the trawlers on the waterways were familiar to me. From above, Cochin had a serenity that I didn't expect to find on the ground.

The *Sunday Times* booking agent had made reservations for us at the five-star Malabar Hotel, though when Barrie

Penrose saw it he wasn't greatly impressed with the best that Cochin had to offer. But the hotel did at least have both telex and telephones.

The journalist first wanted to talk to Jim Howard to get his side of the story, so I explained how he could hire a public rowboat to take him close by the *Steppenwolf* on the short row over to the Bolghatty Hotel. Whether he got invited aboard would depend on his skills as a talker. Before going up to his room to change Barrie Penrose asked the hotel staff to organize a car and driver for his use, while from the main desk I telephoned Maxwell Fernandez. My Indian friend was excited about my being in Cochin again and suggested a meeting that night with S. K. Anantaramin, the editor of the *Indian Express*, and the lawyer Dr Vincent Panikulangara.

A short time later Barrie Penrose reappeared in the lobby, having put on a cravat and his favourite tweed hat, and he now had a camera on a strap around his neck. The image he would try to create for Jim Howard was that of a displaced and eccentric English country squire, a benign character who would offer no threat to the dangerous man. As a part of his disguise the plucky journalist carried a shoulder bag in which he had concealed a small though powerful tape-recorder. He certainly looked a curious sight as we set off from the Malabar Hotel.

From the downtown Ernakulam wharf I pointed out the large ketch with the bright yellow inflatable dinghy tied off the stern. Anchored near the Bolghatty Hotel's jetty, *Steppenwolf* appeared ready to leave at short notice. Wishing him luck I left Barrie Penrose there to do his journalistic work, and took an autorickshaw from the wharf to the bazaar. At the State Bank of India I removed all the documents held inside the safety-deposit box and placed them inside my briefcase. Then the afternoon was free for me to do what I was most anxious to do.

As I sat in the old bus that sped along the rutted serpentine road to Edacochin, memories of the months spent there came into my mind, displacing my anxiety whether I would find *Tiger Rag* in a salvageable state. I got down from the bus at Pambai corner and walked through the crude tea stalls and the few merchant shops before coming to the path that wandered through the trees and scattered houses down to the riverfront. The old men who sat on a log at the corner recognized me and a murmur went around.

The rural people of Edacochin must have been pleased with the monsoon rains that season, I thought as I passed by the still-flooded rice fields. Many village children recognized me and ran to follow behind, and their shrieks of welcome brought more women and children from their houses. The welcome was unanimous, and many asked after Alison. Further along the path I found Shri Anthappam, the boatyard caretaker, waiting outside his house. His wife ran from behind the house and stood two paces behind her husband. Both had broad smiles and each had the same front tooth missing. I shook the old man's hand as he rattled off something in a local language that I couldn't understand, but when I pointed to the room of his house where *Tiger Rag*'s sailing equipment had been locked away, Anthappam wobbled his head to indicate all was well. The same padlock still secured the door and I felt greatly relieved that at least our yacht's essential sailing equipment was still inside. The old man shuffled along beside me, village children fell in behind and I continued down the path.

Tiger Rag stood prominently in the otherwise empty boatyard where two cows were now grazing. I guessed the boatyard proprietors had removed all their items before the monsoon rains came. Later we were to learn that the Mattancherry police officers had looked into the false claims made by the boatyard proprietors and had taken action against them, although the equipment stolen from *Tiger Rag* was never recovered.

By gestures the old caretaker conveyed that a big storm had blown down the awning we had erected from an old sail, so Sri Anthappam had used the torn cloth to wrap the yacht up like a parcel. While he did his best to scoot the noisy children from the yard I unwrapped a section of cloth and climbed up to the yacht's cockpit. On deck and down in the cabins I took stock of the damage. Somebody had been on board after Alison and I had left in June, and deliberately opened the hatches and portholes. The heavy monsoon rains had then come in, completely flooding the engine compartment and ruining the diesel engine. The papers we had left behind had been riffled and were scattered across the navigation desk. Lockers had been rummaged. The timber work inside the cabin had been gouged and stained by ink that had been thrown against a bulkhead, and there were other signs of deliberate destructive acts that presumably had been ordered by the Cochin underworld.

The inside of the yacht smelled musty from the mildew that had grown on the cushions and covers, and there was a definite pong coming from what I presumed were the droppings of water rats. On the saloon table I saw a half-burned candle and I remembered blowing it out almost six months before, on the night we had left the yacht in fear, not knowing if we would ever be able to return.

Later that afternoon I telephoned Alison in Australia and reported that despite the state *Tiger Rag* was now in, it was still possible to patch her up enough to sail her away from Cochin after the legal constraints and trials had been disposed of.

Barrie Penrose was sparkling with good humour when we caught up with each other at the Malabar Hotel. He gleefully told me his ruse had been successful and had got him aboard Jim Howard's ketch. There he had feigned a casual manner and revealed to Howard that a London-based newspaper had sent him to this 'God-forsaken Cochin place' to 'look into these incredible allegations by this strange Australian fellow Milgate'. Adding, 'Cochin was such a hot place and he would be glad to get back to civilization in England.'

Jyl Gocher had responded by opening a warm can of fruit juice which she gave him in a grubby glass. Jim Howard seemed to have fallen for his matter-of-fact style, though I couldn't gauge to what extent when I listened to the tape recording Penrose had secretly made aboard *Steppenwolf*.

Howard's conversation had been capricious, but his drawl noticeably tightened when the English journalist casually mentioned that he had copied 'many of Milgate's documents' and would of course be willing to pass them over to Howard if they met again. The bait had been strong enough to get Barrie Penrose the invitation he needed to return to the ketch the following day.

A knock came at the door of my room before I had finished listening to the recorded conversation. It was the hotel porter, who brought a message that there was a visitor in the lobby for me.

'Hello, Brian. Hello.' The familiar, highly-pitched voice came from the beaming Maxwell Fernandez. I ordered us both coffee while he brought me up to date with what had been happening in my absence, starting by telling me about the pressure that had been put on him to stop him from pursuing his story on the drug network. Maxwell then revealed that an American in the network had suddenly left Cochin after Superintendent Shreedharan and his mainland-based Customs Intelligence Unit began to inquire closely into his activities. A private laboratory which he was thought to have used for heroin conversion was discovered 10 miles out of town, and close by were many acres of opium poppies which were later burned by the authorities.

I told Maxwell about the telex I had read that was sent to Barrie Penrose in Singapore from his London office, revealing that their sources had discovered that one of the foreigners whom Maxwell had met in Cochin was listed on the US authorities' computer as a narcotics dealer.

Maxwell told me that an intelligence officer from the Indian central government had recently interviewed him about Jim Howard. He also related with much animation the circumstances by which Howard had been ordered out of room 44 at the Bolghatty Hotel. It had happened during the first week of November, when Jim Howard began to have uncontrolled bouts of rage. (Maxwell now knew that week coincided with the seizure of the *Hetty*.) During one bout of rage Howard had menaced a security guard with a knife, and the hotel's management, which had had enough of Howard's bad behaviour, ordered him out of the hotel. Despite Howard's fiercest objections, the hotel management had stood fast and would not allow him ever to occupy a room at the hotel again.

I took the Indian journalist to meet his English counterpart. They swopped stories about Howard and other colourful villains they had encountered until it was time for the car to take us to the mainland for the meeting at S. K. Anantaramin's house in Panampilly Nagar.

When we entered the spartan front room of his residence, the white-haired brahmin resident editor rose serenely and conveyed his congratulations. I thanked him for his continued faith in our exposure of the Cochin drug network, and introduced Barrie Penrose to him and to the other gentlemen in the room; P. Krishnaswamy, the owner and publisher of the *Indian Express*, and Vincent Panikulangara, the eminent lawyer and SKA's friend who was due to represent us all in the defamation case brought by Howard in May. Howard was still maintaining his innocence in the drug matter and was continuing with the defamation charge.

Details of the *Hetty*, the aborted customs investigation and the involvement of other Cochin-based persons were repeated to Barrie Penrose, who then described his confrontation with Jim Howard. But instead of praising him for his bluff, his Indian peers were critical of his actions because of the extra risk to me from the exposure of my presence in Cochin. Barrie Penrose seemed put out by this unexpected criticism and, sitting back petulantly in his chair, he suddenly looked a long way from home.

I could understand the conflict of interest between the English journalist and the others at the meeting. Cochin was home for the senior Indians, who were facing the same criminal charge of defamation as Alison and I, and the fight against the many lawyers bought by Howard at great expense, who had guaranteed him results. And for the Indian men there was a moral issue involved which needed to be handled with the dignity befitting their place in society. The English journalist, however, was just doing his job the best way he could. He would be in Cochin only a few days and his strategy was to play a game of wits with the colourful villain Howard. In doing so he hoped to get a good story that would impress his editors back in London.

S. K. Anantaramin paid me a great compliment before I left his house that evening by offering me shelter there. I was at risk of physical attack from revengeful persons in Cochin and there was still an unserved warrant for my arrest. But I knew that Howard's lawyers would be quick to demand that a charge be made against Anantaramin for protecting a wanted person, so I declined his kind offer, assuring him that I knew Cochin well and would be careful not to expose myself to unnecessary risk. I wouldn't spend much time at the Malabar Hotel, I explained; the other hotels that I knew would provide me with a safer place to sleep.

Barrie Penrose kept his second appointment with Jim Howard, and had a third meeting with Howard and Gocher at the Malabar Hotel on Sunday, the third day that we were in Cochin. The journalist got his story and I admired the skill he used to get it. At their second meeting, having heard most of Howard's cover story during the first, the journalist dropped his feigned casual manner for a more direct approach. Howard's cover story was full of contradictions. Barrie Penrose pursued each issue, and Howard didn't give plausible answers. Unknown to Howard, Penrose continued to record their conversations on tape. The journalist cleverly urged Howard into expressing the desire he now had to take revenge on Alison and me. Howard even said that he would have a hard time stopping the mercenaries among his friends from murdering us.

Barrie Penrose was also able to speak with one of the dozen or so expatriates who worked for the large foreign companies which had investments in the Cochin region, some of whom came to the Malabar Hotel on Sundays to use the swimming pool. He was told of a conversation an Englishman had had with Jim Howard in which Howard had bragged of having military connections. The same man had spoken of Gordon Gold, who had surprised him one night when they had gone for dinner and Gold had openly suggested the possibility of smuggling drugs from Cochin. Penrose assessed the information the man had given him as being reliable.

Maxwell Fernandez became the second person to be given the privilege of listening to the conversations discreetly taped during Penrose's sessions with Jim Howard. Maxwell had helped us to follow up some of the loose ends of the *Hetty*'s movements, and he had some very good photographs taken of Howard once when Maxwell had interviewed him. Barrie Penrose asked for prints of the photographs for his newspaper's use back in London.

Early in the morning of our fourth day in Cochin we guarded a position at the head of a queue waiting outside the Indian Airlines Ernakulam office, and when the office opened for business we booked seats on the next scheduled flight to Bombay. Barrie Penrose had a story and was suddenly anxious to be away as quickly as he could from the dangerous man he had put on the spot. Some time around the third day I had noticed a change in Penrose's demeanour. He became very concerned for his own safety, but didn't want to say why. I wondered if the danger of what he was doing had caught up with him, and whether he had been threatened. Had it become known that a story about the Cochin drug network would appear in the international press when Penrose returned to London? Those involved in the network were not the types who would sit back and do nothing. Perhaps this was why Barrie Penrose began nervously to look back over his shoulder on that third day in Cochin.

Before we left Cochin I returned to Edacochin to give Sri Anthappam some money and ask him to watch again over *Tiger Rag*. I took Barrie Penrose to inspect the yacht and to see Edacochin first-hand, but the journalist was unnerved and reluctant to stay more than a few minutes in the isolation of the boatyard.

The flight north took less than an hour and carried us away from the tropical south and to the intensity of the vastly overpopulated city of Bombay. We needed to spend a few days there waiting for a connecting flight to London. At Bombay airport Barrie Penrose ordered a taxi driver to take us to the 'best hotel' and I sat back and looked out at the passing scene on the long drive through congested traffic to the city's Naraman Point district.

Oberoi Towers had more than enough luxury appointments to please Barrie Penrose. It was more opulent than any large hotel I had seen in Australia. Bookings were very heavy, but an efficient desk clerk told us that a suite had just been vacated and would be made ready. All suites had plush furnishings, antique writing desks, silk carpets and leather-covered chairs. The cost of a suite for four days equalled a whole year's pay for the average Indian worker who toiled for six days every week in the real world of India beyond the hotel.

In the days we had to wait for our flight to London, Barrie Penrose hardly left the confines of the hotel to venture into Bombay. Instead he found himself drawn to the exclusive bazaar that filled the hotel's lower floors, where he mingled with rich Middle East Arabs, Japanese businessmen and international flight crews to take part in bargaining over Kashmiri carpets, mink coats, silks, precious stones and other wares and crafts from every part of the subcontinent.

I used my time in Bombay to listen carefully to all the taped conversations that Barrie Penrose had had with Jim Howard. The many hours of recorded dialogue slowly revealed Howard's loss of face as piece by piece his credibility crumbled. At first Howard denied having anything to do with the *Hetty*, and when asked about Zenith Enterprises in London, the company Howard had sworn under oath that he represented, Howard answered, 'Never heard of 'em.' Barrie Penrose had then produced a copy for Howard of his own deputation to Indian customs authorities at the time the *Hetty* was in Cochin, which stated that Howard represented the company, after which Howard had nothing more to say on the subject. Howard had tried to diminish his involvement with the *Hetty*, but Penrose quoted from copies of Howard's own documents which showed that he had received US$10,000 'to represent the ship's interests in Cochin'. Howard had also tried nonchalantly to dismiss his past criminal convictions, although I suspected that being confronted with his past record had bruised his ego. It was chilling to listen to the concluding tapes in which Howard could no longer restrain his passionate hatred for Alison and me over what we had done to him and what we had caused him to lose. Howard took every opportunity to discredit us, even suggesting that I was a spy sent by a foreign government to 'deliberately implicate him in a drug ring' and 'finish him off'. He ended a tirade of insults against us by repeating his gruff threat that it wouldn't be difficult for him to get somebody bumped off.

After listening to the tapes I felt subdued and concerned at the prospect of returning to Cochin to get *Tiger Rag* back. The possibility of removing the yacht by other means had been considered, but the difficulties involved were enormous and the costs far beyond our financial capabilities. Before we could sail *Tiger Rag* from the harbour we had to surrender ourselves to the Cochin chief judicial magistrate's court and face Howard's defamation case. The *Sunday Times* article would help to clear some of the obstacles ahead through the severe blow it would make to Jim Howard's reputation, though my hopes that it would remove Howard from Cochin were slight. The man was a brawler and I knew he would be determined to make it his business to be present in Cochin if we returned for *Tiger Rag*. Then he would have his opportunity for revenge.

22

At Large in London

The British Airways flight to London was full and un-comfortable, but Barrie Penrose was pleased to be on his way home and talked expansively of the country house in Kent he was restoring and of his achievements in a career that had included service with the BBC and respectable London newspapers. By the time the big plane touched down into winter at Heathrow airport I knew something of the *Sunday Times* world, and India seemed a long way behind me.

It rained continuously for the four days I spent in London waiting for the US embassy to arrange my visa and ticket to New York. During my stay the *Sunday Times* provided accommodation for me at a comfortable hotel in Russell Square, from where each day I walked the short distance to the newspaper's offices. Barrie Penrose took a few days off work so in the office I liaised with the senior journalist Colin Simpson, whose open, friendly manner complemented an insight into people that allowed him quickly to establish rapport with them. There was also a mischievousness about him that stopped just short of being devious.

I slid easily into the newspaper world, which at that time was preoccupied with the dismal weather, internal newspaper politics, a rising festive spirit – Christmas was just nine days away – and a terrorist bomb which had exploded outside Harrods department store, killing and maiming shoppers and police. I was pleased to be left alone for much of the time to get on with the busy schedule of calls I had set myself to make after having exchanged notes with Colin Simpson about what I had uncovered in Singapore, and he in London.

Simpson had dug out the background detail of the *Hetty* and had interviewed the former captain, Fred Stanley, and contacted other former members of the *Hetty* crew. From Adrian Impey, the original engineer, he had obtained a roll of undeveloped film, taken aboard the ship in Cochin, which the newspaper had processed – photographs of Stephen Marriott, his girlfriend Shelly Fern and Willie Charlesworth. Two of these former *Hetty* crew members were now under arrest in New York. Stephen Marriott's family lived in Sheffield and at Colin Simpson's suggestion I caught a train to the city to visit them.

Stephen Marriott's mother and married sister lived in a comfortable house which was being extensively renovated. I was invited inside only after the occupants decided I wasn't a journalist. Later they told me that Shelley Fern had sent a telegram from America in November informing them of Stephen's arrest and advising them not to speak to the press. Shelley had also telephoned Stephen's mother from New York and told her, 'Not to worry. The boys are in good hands.'

The Sheffield woman, whom I guessed to be close to sixty, was quite convinced that her son would face only a one-year prison sentence for his part in the drug organization, which shouldn't be too uncomfortable for him, she thought. I doubted if her son in his New York prison cell would agree. 'He's such a good boy,' she confided, 'and he's been very generous to his old mum.' She told me that her son had come home to Sheffield last Christmas, arriving in a chauffeur-driven limousine, his pockets full of money. 'Life in the Virgin Islands has been good to him and Shelley,' she reflected.

I copied down the address and phone number in America that Shelley Fern had given Stephen's mother, after which she and her daughter took me to their regular local pub for just a 'quick Christmas drink' which lasted hours. When I boarded the afternoon train back to London I discovered that Stephen's mother had slipped a five-pound note into the pocket of my jacket when she kissed me farewell at the pub. Perhaps having been able to speak with a stranger about her son had brought her some comfort.

From the *Sunday Times* office I telephoned Hartlepool and spoke at length with Adrian Impey. I also telephoned the secretary of the Durban Yacht Club, which was where Jyl Gocher had told us Gordon Gold had taken his yacht *Honky Tonk* when he left the Maldive Islands in August 1982. The secretary told me that Gold came and went frequently from Durban, but was surprised to learn that Gold had been employed in India as an industrial chemist, since he had only known Gold as a marine-equipment salesman.

Late one afternoon I ventured out into the wet London streets to try to locate Zenith Enterprises, the company Jim Howard allegedly represented, only to find that the information Howard had given to the Indian customs authorities was false – the company did not exist.

Another night I went to the address in Kensington Gardens that Richard Merkley had scribbled on the back of the business card he had given to Captain Stanley. Parked in the street outside was a white Honda Civic car that exactly fitted the description of the vehicle Merkley and Howard had used in London the previous winter when they bought the *Hetty*. At the top-floor I knocked repeatedly on the door until it opened only two inches. I asked if I could leave a message for Richard Merkley, but the woman who had opened the door quickly slammed it shut.

I also followed up a telephone number I had got in Cochin earlier in the year. It was the European contact number of the tall American businessman I had met on the Malabar Hotel jetty, whom we had often seen in the company of Jyl Gocher before the *Hetty* had called at Cochin. The Belgium number rang without answer many times before a heavily accented voice answered. The American was not there at present, I was told; he had recently bought a boat in England and gone off somewhere. The details the man with the French accent gave me were vague, but enough to lead me to Patrick Boyd Yachtbrokers, who had sold the businessman a very large catamaran which they had delivered for him to the Virgin Islands. My next enquiry was to the marine radio station in the Virgin Islands, who located the catamaran at a Tortola marina, the same place from which Richard Merkley operated. The marina's phone was answered from the bar by a barman who confirmed that while the vessel was still at their docks, he hadn't seen the tall New Yorker for a couple of days and thought that he might have flown across to Miami.

On 20 December I pushed the last of the papers into my bulging briefcase, zipped up my travel bag, and went out into the rain and across to the tube station. The crowded train to Heathrow Central rolled on its way below London, then out into the dismal weather; nobody in the carriage smiled and I wondered if they all felt as miserable and fed up with travelling as I did. My vision of myself fell well short of the hero the newspapers were trying to promote me as. I knew I was just a man who had been forced by circumstances to take on an investigative role, the responsibility for which we had unsuccessfully tried to pass along. I knew also that by our action in investigating we were treading on dangerous ground and I was hopeful that in the USA I would finally be able to pass over to an appropriate authority the weight of the responsibility we had been carrying for so long.

23

Winter in America

If the weather had been bad in England, it was worse in America. The temperature when I arrived in Philadelphia was minus 17 degrees Celsius and falling. Blizzards had come with the coldest winter in sixty years, already causing scores of deaths. Worse weather was forecast.

Richard Smith, the Drug Enforcement Administration's agent assigned to the *Hetty* case and to look after me, met me at the airport and installed me in a comfortable hotel with very reliable central heating. The hotel was situated not far from the banks of the Delaware River in the old quarter of Philadelphia, and my room looked out over an old cemetery and a monument housing the Liberty Bell.

Richard Smith, a six-foot, athletically built man in his midthirties, lived in Philadelphia, where he had grown up. Before becoming a federal agent he had been a uniformed cop, and before that a US Marine who had served in Vietnam. He had married a wisp of a girl named Daisy and they now had two charming daughters. Richie, as Richard Smith was better known, worked out of an office in Atlantic City, New Jersey, a forty-minute drive away to the east from Philadelphia. He also worked from a Newark office, a fifty-minute drive to the north. During the many long periods I spent with Richie on my seventeen-day visit to the United States, we got to know each other well.

Richie took me to meet an array of officers from various sections of the law-enforcement communities with whom he worked. He introduced me simply as 'my partner from Australia', which was enough to gain me acceptance without any questions. This introduction took me into a world new to me – a world of high-powered federal agents, assistant district attorneys and computer intelligence.

The first officer I met was quite a character. Bill Braker was a senior Customs Department investigator attached to the Philadelphia office, which now held custody over the *Hetty*. A wise-cracking bull of a man, Braker wore a revolver in an open holster on his hip and a star on his barrel-chested frame. Just the sight of him and the roar of his booming voice must have sent children scampering, but I could sense that beneath the tough exterior lay a much softer man. Braker told me that the *Hetty* lay at a dock in Cape May, a town on the southern peninsula of New Jersey. He explained that the hidden compartment formed by the earlier modifications to the ship, which hadn't been found until after our telephone call to the US Coast Guard in November, was still inaccessible because the timber cargo couldn't be moved until the frozen lifting equipment thawed out.

Work for me in America began as I looked over some of the many items taken from the *Hetty* as evidence. Other items were scattered around various offices in New Jersey and New York and it seemed inefficient that the authorities weren't able to keep the evidence together. I was also confused by the logbook taken from the *Hetty*, which didn't correspond with positions plotted on the nautical charts found on the ship, an aspect overlooked by the policemen, who had neither seafaring experience nor training in navigation. Braker believed that the ship had at one time been used to carry a narcotic substance, probably in the ducting about the main engine's blowers. (This piece of equipment had been removed for 'repair' in Cochin, and again at the shipyard in Singapore where the *Hetty* had gone after leaving Cochin.) Braker's customs investigators had no trouble in understanding the meaning of a film they had taken from a camera found aboard the *Hetty* which, when developed, showed the manner in which Marriott and Charlesworth had concealed a white powdery substance, heroin, in the sole of a thick rubber thong. Braker said he would later have an investigator drive me to Cape May where I could inspect the ship. When I left Braker's office he walked Richie and me to the door and gave me a wink as his voice boomed out, 'Don't worry, son. We'll break their balls.'

The DEA office where I met Richie's boss was situated deep inside a security area on the outskirts of Atlantic City. The large compound was shared with military and other federal offices, and nearby was an airstrip where heavily armed jet fighter planes were constantly ready to take to the air. Jerry Moore, the senior DEA officer, had an assortment of agents to watch over, each one involved in a different case. The agents were of remarkably different ages and ethnic backgrounds to suit their undercover role of detecting drug traffickers.

While I turned out my briefcase, Richie pulled two extra chairs up to his work-laden desk and removed the evidence from the security safe. With Jerry Moore in attendance we began to compile the *Hetty* case.

The paper chase went on for two days as the names of many vessels and suspects were punched into the computer terminal. Each piece of information extracted from the computer was exhaustively cross-referenced as the names of suspects and vessels began to interrelate. I moved between Richie, who was at the computer display, and Jerry Moore, who had pinned an enormous blank sheet of paper on the wall and was building a flow diagram of the connections that made up the international network as we uncovered it. At the top was Richard Merkley, below him a number of powerful distributors, and further down were the traffickers and couriers. All but a few of the names I had brought were already listed on the DEA's computer, although a connection between them had not previously been established. Common haunts for the drug organization's members were Singapore and the Virgin Islands, with the empire reaching into England and Europe, Australia and America. The *Hetty* bust, while involving a huge quantity of drugs, was still only one of many shipments the network was thought to have made.

Both the DEA agents expressed their surprise that the information we had given to the Australian authorities had not been taken up, especially as many of the people operating through Darwin, the major northern port in Australia, could be linked together in the Australian police computer to which the DEA had access.

It took Jerry Moore a few days to read through the mass of papers I had brought, most of which related to our domestic struggle with the Australian authorities. The file was complete and needed no further explanation by me and I was pleased that Jerry Moore took an interest in the matter.

Soon after my arrival in the USA the Australian Federal Police requested permission from the DEA hierarchy to send an officer who could sit in on our discussions. Although I had no objection to this, somebody senior in the administration must have vetoed their request, because the officer never came.

I woke early on the day the US Customs Department had scheduled an investigator to accompany me on the long journey to Cape May to inspect the *Hetty*. The local radio announcer gave the temperature as being minus 25 degrees Celsius, and I looked out through the hotel window onto a cold white scene. The night's fresh cover of snow was as yet undisturbed. When I had left Australia nineteen days earlier I had had to pack clothing for the equatorial weather of Singapore and the dampness of an English climate, but I owned no clothes suitable for this bitterly cold weather, nor could my budget be stretched enough to buy any. I was now suffering the cold-weather blues.

The customs investigators' vehicles were parked in a row behind their Philadelphia office and when I saw them I realized that the US government gave the Customs Department a less generous vehicle allowance than the DEA received. But the small sedan in which the customs investigator drove me to the *Hetty* successfully rattled its way across New Jersey State and finally reached Cape May.

The *Hetty* looked forlorn and neglected in its bleak surroundings. Rust streaks were abundant on the superstructure and I doubted whether the US Customs Department would get many bidders when in due course they auctioned the confiscated ship. Ice crunched under my shoes as I swung up onto the deck, and I knew that I would have to hurry my inspection of the ship before my toes began to ache.

I began in the forward hold and I saw the place where the 14 tons of hashish had been discovered by the US Coast Guard. As I looked carefully at the timber cargo still in the holds I identified it as being muranti, and not the more expensive mahogany which the ship's papers recorded. (This was yet another attempt to cover the ship's movements, as muranti is widely available only in the Southeast Asian region.) I continued my inspection on the lower decks aft where I quickly went through the crew's quarters, noticing as I did so just how thoroughly it had been overturned. Even the cabin linings had been removed. I didn't linger on the accommodation decks, because I knew I had only this one opportunity for inspection, and in the freezing conditions I wanted to spend as much time as I could in the place I most wanted to inspect – the navigation area.

On the port side of the bridge, standing against the aft bulkhead, was the *Hetty*'s navigation area. Under a large desktop were narrow drawers where nautical charts and records were kept. As I removed each drawer I found that its contents related to a different area of the world that the ship had passed through. In order to establish the navigator's methods and habits I read each notation pencilled on the charts, all the while stamping my feet to keep the blood flowing to them. When I came to the charts of the Indian Ocean I compared the daily plottings made on them with those I had copied from the logbook I had read in the Philadelphia customs office, noticing that beneath the pencilled plottings on the chart there were others that had been clumsily erased. I continued my search through the desk, handing to the customs investigator the charts I wanted taken back to Philadelphia for closer examination.

The bottom drawer of the navigation desk was jammed. My frozen fingers pulled savagely at it until it came away in my hands, but I totally lost interest in what the drawer contained when I caught sight of what had been jamming it – a second logbook with an identical cover to the one I had seen in the Philadelphia customs office. Inside this logbook were the genuine plottings and daily records of the ship's movements after it had left Singapore in June with its new captain aboard. For a short while the cold was completely forgotten as I read in fascination.

As the car rattled its way back to Philadelphia I read again from the logbook that I had first thought must exist when I had seen its fabricated imitation some days before in Bill Braker's office. The idea of looking for any other logbook had not been considered by the swarm of trained searchers who had taken the *Hetty* apart, looking for drugs. My pleasure in finding the genuine logbook, which covered the period in which the hashish had been loaded, was doubled by the fact that Richard Merkley's name was recorded several times. A notation of his radio instruction to divert the ship to the northern Indian Ocean had been made, with Merkley's signature on another page.

The trial of the *Hetty* crew was set for hearing on 3 January 1984. By the week leading up to Christmas none of the crew were talking of cooperating and there were even suggestions by their expensive criminal lawyers of entering a plea of not guilty. But the lawyers, all hired through a Miami law firm for a fee rumoured to be close to $200,000, didn't know then of the extensive prosecution case that was being compiled against the crew.

Richie drove me to New York to meet the assistant district attorney responsible for prosecution. He took a freeway that he had travelled on many times, but our journey was made long and treacherous by the icy road surface and for much of the time we stayed close behind a salt truck. The sky was a ceiling of snow clouds, though Richie cheerfully told me that it was too cold to snow.

Daniel Gibbons worked from the Justice Department's offices in Newark, a very run-down suburb within sight of the New York City skyscrapers. The district was littered with junk and still bore the scars of the civil rioting of more than a decade before. Short of forty, Dan Gibbons had a clean-cut American appearance and wore the three-piece pinstripe suit that is the uniform of many in the legal profession. Gibbons also outwardly wore his ambition, and the impression I have of him is one of a man on his way to the top in a big city and didn't care who knew it.

I soon realized that the legal world he moved in was played along lines that might bewilder the uninitiated. The personalities of attorneys and judges often decided the strategy adopted for each case. District Judge Frederick Lacey had been appointed to preside in the *Hetty* case, and he had a reputation as 'a hard man in a drug case'. No animosity appeared to exist between Dan Gibbons and the four opposing defence attorneys, nor should there have been, as the game so far had been played by the rules – the prosecution's evidence had been offered to the court in a routine procedure called 'discovery', to which the defence attorneys had objected that the evidence was inadmissable due to a technicality in the testimony of a Coast Guard officer. However, the technicality had not been backed by a strong argument and the defence attorneys' attempt to have the case dismissed failed. Judge Lacey then ordered the *Hetty* crew for trial.

Out-of-court manoeuvring had begun in the time that remained before the trial commenced, each side trying to feel out the strength of the other. The defence attorneys' advice to their four clients had been not to cooperate with the authorities; such cooperation had a value that the attorneys could negotiate with. But the defence attorneys were not then aware that the identity of the drug boss was now known to the DEA, and therefore were reckoning that their clients' cooperation had a greater worth than it did.

I answered many of the questions Dan Gibbons posed to me and identified two of the *Hetty* crew members from their photographs. There were other photographs taken aboard the ship about which he sought my opinion. We discussed the meaning of the logbook I had found on the *Hetty* and I explained certain points of navigation to him. I looked through the third assortment of evidence taken from the *Hetty* while Richie told Dan Gibbons about the DEA's computer search and its results.

When Dan Gibbons had finished with us we left his office, and in the walk down the long corridor to the security exit Richie expressed his satisfaction with the meeting. He explained to me that the advances in the DEA's collected intelligence on the case since my arrival would now tip the advantage in any negotiation between opposing attorneys in Dan Gibbons's favour. Gibbons might give the defence attorneys' request for negotiation a cool reception for a while, to strengthen further the prosecution's position. The defence attorneys could finally enter a plea of guilty in return for some concessions, Richie speculated; this was how the game of plea bargaining was played. At the end of the corridor we passed through the security check, where I noticed the insignia of the Justice Department – idealistic notions topped by the scales of justice. Somehow I couldn't help feeling a wee bit cynical about it all.

Before we left New York Richie took me to an office Christmas party held for some of the federal agents who worked undercover in the city. Present were agents of all description and seniority. As the night wore on they became more relaxed, some a little inebriated, and as I mingled among them I heard many bloodcurdling stories as they told each other of past experiences.

Christmas 1983 came and went. The festive period would have been a lonely time for me if Richie Smith and Jerry Moore hadn't thoughtfully included me in their family programmes. The holiday break brought for most a respite from the usual hectic pace of American life, and the whole country seemed to slow down.

On Wednesday 28 December I phoned the American correspondent for the *Sunday Times*, Mark Hosenball, who reported to the newspaper's London office from his base in Washington. He told me that he would be coming up to Philadelphia late on Friday night, and suggested that on the following morning I could catch a taxi to the hotel where he usually stayed.

I briskly walked the thirteen city blocks to the address Mark Hosenball had given me. The cold weather continued to keep most people indoors, though I passed by a number of bums and winos staked out across pavement grilles where hot air emerged from nearby centrally heated buildings. Mark Hosenball met me in his hotel suite. He told me that the *Sunday Times* had instructed him to approach Shelley Fern for an interview. From one of the bulging pockets of the very tired suit he wore he pulled a sheaf of cable messages. He had brought copies of the telexes that had gone between him and London. We exchanged notes and I explained that I had traced Shelley Fern to a district west of Philadelphia where she had been recently staying with her sister. The description fitted that of the woman who the DEA knew had visited Stephen Marriott in prison, taking him *Playboy* magazines. Following the *Hetty* bust she had taken a brief trip to the Virgin Islands. The DEA were interested in talking to her.

'We'll doorknock her,' Hosenball decided. The first step in his programme was a stop at the hotel's lounge where he had a large drink to brace himself against the cold. Then we caught a taxi to a car-rental base. From a battered leather wallet, stuffed inches thick with pieces of paper and crumpled money, he found the right plastic card to bring a rental car around to the door.

On the drive through suburbia I realized that Hosenball was an odd character. He had a small, rotund body that looked decidedly lived in. His constantly ruffled hair, tie askew and spectacles balanced on the tip of his nose, gave him the appearance of an untidy schoolboy. As a youth he had received a private education at one of the best English schools, returning to America with a foreign influence in his accent and an eccentricity in his personality. His father was a leading Washington lawyer, specializing in law in outer space. Hosenball's wife was a newspaper person like himself.

The address we had for Shelley Fern turned out to be a

block of apartments. Hosenball questioned the caretaker but it seemed he had no occupancy list. From a nearby payphone Hosenball called the telephone number we had for the address. There was no answer.

We went for lunch at a local diner and then tried again. This time Shelley Fern's sister answered. 'Shelley's not here. She's gone to New York to visit Stephen in prison. She said she might stay over for the court case next week. You might find her at the George Washington Hotel on 35th Street.'

Back at his city hotel Hosenball checked out of his room, while I was allowed only enough time to pack some clean clothes at the hotel where I was staying, then we caught an afternoon train to New York.

The American correspondent was good company for me on our train journey, talking at length about American law enforcement and legal groups. At New York's busy Penn Station Hosenball showed ruthlessness in getting us a cab to the Windsor-Harley Hotel. There he found another plastic card in his enormous wallet and we were each given a room. Another cab ride brought us to 35th Street and the entrance to the George Washington.

Hosenball confirmed with a very tough female clerk behind the George Washington's counter that Shelley Fern was staying at the hotel, but all Hosenball's persistence to get the room number failed to move the woman. A row of house phones in a hallway leading to a tacky refreshments shop was where the correspondent then went to 'doorknock' Shelley Fern. When the phone answered, Hosenball began explaining who he was and why he had come to New York. Shelley did what I expected and told Hosenball she would not talk to the press, but said that if he wanted she could give him the number of Stephen's attorney. The newspaperman was good at his telephone work and he drew Shelley Fern deeper into conversation, telling her that he was in the hotel's lobby with Brian Milgate, the man she had met in Cochin when she was there on the *Hetty*. As Shelley was curious to know why I was in New York, Hosenball responded by handing the telephone to me.

In the ten-minute conversation I had with Shelley Fern I was not able to convince her to meet Mark Hosenball. However, her curiosity to know more about my invitation to the US as witness in next week's court case was much too great for her to refuse my invitation to dinner that night.

'After all,' I said to her, 'New Year's Eve would be no fun alone in your hotel room.'

I returned to the George Washington at 8 p.m. sharp and called Shelley on the house phone. I assured her I was alone, a condition of her agreement to meet me; Hosenball had rugged himself up against the cold and gone off to Times Square. Shelley asked me to wait, saying she would be down shortly.

I recognized her the moment she stepped from the elevator into the busy lobby, but more from the photographs I had recently seen than from my recollection of her in Cochin, when she had been the cook on the *Hetty*. Tall and slim, she looked smart in the knee-length leather boots and the fur jacket she wore. We walked four blocks to a small Italian restaurant she knew. On the way she explained the ground rules the defence attorneys had stipulated to her and the limits of what she was permitted to talk about.

The restaurant was very pleasant, as was the food they served, and the festive atmosphere of the place helped us through a second bottle of wine. Shelley told me a lot more about the organization than I had anticipated she would, stopping just short of incriminating herself. I gathered her position now was that of go-between, keeping a communication line open between Richard Merkley and the defence attorneys, and although she told me many useful things about Merkley I felt sure she had no way of contacting him directly. She said that Stephen and the crew were afraid that the Mafia, who were the buyers of the network's hashish, might execute them in prison if they cooperated with the DEA. She blamed Jim Howard for the trouble they were in now, for having brought too much attention to them in Cochin.

At midnight the band played Frank Sinatra's 'New York,

New York' and the restaurant's patrons belched along to several choruses. I told Shelley Fern that if she wanted a way out from a life of crime she might think about co-operating with the DEA. She said she would consider what I had said and promised to call me in the morning.

Hosenball caught up with my news at breakfast. He had decided it was no longer worth his time to pursue Shelley Fern and would catch a morning train south. Shelley Fern called me to say she wished to talk further, so I planned to take an afternoon train when our meeting concluded.

She came to the hotel where I was staying and met me in the lobby. We went to a delicatessen around the corner on Sixth Avenue where we had many cups of coffee. Later she walked me through the wintry New York streets towards Penn Station, leaving me at Broadway. She told me that her involvement in the organization was too deep for her to pull out, though she seemed sincere when she wished me luck in my efforts to get *Tiger Rag* out of Cochin.

When she walked away I could see reflected in her the beginnings of a hardness that might take her through the tough years ahead, though I felt that the attractive young woman might very soon find herself out of her depth in the society she couldn't step away from.

On Wednesday 4 January Mark Hosenball sent by telex his despatch to the *Sunday Times* office in London. It began:

At a one-hour hearing in Newark, New Jersey, before US District Judge Frederick Lacey all four defendants in the *Hetty* case pleaded guilty to one charge of conspiracy to possess nearly 15 tons of hashish with intent to distribute it.

Peter Jackson, Stephen Marriott, William Charlesworth and Donald Dickinson each now face up to fifteen years in prison and fines of up to $125,000 each for their admitted role in the drug-smuggling conspiracy. Judge Lacey announced he would sentence the men on 14 February. He remanded them in custody till that time. The US prosecutor in charge of the *Hetty* case, Dan Gibbons, said that during the course of the hearing before Judge Lacey, the judge, as a matter of routine, began to question Dickinson in detail about the case, to make sure Dickinson understood the full weight of the government allegation to which he was pleading guilty.

During the course of Judge Lacey's questioning, Dickinson admitted to conspiring to import the hashish along with the other defendants. Dickinson also said in open court that Richard Merkley was part of the conspiracy, although he apparently gave little information as to who Merkley is or what his precise role in the conspiracy was.

The outcome of the proceedings brought a successful conclusion to my usefulness in the USA. The DEA were now on the trail of Richard Merkley. The days of plea bargaining before Judge Lacey's sitting had left the attorneys on both sides agreeing that Richard Merkley was to be implicated in court. However, the *Hetty* captain added a further remark to protect himself from reprisal by the Mafia. By stating that the hashish had been loaded in Oman, he was trying to cover for the Mafia don who had flown to Dubai to inspect the ship's concealed drug cargo. (The *Hetty* had only gone *near* Oman *after* it had sailed from Dubai.)

I booked a seat on a flight back to London on 6 January, two days before the *Sunday Times* was scheduled to go to press with our story. I was very much looking forward to seeing Alison, who was still in Australia, but soon due to meet me in London. She had told me on the telephone that her departure had almost been delayed for several weeks due to last-minute harassment by Foreign Affairs Department officers in Perth who had tried to withhold her passport when she had taken it to be amended. But she had overcome the difficulty and was now on her way.

Richie drove me out to the airport at Philadelphia and arranged my ticket to London, then through to Bombay. The DEA also gave me enough to cover my expenses. Dan Gibbons had said in farewell that any further assistance given to me by the US government might bring embarrassment to the Australian government.

Jerry Moore's farewell was sincere, but also chilling. He took me aside to urge me to be careful since a number of characters in this drug organization checked directly back to the intelligence community – the CIA as well as another foreign government. And if the CIA's business had been threatened, he told me, their wrath would be far deadlier than what might be expected from the Mafia. Richie added his good wishes for my uncertain future. I shook the agent's hand and thanked him. The drug organization which Alison and I had identified in Cochin had at last been fully exposed. Its verification was what we had needed for so long to use against Jim Howard in his defamation case.

24

Clearing the Way

Colin Simpson and Barrie Penrose worked in top gear as they put together, for their editor's approval, their story entitled 'The Cochin Connection'. Alison had arrived in London two days before me and we stayed in a hotel near the *Sunday Times* office, spending many hours at the newspaper watching over the shoulders of those who put the feature article to press. For both of us there was much to catch up on, and while I was in America more information about Jim Howard had been gathered.

As the *Sunday Times* was later to claim, the former UPI photographer was known to police in several countries. His extensive criminal record has carried at least two prison sentences – and he has been deported from South Africa and from the former Central African Federation. He is remembered in the Congo during the civil wars of the 1960s, but more as an associate of mercenaries than a photographer, and is listed by Interpol as a known associate of a particularly active group of drug smugglers.

The publication of the *Sunday Times* feature on 8 January 1984 brought another landmark for us, though those involved in the case thought the story would end there. The *Sunday Times* journalists had summed up their feelings in the final paragraph of the article:

Chief federal prosecutor Dan Gibbons said: 'Thanks to Milgate's brilliant intelligence we have learned more about this particular network than usual.' But for Milgate that can still only be cold comfort. *Tiger Rag* still sits in Cochin, deteriorating with time and the climate, and there seems little chance that he will ever sail her again. A high price for public spirit.

But Alison and I were more optimistic. We had no intention of abandoning *Tiger Rag*, especially as we had worked for so long towards getting her back and now things were going our way. Before we could leave London for India, however, there was a round of official places to call on.

The first call was to Australia House, offices of the Australian Foreign Affairs Department – an imposing corner building in the Strand. Our reason for going there was to ask our government if they had had a change of heart and might now be willing to support us. We were shown into the office of a Mr McCloskey, the first secretary. Sitting in on the interview was a diplomat who mumbled that he was an assistant political attaché, though his manner and the gaberdine trenchcoat he was wearing more suited the mould of someone in the Intelligence Unit of the Australian Foreign Affairs Department.

It was days before an answer was ready for us at Australia House. When it finally came, McCloskey shrugged his shoulders many times as he read for us Canberra's terse words – it was a private legal matter and they would not get involved. 'I can't understand their attitude towards you,' was all the first secretary could say to us in consolation.

Detectives from New Scotland Yard were interested to receive certain facts about the drug organization's connections in Europe, especially about the shipment of drugs from Cochin concealed in shipping containers. We were impressed by the politeness of the detectives we spoke with, and grateful for the short note we had received from the Home Office thanking us for our earlier information which they said had 'proved to be most useful'.

The Indian high commission, a few blocks away from Australia House, was the last official place on our list to visit. We were directed to the office of Mr O. N. Khanna, a senior diplomat, and the official discussions that ensued with representatives of the Indian government proved rewarding for both sides. We were able to pass along information received in America – that the American businessman we had met in Cochin was shortly expected to arrive in India from the Virgin Islands. He had been overheard saying that 'after just one more business deal in Cochin' he could retire for ever.

The Indian officials seemed less interested in the drug aspect than in the covert intelligence operation now uncovered in their sensitive port of Cochin. They had come to their own conclusion that Jim Howard had used his computer to record naval and military training information, and that the floppy disks were subsequently smuggled out of India. They asked questions along the same lines as Additional Collector Venugopalan almost a year before, when he too had concluded that Howard was involved in espionage. Again we explained that we had first learned about Howard's computer from Jyl Gocher, who complained that Jim was up every night operating it. At that time we had only just met Howard and were anchored off Bolghatty Island, but we noticed that the light in room 44 burned for most of the night. On his return to Cochin, when he had bought the *Hetty*, Howard had again spent uncountable hours at his computer. When we spoke to Venugopalan in April we learned for the first time that, after the customs rummage of Howard's room at the Bolghatty Hotel, Howard was suspected by the customs chief of having used the computer as well as the photographic darkroom he had set up in room 44 to record sensitive information. We had only seen a few lines of text, which indeed looked like military information.

There was much we could suggest, however, in answer to the question of how military information could have been passed to Howard. We recalled having given Jyl Gocher a lift in our dinghy from Bolghatty Island to the Ernakulam mainland one afternoon in January 1983, when she told us she was in a hurry to pick up papers from a Cochin lawyer's office which 'Jim needed to put on his computer'. A second link came by chance when we were searching for a sailmaker in Cochin and came across an Indian who worked inside the naval base, and worked with senior officers. Much to our surprise we discovered that he called regularly at that same lawyer's office as Gocher was known to collect documents from. Much later, however, these threads, plus others we were to recall, as well as the confirmation that 35mm negatives of foreign warships were in Howard's possession, led us to the same conclusion as Additional Collector Venugopalan and the intelligence officers of the central Indian government.

Out of our meeting at the Indian high commission came an assurance of the cooperation we would receive from the Indian Government in the future.

When we had done all we could do in London we felt the way had been cleared enough for us to return to India. Our friends tried to dissuade us from going back, and came up with a tempting offer to provide a yacht for me to sail in the 1984 transatlantic yacht race in place of *Tiger Rag*, but we both felt we must resolve matters in Cochin and booked a flight to Bombay for 24 January.

Circumstances lessened our apprehension about returning to India. Despite Howard's continuing defamation case, on 9 January the *Indian Express* published a story on the front pages of many of their publications across India which had been cabled through from their London news service. It was the second time that the alleged Cochin drug organization had made the front page of the national Indian papers, and on this occasion Howard's photograph appeared and he was named as one of the drug organization's principals.

Howard was furious. He had called a news conference at the press club in Cochin's Ernakulam District to declare his complete innocence, and had expressed a renewed determination to pursue the earlier defamation case against the *Indian Express*. After this he announced his intention of going directly to London, where he intended also to sue the *Sunday Times* for defamation. The next day he had flown out of India, but not to London as he had suggested. Indian intelligence officers discovered that he caught a flight to Sri Lanka and understood his next destination to be Singapore.

On the day we flew out of Heathrow airport, Howard

finally turned up on the doorstep of the *Sunday Times* building, puffing at a cigar and breathing fire. The legal people at the *Sunday Times* had told us that his threats to bring a defamation case were just bluff, and they were right. The security man at the desk in the foyer ordered Jim Howard to leave the building or he would call in the bobbies. Jim Howard didn't grace the *Sunday Times* with his presence again.

25

Back in Cochin

India's leading national current-affairs magazine, *India Today*, interviewed Jim Howard early in January 1984.

Howard accuses Milgate of being a real nut, and a member of the CIA. The hashish, according to Howard's version, 'is from Afghanistan and is part payment by the Afghan rebels to the CIA for supplying them with guns'. He threatens to 'sue Brian's pants off'.

India's Republic Day celebrations on 26 January meant a two-day wait in Bombay before Brian and I could get an onward flight to Cochin. It was a time to reacquaint ourselves with India. We took an early-morning beach walk and watched as Koli village women, with saris hitched above their knees and twisted between their thighs, waded out to unload small fishing boats. Brian took me for a birthday lunch at the Oberoi Towers and later we watched a street performance by three ragged children who had trained a hungry-looking dog to do extraordinary tricks. A late-afternoon stroll along Juhu Beach among masses of people brought sights one could only expect to see in India. Some Hindus had buried themselves in the sand so that a small straw was all that was visible where a head was buried, and only a hand or leg was exposed. One man we saw, who had painted himself entirely white, had tied his body in knots. The border between rational and irrational, as the Western person understands it, is distinctly different in India.

We slipped quietly into Cochin. The timing of our return seemed good, since both Jim Howard and Gordon Gold were absent and the warrants for our arrest had expired. Our first move to recover *Tiger Rag* was to patch her up for launching, after which she could be towed away from the

Edacochin boatyard where we had been such an easy target in the past.

After the first seven days back in Cochin we had made significant progress with *Tiger Rag*. A trip to the customs house to have the restraint order on our sailing equipment revoked had revealed many changes – Additional Collector Venugopalan and two other senior officers had been transferred to lesser positions outside Kerala State, presumably the penalty they paid for dropping the *Hetty* inquiry. Superintendent Menon remained in Cochin. The shake-up in the hierarchy had brought a cool attitude towards us at the customs house, but eventually we came away with the official release we had needed. At the workshop, where seven months before they had begun to make a replacement for *Tiger Rag*'s stolen rudder, we had a friendly reception. Work on the rudder had stopped when we had suddenly disappeared in June of the previous year, but after a massive two-day effort the rudder and mechanism were completed. Our third task was to find a suitable and safe boatyard near to the harbour entrance but away from the Ernakulam mainland, where we knew the underworld had influence within police circles. There *Tiger Rag* would be taken for the essential repairs that were required due to damage caused in Cochin the previous year. We had patched up the hull and were ready to launch the yacht when a friend brought to the Edacochin boatyard a man who managed a small slipway at Mattancherry.

We felt great relief at last to be able to get away from Edacochin, but our relief was shattered only a few hours after *Tiger Rag* had been towed downriver to the GKW Corporation boatyard at Mattancherry. Two tough-looking Indians walked aboard the yacht uninvited as she lay against a small jetty awaiting the high tide when she could again be hauled out. They were later identified as part of the Cochin underworld, connected with a local group known to have been the distributors of heroin recently shipped to the UK in tins labelled CRAB MEAT. The spokesman for the two was as tough a character as we had ever seen. He approached his topic with a remarkable bluntness.

'No more publicity about Cochin drugs, or no more you.'

We looked at the second man, who slowly drew his index finger across his throat, confirming what his associate intended. We assured them that we wanted no more trouble, boldly adding, in terms they could understand, that if there was to be peace in Cochin then they must also order Jim Howard to back off.

The visit from the underworld characters left us feeling unnerved. Before the *Hetty* bust had hit the international headlines, Cochin had been virtually unknown as a port for the export of hard drugs. Now every drug trafficker in Cochin had cause to resent us for the attention we had brought on the city.

That evening *Tiger Rag* was hauled out, the slipway trolley removed from beneath her and the hull securely propped. GKW was a small boatyard run by three Christian partners: a devout Franciscan named Francis, an orthodox Catholic known as Sunno, and Mr Joseph, who belonged to an ancient breakaway Christian order. It was situated in the heart of the Muslim district of Mattancherry, across the road from a mosque. A high concrete perimeter wall and heavy timber entrance doors gave the boatyard good security and each night a watchman came with two big Alsatian dogs. Although the equipment in GKW's workshop was antiquated and basic, the workmen were skilled and diligent and after our first day there we were hopeful of completing essential repairs, given fourteen days without interruption. After that we could sail from India.

But on our second day at GKW, Jyl Gocher marched arrogantly into the boatyard and up to where *Tiger Rag* was secured. Behind her came a number of uniformed policemen and two men who we assumed were Howard's criminal laywers. Gocher pointed to the yacht. 'That's *Tiger Rag*,' she said on cue. Two policemen climbed on board and ordered us to get down immediately. The yacht was locked and the key taken by police. We were forbidden any access, and the GKW partners were informed that if further work was carried out on the yacht they would be imprisoned.

Brian and I were taken separately by armed policemen to the local Mattancherry District police station, about two miles away. I was marched up to the desk of a senior officer. Brian was nowhere in sight.

'Your vessel has been attached by the court,' the officer said, then waited for my reaction.

I didn't answer.

'Miss Gocher has ordered your arrest on a defamation charge. You must present yourself to the court within seven days to take bail.' He produced a document he assured me had been issued by the court and told me to sign it. I refused, and told him I would continue to refuse until someone I could trust translated the document into English. The officer became angry and threatened to imprison me for my non-cooperation. But I stood my ground, sensing that Howard's lawyers, who were lurking near the doorway, had enticed the police officer to misuse his authority.

The stalemate lasted for an hour and ended only when the police officer realized he was wasting his time and I was allowed to leave the police station without signing the document. What was written in the document remained a mystery.

It was dark when I got back to the GKW boatyard. A light was burning in Francis's office as I made my way across the earthen workshop floor to the head of the old stone building. The office floor was concrete, the plaster on the walls was cracked, and the window had no glass, only steel bars. A bare timber bench and desk added to the austerity of the room.

Brian arrived soon after me. We sat in the office in company with the GKW partners, all of us understandably gloomy. Brian had been given threatening treatment by a different officer at the police station, but he also had resisted intimidation and refused to sign the document.

I telephoned the home of our lawyer, Dr Panikulangara. 'Vincent caught the morning train to Trivandrum, where his main office is,' I reported with disappointment, 'and his phone there is out of order.' The GKW partners solemnly shook their heads in unison, but Brian suggested that we should go to Trivandrum, too, to see Vincent and perhaps try to arrange a meeting with the state's top police officers.

For our own peace of mind we resolved to go immediately; we could catch one of the long-distance buses that departed Cochin at intervals throughout the evening and sped through the night on their eight-hour journey south to the state capital. But we stood in only our workclothes; our papers and all we needed to take with us were now locked inside the impounded yacht. We looked across at Francis, sitting behind his tidy desk. On the bare desktop he had quietly placed the spare key to *Tiger Rag* Brian had earlier given him. Francis said softly, 'For some minutes I must close my eyes and think about your problem.'

Trivandrum, Kerala State's seat of government, is an inland city laid out in an orderly fashion among low rolling hills. It is a city of trees, gardens and public buildings. We arrived at the bus station just before dawn and took a little autorickshaw to a central area where there were several good hotels. By 10 a.m. another auto had delivered us to the entrance gate of a substantial former colonial mansion a few miles from the city centre. The building was now the state police headquarters.

For two hours we were processed from the reception foyer through a number of waiting rooms, and finally directed to a comfortable room deep in the large building and close to a grand and elegant staircase. Having come without an appointment we hadn't been confident of being given a hearing on our first attempt, thinking that the execution of law and order over the state's 30 million inhabitants would have priority. But the wide publicity our case had received in India had given it political implications that couldn't be ignored. From a source unknown to us, details of the police action at the GKW boatyard on the previous day had been printed in that morning's daily newspapers, which were routinely circulated throughout the building.

The embossed sign above the door read: Inspector General of Police, T. V. Madusudanan. We stood respectfully inside his office door for several moments, taking it all in until he invited us to sit in the armchairs at his desk. The office was very large and impressive, and fitted the man whose quiet authority and apparent efficiency must have helped his rise to the state police's top operational position.

'What do you want from me?' This was the polite way busy Indian people effectively got to the point.

We explained that we had come to seek assurance that there would be fair play towards us by police in Cochin.

'And?'

'Nothing more,' Brian replied.

The inspector general sat quietly at his desk for a moment before the officer who had ushered us into the office appeared in the doorway in response to some hidden signal. When the inspector general had given an order he turned his attention back to us. 'And haven't the Cochin police been fair to you?'

We began to answer his question by outlining the police intimidation of the previous day, following up with a description of events that had occurred in the past year. Before we had finished the telephone rang.

The inspector general's conversation lasted many minutes.

He maintained a calm but serious expression as he put down the receiver; then, to our surprise, he asked how we had come to Trivandrum. What had been the time of our arrival? Had we travelled by car? Had we taken a hotel room? While Brian replied to his questions I remembered that I had slipped the bus tickets into my purse. He read the tickets intently, turned them over and even held them up to the light. Satisfied, he explained, 'A Miss Gocher has reported to our Cochin police commissioner that you attempted to murder her in the early hours of this morning. She claims to have witnesses.'

Brian and I looked at each other, then back at the inspector general, both of us too stunned to comment.

'Please do one thing,' he said. 'Write a statement of what you have told me about police harassment in Cochin. Leave nothing out. Cochin DIG of police, Krishnan Nair, whom you have met, is expected here for a meeting on Wednesday morning. Please remain in this city and return to this building at that time.'

Maxwell Fernandez was first relieved and later amused when we telephoned him from Trivandrum. Jyl Gocher's charge that we had attempted to murder her had been leaked to the press. Rumours had also been spread that we had run away. But no sooner had the reporters rallied at the Ernakulam press club than the Cochin police withdrew the charge. We had been more than 100 miles away at the time that the incident was said to have occurred.

We eventually tracked down Vincent Panikulangara at his Trivandrum residence and discussed the ongoing defamation case as well as the recent development of the attachment of our yacht and the issue of warrants which ordered our surrender to the court within seven days. Vincent told us that it would be difficult for him to advise us fully until he had all the facts, including those detailing under what conditions the yacht had been attached to the court, and what bail requirements would be set. By the time we were due to return to Cochin he was confident of knowing more.

When we went for our Wednesday appointment at police headquarters, a meeting of high-ranking state police officers was being conducted. From our seats in the waiting room we noticed a greater feeling of urgency in the old building as the polished floors in the corridors echoed to the footsteps of the attending district officers. At midday we were ushered into Inspector General Madusudanan's office. He looked us over carefully, his face giving no indication of the fate we might expect. He invited us to sit, and snapped off an order to the officer who had shown us in. We handed the inspector general the statement we had prepared at his request. As he read our complaints about harassment by Cochin police officers, a very stern expression came over his face.

In the silence that followed we heard the faint sound of a

buzzer from beyond the door. Krishnan Nair briskly entered the office and saluted the inspector general. He nodded to us and came across the room to sit in an armchair next to me. The inspector general's voice was unyielding as he addressed a highly nervous DIG Krishnan Nair.

'This man claims to have been held in prison without charge for three days by officers in your district. Is this correct?'

The inspector general's words hung in the air. Krishnan Nair darted a glance in Brian's direction. It would be a big admission for Krishnan Nair to confirm the imprisonment to his inspector general, and for us it was also a tense moment until his reply came. 'Yes, sir. It did happen, sir.'

DIG Krishnan Nair remained in the inspector general's office when the meeting was over. We could only speculate on what the DIG must now face for the misdeeds of policemen in his charge. But for us the outcome of the ten-minute session had been positive. The inspector general had given us his word that no further charges would be brought against us by police without his authorization. Furthermore, he would personally order the subinspector of Mattancherry District police station to provide round-the-clock protection for us.

Indian long-distance buses aren't known for their comfort. By late Thursday afternoon when the bus Brian and I had caught rolled into Cochin we were feeling jolted and tired, but with only one day left for us to surrender ourselves to the court, any rest would have to come later. First we needed to satisfy ourselves that bail would not be set beyond our modest means. The police would now ensure our physical protection, but they wouldn't be able to intervene in what took place inside the courtroom.

Vincent Panikulangara was expecting us when we arrived at his Panampilly Nagar residence directly from the bus station, and Maxwell Fernandez, who had been invited to sit in, was already there. Unfortunately the news Vincent had to give us wasn't comforting; as in the previous year, the chief judicial magistrate would not specify what amount of bail he would set for us. Maxwell looked concerned. Like the rest of us in Vincent's front-room office he was aware of the influence Howard's lawyer, Sukumaran Nair, would exert on Chief Judicial Magistrate Mathew. Outrageous bail requirements could very easily be set. But Vincent wasn't pessimistic, he had a bold strategy he hoped would solve the problem.

My first thoughts as Vincent outlined the unprecedented moves we could take were that it seemed like a reckless idea, but as he explained further, Brian and I saw his logic. The plan was that we should have no formal legal representation, and instead I alone would do all our arguing in court. As Vincent explained it, to have a foreign woman argue the case in court, in place of an Indian barrister, would be a precedent that was bound to baffle the opposition. Such a strategy would bring extra attention from the press, which might assure us a fairer hearing. Tonight we should go to Ernakulam and approach Magistrate Mathew at the boarding house where he stayed during the week.

Maxwell accompanied us in the autorickshaw, which he directed to stop in sight of a three-storey unpainted concrete building in the heart of the commercial district. He left us with uncertain words of encouragement and walked off into the night. Having got the courage to make a start on the bold venture, I led the way into the dimly lit forecourt. The boarding house catered for advocates and public officials whose homes were outside Cochin. Mathew occupied one room at the end of an unlit third-floor corridor.

It was a sultry night and when we reached Magistrate Mathew's door we found it ajar. I hesitated, but Brian reached out and knocked. A grumble came from inside, but nobody came to the door.

'Mr Mathew, we have come to speak with you,' I said in clear English, which must have caused the bewildered expression the magistrate wore on his face when he opened the door fully. After realizing who we were, he reluctantly invited us to enter. It was a large concrete room with an unmade single iron-framed bed standing against a far wall, while mounted on a rod in a corner the magistrate's clothes were hanging. In the centre of the room below a naked electric bulb was a small timber table and a few metal chairs. We had interrupted him in his reading. The *Indian Express* lay open on the table and a stack of folded newspapers lay piled on the floor against the wall.

I took the chair closest to the magistrate's table and offered an apology for our interruption. We hadn't enough money to engage an advocate, I explained. 'In the morning we will be coming to your courtroom. But tonight we would be thankful if you could indicate what bail requirements we might expect.'

Mathew looked hard at me for a long time before he spoke. It was obvious that he was very unhappy to have been put on the spot, and his voice was harsh. 'Do you realize that I could have you arrested? Tell me who sent you here?'

I stiffened. Again I apologized, though I didn't directly answer the magistrate's questions. We were very worried, I went on, and had come in good faith, but if he wished we would leave immediately.

Mathew didn't respond, but sat back and contemplated. He was dressed in a white cotton singlet and *mundu* and looked anything but dignified in his surroundings. I was beginning to doubt Vincent's strategy until Mathew relaxed just a little and began to ask questions. Did we understand the seriousness of the criminal defamation charges we faced? Why had we not taken an advocate? And why had we run away the previous year?

My answers came in line with the strategy in which Vincent had versed me. Mr Mathew was mostly noncommital, while Brian sat back from the table, removing himself from the conversation. The magistrate lived in a close world of legal men and was awkward in communicating on a case with an outsider, especially a well-spoken foreign woman. Although we failed to get him to specify bail requirements, at least the meeting had broken the ice. Now I would be better able to face my morning in court when there would also be Howard's criminal laywers to contend with.

Maxwell Fernandez emerged from the shadows and fell in step behind us as we walked away from the boarding house. An autorickshaw that stood vacant on the corner whisked us off into the night in the direction of Vincent's residence, where I was to receive my instructions for our court appearance the following morning. Vincent's door stood open and an outside light was burning, a warming assurance that we were not without support in Cochin. I suppressed much weariness at the end of a long day and questioned Vincent until satisfied that I was fully briefed. So much would depend on me in court the next day.

26

Alison at Law

The big iron gates of Ernakulam's court complex were open when Brian and I arrived an hour before the court was scheduled to begin. The court buildings were set well inside the grounds beyond several huge fig trees, and their distance from the busy roadway outside helped to reduce the incessant blaring of air horns from trucks and buses. All that disturbed the noisy black crows was the occasional worshipper passing along the swept earthen paths between the court buildings on their way to and from an ancient Hindu temple; its spire, which stood above the complex, was said to be made of gold and in the morning sunlight its radiance was spectacular.

The chief judicial magistrate's court was easily found. Prominent in the centre of the complex, it was a two-storey timber building with a vast number of doors, most of which had been left open after the sweepers had finished their duty. All things combined to give us a feeling of solitude, something rarely experienced in the heart of an Indian city.

When the clerk of the court arrived and began to prepare the lists for the day's session we informed him of our intention to surrender ourselves and take bail. The necessary papers were filed and we sat and waited in the small, unelaborate courtroom. After a while the advocates and their clients began to gather on the wide veranda beyond the courtroom doors; the usher's bell would bring them inside when the magistrate was ready to sit. As that time neared our tenseness grew. Someone tapped Brian on the shoulder and he jumped in alarm. It was the clerk of the court. 'Mr Mathew wants to see you both in his chamber.'

We were shown through rooms where clerical staff were now working and into a second room where a black curtain was hanging across a doorway. The clerk disappeared behind it, but a second later his small hand emerged to wave us forward. Mr Mathew didn't invite us to sit. He questioned us. 'Will you be represented by an advocate today?'

Brian shook his head and looked across at me. The magistrate began to suggest that there were many advocates available from those who came to his courtroom each day who would be willing, but his words trailed off in midsentence. He must have realized we were smart enough to know what we were doing and I guessed that he had now resigned himself to what we wanted – our self-defence was going to be allowed. He grudgingly asked what funds we had between us in India. When I told him 6000 rupees, he looked appalled and told us to go.

Case 63 of 1983, criminal defamation, was left to the end of business. Our presence in the courtroom had disrupted normal routine and as the morning progressed, a number of court journalists slid into the seat behind us to whisper questions, curious to know what was going on. Two of the black-gowned advocates had likewise moved into positions where they might find answers to satisfy their curiosity. These actions brought frowns of consternation from Magistrate Mathew as he sat sternly at his bench some 10 feet above the small courtroom. When a swarthy-looking advocate in a black silk gown glided into the courtroom and a voice close by whispered, 'Sukumaran Nair', we knew that the case would soon be heard.

From the moment we were called to stand, courtroom discipline was strained. At least as many as were already inside crowded in from the veranda. The disorder was increased by many eager voices all telling us at the same time that as accused we must stand in the dock at the rear of the courtroom. Mr Mathew's voice could be heard above the noise. 'Please state your name and your purpose in coming here.'

The babble in the courtroom died down as I began to speak, but although my voice was clear and loud, it was soon apparent that the chief judicial magistrate was having difficulty in hearing me. Accused who stood in that rear dock were seldom asked to answer questions; instead, advocate would speak from the front of the courtroom. Mr Mathew solved the complication by asking me to go forward and join the advocates. Sukumaran Nair appeared dumbfounded at this unorthodox situation; he now had to argue face to face with the woman defendant herself.

Having heard my request to be allowed bail, Mr Mathew specified the requirements – 6000 rupees to be deposited with the court, a further 10,000 rupees as personal bond, surrender of our passports and the attachment order over *Tiger Rag* to remain in force.

Sukumaran Nair stood to object, but my response was quicker.

I objected to an irregularity in the magistrate's ruling, pointing out that under Indian law a person's home cannot be attached in a defamation case, and *Tiger Rag* was our home. Mr Mathew, surprised by my counter, looked in the direction of Howard's advocate.

'I object,' Sukumaran exclaimed testily. 'They have other passports and unless the attachment order remains they will run away in this boat.'

I assured Mr Mathew we had no other passports and to deny us access to *Tiger Rag* would cause us extreme hardship. Instead the court could order the Cochin Port Authority to restrict the yacht's movements.

Sukumaran Nair argued that such a restriction wasn't possible. Mr Mathew clearly wasn't aware of Indian maritime law, and the courtroom became animated as other advocates joined in to discuss the technicalities of attachment orders. Sukumaran Nair had lost the initiative, but Mr Mathew was losing his patience. He banged down his gavel and made his order – the bail originally specified was amended to allow our access to *Tiger Rag*, though a restriction on its movements within Cochin port was to be imposed. Case 63 was set for a next hearing on 24 February, one week later.

We felt jubilant. Dr Panikulangara's wise legal counselling had allowed us to win our first round in court, and my bold courtroom work would enable repairs to recommence on *Tiger Rag*. We planned to get as much work as possible done on the yacht before the court was scheduled to sit again, at which time we presumed Jim Howard would have returned to Cochin. As we left the court complex our first priority was to find a good restaurant. Due to the urgency of our situation it had been more than twenty-four hours since we had last eaten.

It wasn't until we had tucked away a late lunch and emerged from a café in the bazaar that we noticed we were being followed. The same three men had been waiting on the veranda outside the court sheriff's office when we had lodged our bail money. Two of them were just big and brawny, but the third had an appearance so distinctive as to make him unmistakable. His face was unlined, although the complete greyness of his hair suggested an advanced age, but his most remarkable feature was an extraordinary bristling silver moustache which grew across his cheeks to his ears. Once out in the street, Brian and I quickened our pace and the three men dissolved behind us into the crowded bazaar.

On that Friday afternoon when we returned to our hotel the reception clerk handed us a printed card which caused us alarm. The card read: 'Bruce Rae, First Secretary, Australian High Commission, New Delhi.' On the reverse side was handwitten 'Malabar Hotel', and the date. Why this man had come to Cochin was itself a mystery, though how he had traced us to a hotel we had taken only on our return from Trivandrum the previous night was what really worried us. A telephone call to the Malabar Hotel brought Bruce Rae a second time to our hotel. When we spoke to him his attitude towards us was cool. He told us tersely that a complaint had been made that we had attempted to murder Jyl Gocher, an Australian citizen.

We weren't about to discuss that topic with him, and suggested he speak instead with police officials. Throughout our conversation he remained guarded, and before he left the hotel he requested we attend a further meeting with him on the following Sunday at the Malabar Hotel.

On Saturday morning we began early. Refreshed from a good night's sleep we looked forward to reoccupying *Tiger Rag*. It was most important that we put aside recent intrusions and concentrate on the task of repairing our yacht. Jim Howard had sworn publicly that he would never allow us to leave Cochin harbour aboard *Tiger Rag* – that was to be his revenge; however, we weren't about to leave without her. Howard's public statement to the press had challenged us to return to Cochin and face him, and with each day we spent in Cochin there was risk of fresh attacks against us.

The moment Brian stepped from the hotel entrance he spotted the three Indian men who had followed us the previous day. He quickly turned to re-enter the lobby before the door closed, almost knocking me over as he did so. 'Long grey moustache and his two heavies are across the road,' he explained. It was getting ridiculous, we thought, as we headed for the hotel's ice-cream parlour which we knew had a separate street entrance.

We had to wait at Mattancherry District police station for almost an hour before the officer who could release the key to *Tiger Rag* was summoned. The no-nonsense, single-storey concrete building was situated on one corner of an out-of-the-way square which the police station shared with a local bus terminus, a small public hospital and a ferry wharf. The Mattancherry District was first settled by the Portuguese four centuries ago and along the riverfront there remains a maze of narrow cobblestone streets crowded with ancient two-storeyed stone dwellings and small spice warehouses. The smells of the spices that have been traded in the same way for hundreds of years continue to permeate the streets and houses where a multiracial community now lives. The Mattancherry District, rich in history, is also infamous for its record of crime and sectarian violence. Two vintage police buses stood outside the station, and shields, lathis and whips lining the walls of the muster room were a reminder that trouble was never far away.

The subinspector in charge of the station was a big man, over six foot, and his almost black eyes and opaque complexion gave him a fearsome appearance. His authority was absolute, and when he entered the building each man stood frozen to attention. We were called to a very large, bare room with a desk and two chairs. There was a whip on the wall. From the desk he took out the key to *Tiger Rag*, examined it ponderously, then placed it on his desktop before clapping his hands together four times. An officer entered, orders were spoken, and shouts of further orders came from outside. To our surprise the slightly hunched man with the long silver moustache shuffled in, his left hand clutching the lower half of his lungi, his right hand raised in salute.

PC 1649, A. K. S. Naidu, was the most unlikely plain-clothed policeman we had ever seen. He listened intently to the long talk his subinspector gave him, from time to time inclining his head to either side. He turned to us.

'We must be protecting you,' Naidu said slowly in a singsong voice. 'Instruction has come through the air.'

The subinspector nodded his head in agreement and formally passed the key to us. Outside the station PC Naidu solved the puzzle – two days before, the subinspector had received an order over the police special radio from state police headquarters in Trivandrum. Inspector General Madusudanan himself had spoken on his police-car transmitter. Never before had such a thing happened in their small station. Naidu, who spoke to us in self-taught English, had been delegated the responsibility for our round-the-clock protection. But so far we had been too elusive.

'For two days my old feet have been running to keep up with you,' Naidu said.

With two heavyweight policemen in tow, Naidu accompanied us on Sunday afternoon to the Malabar Hotel where we kept our appointment with Bruce Rae. We hadn't known just what to expect when we were asked to his hotel, but certainly what we found when we were directed to the hotel's garden disturbed us. The senior Australian diplomat was sitting with a woman. Her shoes were off and her long legs stretched lazily in the sun. On the table were beer bottles, glasses and a full ashtray. Jyl Gocher looked very relaxed indeed. When Bruce Rae noticed our approach he made moves to draw up extra chairs, but Brian and I stood back from the table.

'How can you expect us to be seen socializing with this woman, here in a public place?' Brian asked frostily, pointing directly at Gocher. The diplomat tried to smooth over the situation, insisting that we sit down and discuss this affair like intelligent adults, but we would not yield.

Before coming to this appointment we had reread the documents and memoranda we had extracted from the Australian government under their Freedom of Information Act, again concluding just whose side Bruce Rae was on. The defamation case Jim Howard had brought was a serious matter and we had no intention of discussing our defence with Jyl Gocher at a hotel drinking party.

When Brian suggested that a more private place to talk might be found, Rae brusquely strode off towards the hotel. Naidu shuffled out into his path, interrupting his pace, and faded once more into the bushes. Rae was bristling with annoyance when finally the three of us sat down to talk.

He told us that we had been wrong to make public allegations about Jim Howard. Rae's words reflected his mood. In reply Brian told the diplomat that we stood by our allegations and that this matter would not be decided except in the courts of India, adding, 'Jim Howard had a criminal record and his recent association with international drug smugglers can be proved. Do you deny this?'

Bruce Rae looked hostile and told us that he would deny that the Australian high commission had ever made the statement reported by Maxwell Fernandez in the Indian Press in an article on 22 January:

> . . . What has the Australian high commission got to say about Jim? Here is the exact quote from a secret document police liaison file 70/1/1: SUBJECT JAMES CHARLES HOWARD WAS SUBJECT OF ENQUIRY FROM DRI TO AUSTRALIA THROUGH INTERPOL CHANNEL.

AUSTRALIA RESPONDED ... REF IP/5373/83. SUB-
JECT APPARENTLY HAS 17 CRIMINAL CONVICTIONS
IN AUSTRALIA

Bruce Rae repeated the denial, saying, 'It is not the role of an
Australian high commission to issue any such statement.'
But was this denial going to be used in court to protect Jim
Howard? We didn't know.

It was obvious that we had nothing further to discuss
with Bruce Rae; however, he still had something to say to us.
Losing his reserve he told us that because we had made
public allegations about Jim Howard we should expect the
maximum punishment – prison.

The remaining four days before the court was due to sit we
spent at Mattancherry in the GKW boatyard working on
Tiger Rag. The yard had hauled up trawlers on the slipway behind us for small repairs and many tough Muslim
fishermen came and went. But when the heavy boatyard
doors shut each night we felt quite safe. Francis, the GKW
partner who managed the yard, was a rare and gentle person
who invoked respect from all who knew him, and his personal efforts ensured all work ran smoothly for us. Naidu
established himself as a constant presence and our trust in
him came quickly as well. Despite his frail frame Naidu
proved to be an efficient bodyguard, effectively utilizing
India's greatest resource – its people. He was also good
company and we often laughed over his quaint homespun
philosophies. At the GKW boatyard we were among good
men.

On the eve of our court case we visited Vincent Panikulangara at Panampilly Nagar for a last briefing. Vincent
would be present in court formally to represent accused
three and four, the resident editor and the publisher of the
Indian Express, but would speak on behalf of all four defendants. Jim Howard was to be examined first and Vincent
was eager to confront him. His legal preparation had been
thorough and he was finishing his explanation of the new

evidence to be filed in the case when Maxwell Fernandez knocked on the door. Vincent had asked him to establish whether persistent rumours that Jim Howard was back in Cochin were correct, but Maxwell's sources had been unable to confirm or deny this.

The chief judicial magistrate's court was already crowded when we arrived the following morning. Jim Howard was nowhere to be seen, but Vincent stood on the veranda surrounded by newspaper reporters. They parted as we approached.

'The Australian government man is in Magistrate Mathew's chambers,' Vincent told us, frowning.

I shrugged my shoulders, unable to comment, nor could Brian. The court usher's bell interrupted our speculation and we moved inside. Bruce Rae appeared on the veranda with Howard's barristers. But there was still no Jim Howard.

Press coverage of proceedings appeared on the front page of the *Indian Express* the following day, Saturday 24 February:

James Charles Howard, the Australian who figured in the newspapers as a prime suspect in the $200 million hashish catch by the US Coast Guards, did not turn up for the sixth time in a row in the chief judicial magistrate's court, Ernakulam, when the defamation case he had filed against the *Indian Express* and two fellow Australians came up on Friday. [Howard's five previous failures to appear had been when we were in Australia.] The magistrate, Mr P. A. Mathew, however, refused the plea of counsel for the *Indian Express* that the case might be thrown out . . . Opposing the request for another postponement, counsel for the *Indian Express* Dr Vincent Panikulangara argued that it was evident that Howard was not serious in pursuing the case but actually evading the court.

Miss McGuinness, the second accused in the case, arguing for herself and Brian Milgate, opposing further postponement, said that any delay would bring them undue hardships. They were short of funds after depositing Rs 6000 in the court as security. Further, their voyage in their yacht would be in jeopardy after the monsoon season set in, she argued.

The magistrate suggested that they engage a lawyer which might be helpful to expedite the case.

She contended they had no money for this.

The case was finally adjourned to 6 March.

We never saw Bruce Rae again, but the mystery of Jim Howard's whereabouts was solved that same Saturday when he was observed emerging from Superintendent Menon's office at the Cochin customs house.

27

The Trial

———

'I will not allow a Milgate to spoil my image. Come forward, Milgate. Meet me in court.' Jim Howard made this statement to the Express News Service in January 1984. However, it was the need to ensure formal protection for *Tiger Rag* that took us to the highest court in Kerala State.

Alison sat with me at one end of a reading room near windows screened by a latticework that threw patterns of sunlight on a polished timber floor. The room was furnished with armchairs and low tables, and shelves of books lined the walls. Dr Vincent Panikulangara stood at the far end of the huge room watching the man who was typing out the third and last foolscap page of a petition. Milling past him on their way to and from a refreshment room or to various duties around the high court of Kerala were Vincent's fellow advocates. Occasionally one would pause to talk with him. The petition to be presented to the high court that morning hadn't been kept confidential from the men who practised alongside Vincent; the affair had become a public topic.

Vincent hurried towards us, scanning the petition for errors. Alison signed it and I followed, adding the date, Friday 2 March 1984. Then Vincent left the room and quickly made his way through the well-kept gardens towards the imposing granite building of the high court. The barrister's reading room was a pleasant place in which to bide our time, an escape from the strain of the last few days during which another sinister plot had unfolded. We had learned that another move was afoot to hide a small quantity of narcotics aboard *Tiger Rag*. The Customs Department Rummage Squad were due to come a few hours later for their 'hit'. We would be imprisoned and discredited, and *Tiger Rag* confiscated. But an indiscreet telephone call to the

GKW boatyard had brought us a hint of suspicion. Maxwell
Fernandez, checking sources close to the syndicate, had heard
that before the chief judicial magistrate's court sat on 6
March something big was planned. But the details of the
plot were only revealed after a friend whom we had met
through Cochin Marine Corporation had led us, two nights
before, to a sleazy waterfront character who owed him a
favour.

We had found the man sitting on a downtown ferry wharf.
His eyes were glazed from heavy drug use, and the English
speech he had learned from tourists was littered with profanities. He had led us through the darkness across a number
of unused tourist ferries to a rundown launch, needing to be
on his own territory before he would talk freely. He told us
he lived on Bolghatty Island and that he had been approached
to be a 'witness' in Jyl Gocher's attempted murder charge.
After the charge was dropped he had been offered a sum of
money to take a package of heroin to the GKW boatyard and
plant it on the yacht. But he had turned the offer down. He
talked at length about the network, and how the underworld
controlled the distribution of drugs from Cochin. We learned
that in recent years laboratories had sprung up in the district
inland from Cochin, and now heroin was being processed
for organized smuggling networks in India itself, instead of
overseas. This explained the abundance of refined heroin on
the streets of Cochin.

In the darkness of the squalid launch that night the waterfront drug dealer had felt secure. We were sure that what he
told us was true, but unfortunately in a courtroom he would
have been seen as unreliable and lacking in credibility.

Vincent was beaming with success when he re-entered the
barrister's reading room. The petition, asking for protection
on the grounds that an attempt might be made to plant
drugs aboard *Tiger Rag* or sabotage the vessel, and referring
to Jim Howard as a criminal and Jyl Gocher as a person who
concocted false charges, had been accepted by the high court.
The judge had handed down his response to the state's
principal police attorney – order 1731 of 1984 ensured the

continuation of our police protection, with that protection extended to cover *Tiger Rag*. The judge had further ordered that neither Jim Howard nor Jyl Gocher be permitted within twenty paces of us. Vincent felt confident that as long as the high court order stood the Customs Department would not approach *Tiger Rag* without first obtaining the consent of the police, and any intended action needed to be first cleared with the inspector general himself. Vincent explained that copies of the petition would be served on both Howard and Gocher, and expected that they would challenge it, since it was damaging to them both.

Safe behind the high stone walls of the GKW boatyard, we were not much disturbed by the outside world, though a police squad had to be called out one night when Jim Howard was discovered in a motor car parked in the shadows near the boatyard. The car sped away when police arrived.

On the eve of the defamation trial, 5 March, the three GKW partners, Naidu, Alison and I gathered in Francis's little office to share a small bottle of spirits and celebrate the successful high court petition. Word had been leaked from Sukumaran Nair's office that no challenge was to be mounted by Howard or Gocher. Francis tittered with delight as he translated news of us that had appeared in the local-language newspaper in the past week. And Naidu surprised us all by revealing that he had gone to Ernakulam during the week and waited for Jim Howard. 'Just to look at his face,' Naidu confessed. Although Howard's photograph had appeared several times in the press, Naidu had been driven by his policeman's inquisitiveness to see the man for himself.

Alison and I had not seen Howard for ten months, though we expected to see him in court the following morning when the defamation trial began.

'Don't let your mind be dancing, Miss Alison,' Naidu advised as he walked with us through the Ernakulam court complex. The old man's expression reflected the anxiety we all felt.

From the corner of the timber courtroom ahead a man gave Naidu a hand signal. 'Big Jim has not yet come,' he translated.

Dr Vincent Panikulangara hadn't arrived either, nor could Howard's witnesses or advocates be seen among the many people already on the wide veranda. Sitting inside the courtroom was a solitary European man I had never seen before. Dressed in a safari suit he looked quite out of place. Alison recognized him immediately – Ian Tricks, consul general of the Australian consulate in Bombay. (Alison had last spoken to him almost twelve months before in his Bombay office when our problems had just been beginning.) Tricks informed us that he had been instructed by the Australian government to fly to Cochin and sit in on the trial.

The many journalists and photographers who had been sent to cover the important trial surrounded Vincent the moment he arrived. Mr Jacobs, witness for Jim Howard, arrived in a motor car with Raman Pillai, the junior barrister to Sukumaran Nair. Next to come was Captain Thomas, second witness for Jim Howard, a big man whose recently acquired flashy gold jewellery set him apart from those on the veranda. All but these two of the original five witnesses named by Jim Howard had withdrawn.

As the usher began to ring his bell we took our seats, looking at Naidu posted at the door. He was to give first indication of the last-minute arrival of Howard with his advocate, Sukumaran Nair.

Magistrate Mathew made his entrance and those in the courtroom stood. He sat and the assembly sat. An air of expectation was evident. He read to himself some document on his bench while we sat in suspense, watching the door and waiting for Howard's entrance. Mathew cleared his throat, adjusted his heavy-framed spectacles and slowly looked around the courtroom before asking, 'Is case 63 ready to proceed?'

Raman Pillai stood, all attention on him. But where was Sukumaran Nair? Pillai shuffled through some papers on the table in front of him without looking up. Pillai was grossly overweight and in the stuffy air of the crowded courtroom beads of sweat had broken out on his forehead. From some distant place a drumbeat could be heard.

'The petitioner James Howard begs your honour's forgiveness,' Raman Pillai began. 'He suffers a grave illness and has been ordered not to move. He prays for an adjournment.'

The sound of drums was moving closer, and with it chanting voices could be heard. Vincent was on his feet seething with outrage. 'Your Honour cannot possibly allow this.'

Before he could continue, Mathew raised his hand to silence him and turned to address Raman Pillai, who was studying the floor. 'Does the petitioner provide a medical certificate to the court?'

Pillai's apologetic reply was drowned out by the sounds of loud chanting. Through the courtroom doorway we could see the first rows of a procession of men marching along the earthen path which twisted between the buildings in the court complex. A militant voice chanted a remark we could not understand, and the procession followed with a chorused reply. Again and again this procedure was repeated by the marchers, who sounded hundreds strong. The drummer seemed to be coming with the tail. Whether their cause was political or a union-inspired dispute we couldn't tell, but the mantra of the marchers mesmerized those in the courtroom for minutes until the chants of the last line of protesters faded into the distance.

The lingering spell in the courtroom was only broken when Vincent, stoked up and ready to go, jumped to his feet and began to heap argument upon argument. 'Howard has not appeared seven times to face the court, Howard is making a mockery of the Indian legal system, Howard is afraid to face my cross-examination, Howard insults the dignity of those who practise in this court, Howard exploits the system in order to carry out his reprisals.'

Shouts of agreement came from the floor, spurring Vincent on. With each outcry Mathew winced and Raman Pilla sank lower into his chair. Mathew gathered his wits and instructed Vincent to pause long enough for him to hear from Raman Pillai when the petitioner might be well enough to face the court. But Vincent, who practised in the supreme and high courts of India, wasn't about to be dismissed.

'With respect,' Vincent barked, 'the procedure of this court is no different from any other in the Indian legal system. A medical certificate must be produced.'

Magistrate Mathew held up his hand for silence, and waited till it came. Vincent was still on his feet, eager to go on. Raman Pillai remained seated. The magistrate's ruling followed the sound of his gavel. The preamble was lost in his muttered words, though his last sentence came through loud and clear.

'Under section 256 of the Criminal Penal Code all four accused are acquitted and set at liberty.'

Although there was other business on the day's lists, most of those in the courtroom moved outside. Slaps on the back, handshakes and congratulations were captured by clicking press cameras. We were euphoric. We had won. Ian Tricks found his way through the crowd to shake our hands. Vincent was awash with the admiration and praise of his fellow advocates.

On that same morning, less than one mile away, aboard his luxury ketch, Jim Howard was putting the finishing touches to his next move – a new legal case intended to take *Tiger Rag* away from us.

Witnesses who saw Jim Howard go with his new advocate to a poky little subcourt at Ernakulam less than twenty-four hours after he had failed to appear in his defamation case told us he didn't look ill at all. The Indian government agents appointed to keep surveillance on him since his return to Cochin had no doubts about the mood he was in, and reported that Jyl Gocher had moved off the ketch. The government agents had followed Howard when he too had moved off the ketch and into a downtown Ernakulam hotel. But it wasn't until they had tracked him to the subcourt the next day that they realized why he had been travelling back and forth the fifteen miles to the rundown office of a small-time civil lawyer.

The face-to-face confrontation with Jim Howard that we began to think might never happen came only two days after our acquittal. Alison was out on the first of many excursions to buy the provisions needed for our impending crossing of the Indian Ocean, and I was busy with preparations to *Tiger Rag*, when Naidu called to me to come quickly. I followed him to Francis's office, from where raised voices could be heard.

There were about ten men in the office; all were standing and the atmosphere was tense. Two men in the centre of the room were shouting at Francis, though he appeared to be calm. Behind him were the GKW carpenter and a beefy Muslim fisherman, both ready to spring to Francis's side should violence erupt. The other two GKW partners were standing back from the uproar, discussing something between themselves. A gross-looking character was slouched against the wall – Howard's new lawyer. He wore tight pinstripe trousers and a matching waistcoat fastened with a gold chain that stretched over his large belly. When I came into the room Jim Howard moved behind the desk and was now sitting lordly in Francis's chair.

'They say we must launch *Tiger Rag* at once. The subcourt has attached it and ordered it towed away,' Francis stammered, turning his back on the two men. One man was still waving a paper about, the other shouting.

While the tumult about me continued I telephoned Vincent's residence, only to learn that he had left an hour before for Trivandrum. I was putting the phone down when Naidu hurried from the room and I could hear his singsong voice pleading, 'Miss Alison, Miss Alison.' Her steps didn't falter when she entered the office. She took three bold paces up to where the smirking Howard was sitting, arms folded, and spat squarely in his face.

Naidu pulled her back, for her own protection. Then the

sound of boots running on an earthen floor carried above the general commotion and several policemen burst menacingly into the office; Naidu had had the sense to send a runner to Mattancherry police station for help.

'Get out of here.' The order, from a senior police officer, was directed at Jim Howard. Howard's new lawyer, still slouching against the wall, finally stirred. The two shouting men slowly became still, but Howard sat smugly considering the end of his cigar. The officer moved to the desk and stood over Howard. 'Get out,' the officer repeated, clicking his fingers as a signal to two rugged constables. As they moved towards him, Howard turned pale.

When the police officer walked back into the boatyard after having escorted Howard off the premises, the two men who had been at the centre of the commotion approached him. The officer listened patiently as the men, who stated they were court employees, insisted that the subcourt had attached the yacht after Mr Howard had lodged a civil complaint. The yacht must be taken at once to the Ernakulam ferry wharf where it would be closer to the court complex. The officer looked first at *Tiger Rag*, then in the direction of the water. Between the two were three fishing trawlers, one with a number of planks removed from its underside. Even his untrained eye could see it would be days before the way could be cleared to let *Tiger Rag* through.

The ranting and raving of the two men hadn't eased at all and we were wondering how long the officer would suffer them when he again spotted Jim Howard, who had sneaked back into the boatyard and was measuring the keel under *Tiger Rag*. A number of policemen moved forward at once and Howard bolted for the boatyard gate, but caught the heel of his cowboy boots on a steel spike and sprawled headlong in the dust. The two court employees, who seemed to owe some allegiance to Howard, went to his aid and together they drove off in Howard's car. The police bus disappeared after them.

This latest attack left us stunned. Jim Howard had taken out a civil case against us the day after our acquittal in the defamation trial, claiming that we had stolen money from him. Though we felt angry and bitterly disappointed, long faces weren't going to help us so we decided on a course of action that would divide our energies – I was to travel to Trivandrum to speak again to Police Inspector General Madusudanan while Alison, who now had Naidu to watch over her, would do whatever she could the next day in court.

28

The 'Money Sack'

A serious traffic accident in the district south of Cochin had blocked most of the carriageway and reduced the progress of the long-distance bus I had caught from Trivandrum back to Cochin to a walking pace. I tried not to feel agitated, but the all-night bus journey south, the all-day ordeal of waiting rooms and officialdom, and now the long journey northward had exhausted me.

From the bus window I could see the sun setting somewhere beyond the coconut trees, throwing brilliant colours onto the heavy clouds – clouds which brought the first indication of the approaching monsoon season. Before the rains came Alison and I planned to be sailing westward into that sunset, just as we had intended to do one year before. Adding to my despondency, our dwindling finances wouldn't be able to hold out much longer. I swung down from the bus before it reached Thoppumpady Bridge and hailed an autorickshaw. The fresh air rallied me and I determined to leave my gloomy mood behind before I spoke to Alison.

Despite my weariness from travelling we talked till late into the night. I told Alison of Inspector General Madusudanan's reaction when I had presented my protest stating that Howard's recent reprisals were contrary to the spirit of the high court order intended to restrain such actions. Madusudanan had finally showed his emotions and I quoted the senior policeman's hostile words, 'I have a plan to smoke out that bastard Howard.'

Alison had more to tell about her day, most of which had been spent in court. Faced with the daunting complexities of the Indian legal system she had enlisted the help of our friend Maxwell Fernandez. He had introduced her to his uncle, an advocate who took civil cases, while he in turn introduced Alison to his junior barrister. Together they trudged the labyrinth of legal offices and found the facts, and later prepared a petition which won them, from a higher court, an amendment to the subcourt's order to remove *Tiger Rag* from the GKW boatyard.

A small bribe was paid to a court official and Alison was able to see the evidence Jim Howard had submitted to the court. The judge had accepted Howard's word that he had recently remembered lending us 20,000 rupees about one year before, the only evidence consisting of a sheet of paper supposedly written by us to him, dated at a time when Howard wasn't even in India. The signatures at the bottom didn't bear any resemblance to either of ours. On this claim by Howard, a prima facie case against us had been established.

'It's totally outrageous,' Alison summed up, 'and smacks of corruption.' The judge's order to remove *Tiger Rag* from the GKW boatyard contradicted Port Authority and Customs Department regulations. On Tuesday we would have to go to court, to battle our way through another legal nightmare.

We had hoped to spend Saturday quietly working on *Tiger Rag*, her repairs being almost complete, but late in the morning our work was interrupted by a well-spoken young man. Naidu, never far away from us, sidled up from behind the young man when he was introducing himself and whispered very loudly, 'Intelligence wing, Indian central government.' With a glint in his eye the old man shuffled away.

The intelligence officer, a serious-looking fellow, had come to ask us questions about Jim Howard, and a Cochin lawyer. He was following up the discussions we had had with the Indian officials at their high commission in London the month before, when the main topic had been espionage. The young intelligence officer told us he had interviewed Jim Howard and found his answers unacceptable. His report had been sent to New Delhi. 'Perhaps the cogs will slowly turn to remove him from India,' he said frankly, adding, 'Howard is a desperate man. My advice to you is to leave India without delay.'

Francis and Naidu had their heads together for most of the afternoon and Naidu made several phone calls. We downed tools as twilight came on, but they still hadn't emerged from Francis's office. We found them in darkness, both deep in thought. Francis sat with his elbows on his desk and his chin cupped in his hands, Naidu opposite, pulling slowly at the end of his long moustache. They had been trying to solve a problem, Francis told us, but they didn't have enough clues.

The mystery had been uncovered through Naidu's detective work – he had heard that Howard had yet another plan to have *Tiger Rag* taken away. We had come to realize just how efficient Naidu was at his job, for not only could he learn when Jim Howard opened what Naidu described as the 'money sack', but often he knew how much had been taken out. This time Howard had opened his 'money sack' at the Cochin Electricity Department. Naidu tried to explain. 'We are knowing where big Jim's feet are going, but we are not knowing what his head is doing.'

In the early hours of Monday morning we were woken by the barking of the GKW watchdogs. I clambered to the deck, grabbing the torch from its place by the companionway as I went. The dogs were jumping at the wall directly in front of *Tiger Rag*, snapping furiously. The watchman was shining his torch through the crack between the heavy doors, trying to see what was exciting the dogs.

'Let them out,' I yelled at him. But I had spoken too fast and he hadn't understood me. I tried a second time. As the door opened a few inches the dogs jumped through it. From outside came shouting, an engine raced, somebody screamed and a car drove away. A few minutes later the dogs returned and scratched at the closed gate. A crowd had gathered outside, and some of them were talking to the watchman through the crack.

When the police bus arrived, an officer came to the

boatyard to tell us that the disturbance had been caused by a big foreign man. Somebody from the mosque opposite had recognized him as the man whose photograph had been in the newspapers. Apparently Howard had been using a tape measure against the boatyard's stone walls, and the dogs had chased him to his car. We couldn't understand what to make of it all and wondered if it might be another piece for Naidu's puzzle.

The two court employees, still trying to serve the sub-court's attachment order issued six days before, came to the boatyard again on Monday afternoon, again in Jim Howard's motor car, but this time Howard didn't accompany them. Neither man from the court spoke English well enough to make himself understood, but that didn't stop their incessant loudness, arm-waving and general theatrics. We stood calmly to wait out the first act of their performance, before Francis could get close enough to the boisterous duo to speak with them.

There was a paper we must sign, Francis translated. We asked if it was written in English. Francis replied that it wasn't. Nothing would be acceptable that wasn't written in English, Francis communicated to them. This brought a second outburst of theatrics from the pair, who suggested we would immediately be thrown into prison if we didn't sign this document, but we would have none of it. Francis conveyed our last word – on the following morning we would be in court, and unless the document could be translated into English before then, this matter must wait.

We didn't rid ourselves of the raving pair until Francis feigned a call to the police.

When we arrived at the designated subcourt in good time for our case, we found the courtroom empty. Nobody was to be seen. Alison checked the sign above the door, but we hadn't been mistaken. While we discussed what we should do next, Naidu stuck his head around the corner. 'The lady judge will come only tomorrow. She is taking leave.' Feeling confused and a trifle annoyed that the case was now to be heard in yet another court, we set off to find somebody who could explain.

Principal Judge Sankara Narayanan's courtroom on the second floor of the largest building in the court complex was spacious, though it provided few chairs. The day's business had already begun when we joined the people and advocates gathered by the doorway of the crowded courtroom. In addition to his own court's business the principal judge was to hear, in the absence of the subcourt judge who had accepted Howard's civil complaint about us, matters arising from her court's business. Our case had been noted down near the bottom of the day's list. We were to wait outside until we were called.

'Naidu wants us,' Alison whispered. 'He's over there by the window.'

I turned and followed her to where the old policeman stood looking down from the second-floor window. Jim Howard was standing outside talking with the fat man we now knew was his latest advocate. They were deep in conversation. We guessed that when the usher eventually called the case they would both come thumping up the wooden staircase.

In the afternoon, when the matter was finally called, Howard didn't come to the courtroom. The usher ordered us to stand beneath the bench to wait for the judge to finish writing a previous judgment, after which the judge, a middle-aged man greying at the temples, gave us his attention.

'Why have you refused to accept the subcourt's order to attach your property?'

Alison told him that we hadn't been able to understand the document because it wasn't written in English.

The principal judge didn't acknowledge her explanation, instead he looked around the courtroom. 'Is James Charles Howard represented here?' The judge was looking somewhere over our heads.

'Yes, your honour.' Howard's advocate had slipped into the courtroom and was standing several paces behind us. The judge addressed him.

'Are you aware that the attachment order expired this morning?'

Alison and I looked at each other in utter surprise.

'Yes, your honour,' the fat advocate answered.

'Then do you wish me to extend the subcourt's attachment order?'

'No, your honour,' the advocate replied. 'My client will be seeking a revised order when the subcourt resumes tomorrow morning.'

The judge raised his eyebrows, but made no comment. He lowered his head to make a note on his papers. We were told that if we wished to contest the reissue of the attachment order, we should present ourselves at the subcourt at ten o'clock in the morning.

We pushed our way through the people still waiting outside the courtroom and walked a short way along the hallway to find a place where we could talk. I looked around for Naidu but couldn't see him.

'If the attachment order has expired,' I asked Alison, 'then what is to prevent us from leaving India?'

'Legally nothing,' Alison answered slowly, realizing the opportunity now open to us. 'At least not until the subcourt resumes in the morning and Howard gets whatever revised order he's after.'

We looked at each other, the same questions going through our minds – could we launch *Tiger Rag*, step her mast, buy the necessary provisions, satisfy Port Authority regulations, clear customs and sail away from India, all in less than twenty-four hours?

Alison followed me down the narrow wooden staircase and out into the grounds. A few people were wandering about, but Naidu wasn't among them. We walked away from the building and out to the road which led through the court complex. A car parked a good distance inside the grounds began to move. Alison recognized it. 'Jim Howard's car.'

I grabbed her hand and pulled her off the roadway, back in the direction of the court building and away from open ground. The car veered towards us. I thought of hailing the autorickshaw I noticed coming from the building opposite, but it already had a passenger. We hurried on, but Jim Howard's car was moving quickly now. As the little autorickshaw crossed in front of us, its passenger leant out of the open cab and shouted at us. It was Naidu. The auto stopped near us just before the big car swept by, Jim Howard's face clearly visible through the open window.

'What burns inside him?' Naidu growled as he squinted at the car disappearing through the gateway.

We slowly regained our composure as the autorickshaw turned into the busy roadway and started to jerk in and out of the heavy traffic. Although we were not sure of our direction we were pleased to be moving. Naidu told us he had been talking with the court policemen who had used their influence to help him discover the details of Jim Howard's revised attachment order. At the same time Naidu was keeping his eye on Howard whom he had observed sitting in the big motor car. The autorickshaw turned into Hospital Road, where the afternoon traffic snarl was beginning. As we zigzagged between the buses, trucks and honking vehicles, Naidu revealed what he had learned at the court.

The advocate Howard had engaged on this case was considered a 'small man' in the legal world, Naidu explained, but the fellow had been claiming around the court that he was being paid a lakh of rupees for his special services. Tomorrow he planned to tell the subcourt judge that we were dangerous people, that we had attacked and violently driven off the two court employees sent to carry out her orders, that we would likewise defy the police, customs and port authority, even the Indian navy itself, and that we would abscond with the yacht to evade the justice of her court. Howard's lawyer would ask for an order to give the court employees special powers, Naidu revealed – authority to attach the yacht by whatever means they chose, authority to take the yacht to the court complex where it could be bound for ever by the intricacies of the Indian legal system.

'But how?' I asked, interrupting Naidu's narrative. With his answer the missing pieces of the puzzle fell into place.

'The big crane from the Electricity Department has been bought for 20,000 rupees with the "money sack". Tomorrow the yacht will be lifted over the boatyard wall, taken through the streets of Ernakulam and dropped inside the court complex alongside other confiscated property.'

Naidu fell silent. Alison sat beside him, her head in her hands, distraught by the news of Howard's final plan. The traffic began to move again and we drew nearer to the main north-south road. I shook Alison gently.

'There isn't much time left. Take the auto to the boatyard. On the way tell Naidu what we must do tonight. I'll join you as soon as I can.'

Alison looked up at me, her face showing that she was a long way from being defeated. I stepped out of the auto and into the crush of people.

When I arrived at Vincent's residence at Panampilly Nagar the house appeared shut up. I rang the bell and Vincent's head emerged from an upstairs window. As he opened his front door he told me he had only returned from Trivandrum on the morning train. Very quickly I brought him up to date with the latest developments. He listened intently, checking the important legal points until each one was clear in his mind. Eventually he came to the same conclusion Alison and I had.

'You are free to leave India,' Vincent confirmed. 'But can you launch the yacht tonight itself?'

I couldn't answer, my mind was running too fast over the many problems involved.

29

Angels at Work

Offices were closing and the afternoon rush hour was at its
height when I left Panampilly Nagar. Not one vacant autorickshaw was to be seen. On busy MG Road I caught the
first bus that would take me over the one-lane Thoppumpady
Bridge, always the site of the worst traffic congestion. The
bus was cram-packed with people. Somebody kept standing
on my toes and I felt extremely irritated – it had been
altogether a lousy day. Curse the traffic, I thought as the
bus's pace slowed and slowed. It came to a halt a mile short
of the Thoppumpady Bridge and I got down and walked. I
moved as fast as I could on the loose stones that made up the
verge of the narrow bitumen road which had a smelly drain
running beside it. As I got closer to the bridge the number
of people getting down to walk increased. The hot, clammy
afternoon air reeked of the traffic's exhaust fumes but my
determination carried me on. Time was important now and
every minute would count.

The GKW boatyard was not the scene of activity I had
expected to see when I eventually arrived. The expression
on my face brought Francis forward to explain, but Alison
got to me first.

'They won't do it,' she deplored.

'Why not?' I demanded, glaring at Francis.

'It's not Francis,' Alison clarified, 'the other two partners
are frightened.'

For over an hour Alison had been trying to get the partners
to agree to launch *Tiger Rag*, but without success. Francis
and Naidu had likewise failed. Thoughts of Howard's possible reprisals against them had filled their minds and
couldn't be dislodged. From the office telephone I called
Vincent. He spoke in turn with each of the two reluctant

GKW partners, assuring them that *Tiger Rag* was legally free to go from India. If there should be any repercussions he offered to represent them without fee.

It was growing dark and I turned on the electric bulb. The workers who would be needed for the big task of launching the two remaining fishing trawlers to let *Tiger Rag* down the slipway were leaving for home.

'Will you do it now?' I begged of Mr Joseph.

'We have too much to fear, Mr Brian,' he replied, his agitation equalling mine. Emotion showed in his voice as he went on, 'How can we defend ourselves when these drug-smugglers want to punish us? You won't be here to help us.'

I slumped into a chair just as the electric light went out. The Cochin electricity supply was subject to intermittent daily shutdowns. Francis came into the office to light a candle. Its flickering flame sent dancing shadows across the cracked plaster walls, increasing the tension in the office. Alison came inside, followed by Naidu, who would have heard the GKW partner's criticism of the police. Though Naidu knew better than to comment, like everyone else in the room he understood that Howard's 'money sack' could corrupt officials at even the highest levels. The GKW men had every reason to be afraid.

Suddenly an idea came to me and I asked Alison if she had the inspector general's number in Trivandrum.

Naidu sat by the telephone ready to assist Alison should she encounter any non-English speakers in her quest to contact the inspector general, while I paced the floor. When finally she spoke to the IG a hush fell on the room. She carefully outlined the circumstances by which the attachment order on *Tiger Rag* had lapsed, and how we wanted to launch the yacht before further legal restraints could be imposed. I heard her speak of the refusal of the two GKW partners. She paused in her conversation, and listened. 'Yes,' she said finally, 'thank you, inspector general.'

Everybody in the office looked at her, waiting to hear the

outcome, not aware the IG was still on the line until Alison handed the receiver to the GKW partner closest to her. It happened to be Sunno.

'The IG wants a word with you.'

Sunno hesitantly lifted the receiver to his ear. When he realized just whom he was speaking to he jumped to attention. 'Yes, sah,' he yelled crisply. 'Yes, sah,' he repeated, the utmost respect in his voice. He seemed relieved when he replaced the receiver and announced, 'The IG says we are to launch the yacht.'

Francis, who had been wringing his hands in anguish, looked at Mr Joseph, the remaining obstacle. Mr Joseph was resolute. 'How can we believe that these big men in Trivandrum will protect us in Cochin? We are nobody to them.' With these defiant words he left the room.

Precious time was slipping by. Reason told me this was our last chance to save *Tiger Rag*. How could we ever forgive ourselves if we failed? We followed Mr Joseph outside and tried to talk him round, pleading with him to come to Mattancherry District police station to hear what they had to say. But he refused. Finally Sunno volunteered to go in his place and a compromise was struck – Mr Joseph would agree to launch *Tiger Rag* if the police gave a written assurance that GKW would be defended.

The Mattancherry police station was also without electricity, candleflame alone lit the big building. Sunno and I were told to wait in the subinspector's room while he was summoned. The station was a spooky place at night, with men noiselessly gliding about the rooms like apparitions, and I realized that the policemen had removed their boots so as not to disturb the men asleep in the muster room.

When the subinspector strode into the room, he ignored Sunno and invited me to sit. In the feeble candlelight the subinspector's face was more awesome than ever.

'Why have you come here?' he asked harshly.

I gave him my reasons, emphasizing the earlier phone call to the IG in Trivandrum. He clapped his hands to bring in his orderly. A lighted match was put to three tapers around the room. I watched them burst into flame, each one crackling and giving off an acrid smell.

The crack of a whip shattered the spell, startling me. I hadn't noticed the subinspector move to take the whip from the wall. A second crack resounded through the station. Sunno stood rigid with fear, the whip having passed within inches of his face. The subinspector didn't address Sunno in English, though that didn't lessen the impact of the dramatic scene. The brutal method used to enforce his obedience made me feel sorry for the terrified man standing behind me. Sunno was my friend.

When the subinspector was finished he gave me his edict. 'This man now understands that if the yacht is not launched tonight it is me he has to fear, not Jim Howard.'

It was 10 p.m. as I hung on behind Sunno for the ride back to the boatyard on his motor scooter. The three partners went immediately into discussion. Mr Joseph's plaintive voice could be heard above the others, but the still-nervous Sunno had the last word. Francis came to us with their decision.

'We are going to leave you here now,' Francis began. 'We must bring back the workers. Then we will try.'

By midnight the first trawler had run down the slipway. Only one trawler now stood between *Tiger Rag* and the water. But the task ahead was still enormous. A dozen men had come from their homes, each giving his total effort. The second fishing trawler was raised on jacks and the slipway trolley rolled under it. In unison the men chanted a rhythm as they heaved on the lines attached to the heavy trolley. Alison and Naidu went out in search of hot tea and snacks for the workers, returning in time to watch the second trawler go down the rails, splashing gently into the darkness of the river. It was then 2 a.m. and eight hours remained before the subcourt was due to sit.

Tiger Rag, with her lead-ballasted fin keel, presented a far more difficult task. The yacht had to be moved an inch at a time, a painfully slow process that couldn't be hurried. I toiled alongside the men while Alison and Naidu made repeated trips to bring back whatever provisions they could find from the few night stalls set up near the entrances to hospitals or bus stations. Each time they returned, *Tiger Rag* was a few inches closer to the water. The unspoken risk that Jim Howard might be alerted to our desperate efforts was constantly with us. The same thoughts might have been passing through Naidu's mind when he made the comment, 'Jim Howard sleeps tonight, but the angels are all at work.'

For two long hours the native rhythm of the workers' chanting continued. The receding tide made us hasten our race against time, because by dawn the water level would be too low to float *Tiger Rag* off the slipway trolley. Twice the yacht moved precariously off balance. Each time willing hands jumped forward with timber props.

At 4.30 a.m. *Tiger Rag* stood atop the short incline, ready at last to roll down into the water. I looked around the muddy and grease-smeared men, all drenched with sweat. Theirs had been a Herculean effort. I climbed aboard *Tiger Rag* and readied her docking ropes. The trolley lines were released, the yacht began to move, and cheers of triumph went up.

But the trolley gathered more speed than any of us had anticipated. When it hit the water *Tiger Rag* came alive and slewed off to port, crashing stern first into a derelict trawler. Sounds of splintering timber made my heart leap, but fortunately there was no damage to *Tiger Rag*. The next task was to load aboard the equipment removed to lighten the yacht before it was launched. A human chain was formed and items of equipment passed from hand to hand through the darkness and across the decks of several trawlers – anchors, bags of sail, spars, boxes filled with provisions and bucket after bucket of water till the yacht's stainless steel tank was filled. Last of all came the mast, a ravel of rigging wire and rope, all to be sorted out in darkness. The approaching dawn would quicken the work, but only a few hours would then remain for us to tackle the obstacles yet to come – the Port Authority formalities and the official clearance, which had to be obtained at the customs house.

At eight o'clock we were finally ready for the workboat to take our line for the tow downriver. The stepping of the mast, now securely in place, had taken most of our time. The spars had also been rigged and the sails hanked on. *Tiger Rag*'s engine had been ruined at Edacochin during the previous monsoon season so now the yacht would rely solely on the wind and our sails to clear the harbour if finally we were given our official sailing papers. Alison stood at the helm during the tow downriver while I made the final checks. Our crossing of the Indian Ocean might be expected to take four to five weeks, this late in the season, and all must be in readiness for such a long passage.

I came back on deck as the Malabar Hotel and the Port Authority building came in sight. Standing behind them was the customs house. The prominent clock tower on the Port Authority building showed nine o'clock as the workboat cast off our towline and we let go the anchor. The subcourt would begin to sit in exactly one hour. Alison chose to stay on board while I faced the final formalities.

The clerk at the Port Authority refused to stamp *Tiger Rag*'s sailing papers. He pointed to an instruction in his ledger to restrain the yacht's movement. The instruction had come from the harbour master. I took the stairs to the upper floor two at a time and went directly to the harbour master's office, only to be informed that he wasn't expected till the afternoon. Captain George, chief pilot of the Cochin port, had his office further down the corridor. It, too, was empty. I went to the window to check on *Tiger Rag*, not sure quite what to do next. An official launch on its way to the Port Authority wharf was passing close to the yacht, and by chance I recognized Captain George standing on the launch's bow. I ran down the stairs to meet him, desperately hoping he could help clear our papers. For over one year both the harbour master and Captain George had known of our battle against the drug syndicate; from the beginning they had helped us by giving information on movements of ships and yachts.

'Only this week the chief judicial magistrate's release of our obligation to detain *Tiger Rag* in Cochin port came through,' Captain George told me. 'And it will be my pleasure to personally expedite your sailing papers.'

With growing trepidation I crossed the road to the customs house to face the final obstacle. It was now 9.30 and I guessed Jim Howard would be on his way to the subcourt.

'Mr Brian.' It was Naidu calling me. He was standing on the corner under a huge oak tree with Mr Francis. A strong young policeman who often assisted Naidu was with them. 'Take this man along. I will wait here with Francis,' Naidu said, waving me in the direction of the imposing customs house.

I soon realized Naidu's wisdom in bringing the young policeman to help me with the official papers: it often took many hours to negotiate the bureaucratic red tape, and since this particular policeman was a district football star and the sport was followed enthusiastically by customs staff, his presence was just what was needed. The official clearance document grew before my eyes. As we hurried from section to section the clearance got a stamp here, a few words there and a signature somewhere else. All that remained was its authorization by the superintendent of the preventative section – Archutha Menon.

I hadn't seen the superintendent for almost a year, not since the night we had surprised each other at a bus stop in Tamil Nadu State, that night Menon had had a heart attack.

He was on the phone and I was told to wait. It was ten o'clock, the subcourt was now sitting. I dreaded this confrontation with Menon. Just how much the superintendent knew of our situation I didn't know, though certainly his network of spies and his familiarity with Jim Howard would have kept him in touch. I heard him replace the telephone receiver, then heard his chair scrape across the floor. He emerged from behind his office partition with a smile on his face. But his manner told me nothing.

'Welcome, Mr Brian,' Menon said formally as he shook my hand. 'Shall we walk together?'

We walked along the corridor that led past the offices of

the senior customs officials, Menon setting a slow pace. All the time he spoke too loudly to me, laughing and joking as if I were his long-lost friend.

'You devious old bastard,' I said to him, at last understanding his strange behaviour. 'This is just a big show for your new superiors, isn't it?'

Menon couldn't contain the broad grin on his face. I had correctly guessed that he had only narrowly escaped the Customs Department purge after the *Hetty* bust had vindicated our allegations. Now Menon wanted to be seen to be 'on the right side', and the sight of him respectfully accompanying me from the building wouldn't be missed.

'I've always thought you to be a most intelligent man, Mr Brian,' Menon said to me when at last he put his signature to *Tiger Rag*'s official clearance. 'Go quickly, while you still have time.'

I made a hasty exit from the customs house, waving the official clearance above my head as I came. Even from a distance I could see the joy on the faces of Francis and Naidu as they hurried towards me.

'Make haste,' Naidu insisted. 'Old legs will follow behind.'

I ran through the grounds of the Malabar Hotel to the jetty where I had left the rubber dinghy, anxious to relieve Alison's worry. I could see her leap with excitement when she realized I had succeeded, then she pointed vigorously at the clock tower which now read 10.20 a.m. But I waited for Francis and Naidu. It was a fair distance for the old policeman to run and as he bobbed through the gardens I could see he was doing his best to hurry.

'Don't waste your time on goodbyes to an old man,' he gasped, out of breath.

But I took no notice of his words and gripped his hand in farewell. 'We will never forget you, Naidu.'

Francis, too, was overcome with emotion and unable for a moment to speak. 'God bless you,' he finally said.

I took his hand. 'We owe you so much, Mr Francis.'

Tears were in my eyes as I pulled on the oars, stroking

hard towards the yacht which lay a short distance out in the channel.

'Take good care of Miss Alison,' Naidu called after me.

The morning offshore breeze was fading but the tide was still ebbing as I hauled up the anchor. As *Tiger Rag*'s sails filled in the light breeze, the figures of the two men standing on the Malabar Hotel jetty slowly receded. Our loyal friends were still visible when we glided past the ancient Chinese fishing nets off Fort Cochin, and out through the harbour entrance. It was 11 a.m. Where was Jim Howard now?

Armed with his subcourt order he might be speeding in his car towards the GKW boatyard, only to find the two fishing trawlers again in their place on the slipway. Men would be busy, caulking hammers would sound out, work would be going on as normal. The only thing different was that *Tiger Rag* had vanished. Jim Howard might wonder if he wasn't going mad.

EPILOGUE

15 March 1984 to September 1986

The Connection Is Broken

For us the ordeal in Cochin was over. However, it was some time before Jim Howard finally accepted that we had eluded him. He hired a light aircraft from the airfield on Willingdon Island and, thinking that *Tiger Rag* couldn't have been seaworthy enough to cross the Indian Ocean, began a systematic air search of the coastline north and south of Cochin.

The last report we received on Jim Howard and Jyl Gocher told us that they had been expelled from India some time in 1984, and had taken *Steppenwolf* to the Republic of Maldives, about 400 miles southwest of Cochin.

The US authorities have ordered Richard Merkley to be arrested on sight. Someone will be keeping watch on his substantial bank accounts in Mexico. However, Merkley can afford to remain in hiding indefinitely, knowing that while he remains outside the United States he is virtually free to do as he wishes. But if Merkley is arrested we expect that he will offer to incriminate his associates in the drug network in exchange for plea bargaining or other concessions.

When Gordon Gold suddenly left Cochin after the CIU unit had begun their inquiries into his affairs, he returned to Durban, South Africa. There he may have thought that he too had distanced himself from the *Hetty* investigation, since no formal ties exist between India and South Africa. However, in January 1984, the *Rand Daily Mail* exposed Gold as a prominent part of the Cochin smuggling ring. Gold engaged a lawyer and threatened to sue the newspaper for defamation, but at the same time he made all haste to prepare his yacht *Honky Tonk* to sail within days for the Caribbean, and the Virgin Islands. The *Rand Daily Mail* rechecked their facts about Gold, then told him they would fight the case in court rather than print a denial. Gold dropped the case and his present whereabouts are unknown.

In Cochin a few things have changed. CIU Superintendent Shreedharan has been promoted to a higher position in Calicut District. Maxwell Fernandez resigned from the current-affairs magazine *The Week*, and is building on his good reputation as a journalist. S. K. Anantaramin, editor of the *Indian Express*, retired and went to Madras to live with his children. K. T. Jacobs, former manager of the Cochin Marine Corporation, bought himself a large marine company on Vypin Island in Cochin harbour. Nobody we spoke to, including Jacobs's brother, could understand how he had got the money together to make such a purchase. Joseph Vellapally, Howard's lawyer, faded back into his wealthy background. No doubt he still dreams of the time in the near future when he will retire to Europe.

So the Cochin connection is broken. The considerable newspaper reports, editorials and attention from many angles to Cochin's drug-smuggling connections slowly brought its illicit role into focus. For the next group of major drug traffickers who choose Cochin as their smuggling base, the risks will be greater or, more realistically, the bribes will need to be higher.

And what of us? It took us four weeks to sail *Tiger Rag* across the Indian Ocean, from Cochin to Aden. Wind conditions were mostly light. The first day was spent bolting on the self-steering unit, compass, lifelines and other things left unfinished in our hurried preparation to sail. Because we hadn't the time to be as fully provisioned as we normally would have been for an ocean crossing, we found it necessary to ration both food and water severely. From Aden we sailed to Port Sudan, midway up the Red Sea, and then suffered through fierce headwinds for 1000 miles to Port Suez in Egypt. Once through the Suez Canal we set sail across the Mediterranean Sea to the island of Cyprus, where *Tiger Rag* was repaired and this book was written.

We still have much to fear from those who may seek

reprisals. Because we have been outspoken about the Australian government's attitude towards drug smuggling, as we experienced it, we expect some elements within the government will seek to discredit us.

However, we felt that it was in the public interest that we should write our story. At least we have exposed some of the methods by which international crime syndicates can operate virtually unhindered, and we have exposed Cochin as a burgeoning drug port. We have also challenged the widely held belief that sound cooperation exists between individual countries in the fight against drug smuggling.

If the drug problem is as important as the Western media would have us believe, then many things need to be changed. But while the superbosses stand beyond accusation, and major drug traffickers can cheat the justice system, those who point the finger can expect only suffering instead of reward – and possibly death.

BURTON

The man behind the myth

PENNY JUNOR

He was born Richard Walter Jenkins on 10 November 1925, a miner's son. But by the age of seventeen he had a new name, a new father and a new life before him. By twenty-seven he was in Hollywood, by thirty-seven he was the most acclaimed young actor of his time.

He could have been the greatest actor of his day, the successor to Olivier, but he squandered his talent in second-rate films, threw away his career on drink and women and his own legend.

What went wrong? The question has been asked a thousand times . . . now Penny Junor gives us the answer.

BIOGRAPHY   0 7221 5212 4   £2.95

A CANDID PORTRAIT OF BETTE DAVIS BY HER DAUGHTER

My Mother's Keeper

─── B. D. HYMAN ───

Bette Davis was never a typical Hollywood star. She was tough, smart, aggressive, gifted and bitterly determined. It was those qualities that made her one of the most legendary and charismatic actresses of her generation.

But the stormy personality that drove her to the top knew no rest behind the scenes, and those same qualities damned her personal life right from the start.

The broken marriages, the domestic violence and unhappiness, the vicious battles with The System – all of it is here, told by the only person who knows Bette Davis well enough to tell it, her daughter, B. D. Hyman.

Written with compassion, humour, understanding and searing honesty, this is the story of the real Bette Davis – more controversial , more shocking and more moving than any character she ever played
on film.

BIOGRAPHY   0 7221 4837 2   £3.50

As Time Goes By
The Life of Ingrid Bergman

LAURENCE LEAMER

In a career that spanned forty years, Ingrid Bergman brought her astonishing screen presence to star in a string of classics – *Casablanca*, *Joan of Arc*, *For Whom the Bell Tolls*, *Notorious*. She was adored for her transcendent beauty, her devotion to her family, her vulnerability.

Yet, of all Ingrid Bergman's stunning roles, none was as dramatic as her own life. Behind her idealised Hollywood image was a passionate and daring woman who craved excitement and adventure, a woman who had many affairs, a woman who followed her heart into the biggest celebrity scandal in post-war film history.

AS TIME GOES BY is the riveting and sometimes shocking story of a woman of fierce ambition and strong desires, a story of love and lust, of public image and private truth.

'At once chilling and fascinating. No film of Ingrid's will look quite the same again' Sheridan Morley

0 7221 5493 3   BIOGRAPHY   £3.95

TREVOR
HOWARD

A GENTLEMAN
AND A PLAYER

VIVIENNE KNIGHT

Trevor Howard, perhaps the greatest British film
actor of his generation, famed for his compelling
roles in films ranging from the classic BRIEF
ENCOUNTER to the contemporary WHITE
MISCHIEF, is a man of intriguing enigma and
contradiction. A hell-raiser and drinker, but
always the perfect gentleman, he considers acting
a game and plays it for the highest stakes.

In this definitive and entertaining biography,
Vivienne Knight reveals the truth behind one of
the most popular and well-loved actors Britain
has ever produced.

0 7474 0055 5   BIOGRAPHY   £3.50

'Not since **THE DIARY OF ANNE FRANK**
has a young girl's chronicle recorded
such an appalling story'   MAIL ON SUNDAY

THE STONES CRY OUT
A CAMBODIAN
CHILDHOOD 1975-80

Molyda Szymusiak

Molydan Szymusiak was 12 years old when the
Khmer Rouge took over Phnom Penh and the long
agony of the Cambodians began – an agony in
which one third of the entire nation disappeared,
either murdered or dying of exhaustion and
starvation. Her extraordinary and moving story is
a tribute to the courage and resilience of
humanity in the face of unspeakable atrocity.

'*Compelling . . . the author tells us what it was
really like from the inside*' LITERARY REVIEW

0 7474 0050 5   AUTOBIOGRAPHY   £3.50

FOR THE FIRST TIME EVER, A MEMBER
OF THE KRAY TWINS' FIRM SPEAKS OUT

MURDER
WITHOUT
CONVICTION

JOHN DICKSON

Ronnie and Reggie Kray were a formidable
partnership, possessing a charisma that was
glamorous but deadly. Celebrities, film stars,
con-men and killers were attracted by the Twins'
curious mix of charm and violence, whose reign of
terror in the mean streets of London's East End
continues to exert a compulsive fascination.

Now, John Dickson, a close and trusted henchman of
the Krays for many years, tells the inside story of their
notorious gangland underworld. He describes the
murders, the extortion, protection and gambling
rackets; the Mafia connections; entertaining the
famous; the increasingly erratic and senselessly
violent behaviour of the Twins and their final
dramatic arrest at a time when they had built up so
fearsome a reputation that they were convinced they
were invincible.

This, the first inside account of the gang that
dominated the East End of London for most of
the 1960s, reads like a thriller, but is based
entirely on fact.

0 7221 2948 3   TRUE CRIME   £2.99

A selection of bestsellers from Sphere

FICTION

THE LEGACY OF HEOROT	Niven/Pournelle/Barnes	£3.50 □
THE PHYSICIAN	Noah Gordon	£3.99 □
INFIDELITIES	Freda Bright	£3.99 □
THE GREAT ALONE	Janet Dailey	£3.99 □
THE PANIC OF '89	Paul Erdman	£3.50 □

FILM AND TV TIE-IN

BLACK FOREST CLINIC	Peter Heim	£2.99 □
INTIMATE CONTACT	Jacqueline Osborne	£2.50 □
BEST OF BRITISH	Maurice Sellar	£8.95 □
SEX WITH PAULA YATES	Paula Yates	£2.95 □
RAW DEAL	Walter Wager	£2.50 □

NON-FICTION

FISH	Robyn Wilson	£2.50 □
THE SACRED VIRGIN AND THE HOLY WHORE	Anthony Harris	£3.50 □
THE DARKNESS IS LIGHT ENOUGH	Chris Ferris	£4.50 □
TREVOR HOWARD: A GENTLEMAN AND A PLAYER	Vivienne Knight	£3.50 □
INVISIBLE ARMIES	Stephen Segaller	£4.99 □

All Sphere books are available at your local bookshop or newsagent, or can be ordered direct from the publisher. Just tick the titles you want and fill in the form below.

Name _____

Address _____

_____

Write to Sphere Books, Cash Sales Department, P.O. Box 11, Falmouth, Cornwall TR10 9EN

Please enclose a cheque or postal order to the value of the cover price plus:

UK: 60p for the first book, 25p for the second book and 15p for each additional book ordered to a maximum charge of £1.90.

OVERSEAS & EIRE: £1.25 for the first book, 75p for the second book and 28p for each subsequent title ordered.

BFPO: 60p for the first book, 25p for the second book plus 15p per copy for the next 7 books, thereafter 9p per book.

Sphere Books reserve the right to show new retail prices on covers which may differ from those previously advertised in the text elsewhere, and to increase postal rates in accordance with the P.O.